# A History
## *of*
# MANITOWOC COUNTY

## WISCONSIN

—*Complete and Illustrated*—

*Ralph G. Plumb*

HERITAGE BOOKS
2011

# HERITAGE BOOKS
*AN IMPRINT OF HERITAGE BOOKS, INC.*

Books, CDs, and more—Worldwide

For our listing of thousands of titles see our website
at
www.HeritageBooks.com

A Facsimile Reprint
Published 2011 by
HERITAGE BOOKS, INC.
Publishing Division
100 Railroad Ave. #104
Westminster, Maryland 21157

Copyright © 1904 Brandt Printing & Binding Co.
Manitowoc, Wisconsin

— Publisher's Notice —
In reprints such as this, it is often not possible to remove blemishes from the original. We feel the contents of this book warrant its reissue despite these blemishes and hope you will agree and read it with pleasure.

International Standard Book Numbers
Paperbound: 978-0-7884-1248-6
Clothbound: 978-0-7884-8850-4

BENJAMIN JONES

## PREFACE

A brief explanation as to the purpose of this book may not be out of place. Some years ago when the author first resided In Madison, his attention was attracted to the vast accumulated material on the subject of local Wisconsin history, gathered together in the State Historical Library at that city, and particularly to the hundreds of bound files of newspapers. At first he was led to a cursory browsing in the early volumes of certain Manitowoc county weeklies and the discovery of much interesting and generally forgotten information led to a more detailed and systematic reading of the files. The interest in the pioneer existence of the lake shore region thus aroused became more and more intense as this study progressed and the final result was the determination to gather from all possible sources as much material relating to the history of Manitowoc County as could be found and the condensation and combination of it into a fairly readable account. Old records, interviews and miscellaneous works have been valuable adjuncts to the newspaper files in furnishing the basis of the work and, although the problem of selection presented was often a most difficult one, an attempt, at least, has been made to follow approved historical methods in the recording and interpretation of facts.

This, then, is the aim of this history. No claims are made for its literary merits. On the other hand the author has more largely devoted his efforts towards securing correctness in point of fact than elegance of style. Different phases in the county's history are treated topically also, instead of an attempt being made to write one connected story of the entire existence of the county, as it was thought true prospective would thus be better afforded. It may be objected that too many dates have been inserted. From the literary standpoint this is doubtless true, but it must be remembered that above all the idea in writting this work was the recording in some permanent form of many facts which in future years may be useful as well as interesting, in regard to the beginning and progress of the county. The older generation is rapidly passing off the stage of action and the original evidence of historical value, such as landmarks, is being obliterated year by year. To preserve at least a partial account of the changes made by the course of time was the task the author set before him. Without further apology he submits the result to the reader.                    RALPH GORDON PLUMB.

## TABLE OF CONTENTS

| CHAPTERS | | PAGE |
|---|---|---|
| I. | Descriptive | 1 |
| II. | The Indians | 8 |
| III. | Early Settlement | 16 |
| IV. | Growth and Foreign Immigration | 32 |
| V. | Means of Communication | 42 |
| VI. | Marine | 55 |
| VII. | Railroads | 85 |
| VIII. | Military | 112 |
| IX. | Politics | 133 |
| X. | Village and City Government | 167 |
| XI. | Churches | 183 |
| XII. | Societies and Organizations | 227 |
| XIII. | Education | 243 |
| XIV. | The Press | 255 |
| XV. | The Professions | 278 |
| XVI. | Banks and Banking | 281 |
| XVII. | Business and Industry | 288 |
| | Appendixes | 293 |
| | Index | |

## DEDICATION

To the pioneers who made Manitowoc County what it is to day this work is dedicated by the Author.

## CHAPTER I.

### DESCRIPTIVE.

The territory embraced within the present limits of the county of Manitowoc is situated as follows:—from the shores of Lake Michigan on the east to Calumet County on the west and from Sheboygan County on the south to Brown and Kewaunee Counties on the north, all of the boundaries being regular with the exception of the lake line and also the northwestern corner where Brown County makes an indentation. The county lies in 44 degrees, 36 minutes, north latitude and its area is 612 square miles. It is divided into eighteen townships, the northern row being composed of Cooperstown, Gibson, Mishicott and Two Creeks, that next south of them, Maple Grove, Franklin, Kossuth and Two Rivers, then a tier composed of Rockland, Cato, Manitowoc Rapids and Manitowoc, south of them another, composed of Eaton, Liberty and Newton and the tier furthest south being made up of Schleswig, Meeme and Centreville. The largest of these is Kossuth which comprises forty sections of land, while the smallest are Two Creeks and Manitowoc, which contain about fifteen sections apiece. Cooperstown, Maple Grove, Franklin, Cato, Rockland, Rapids, Liberty, Eaton, Meeme and Schleswig correspond in size to the legal township, viz., thirty-six sections.

The county is all within the territory covered by the Lake Michigan glacier in prehistoric times, this fact having had its effect upon the conformation of the land. The latter is gradually sloping from the western boundaries to the lake, the Kettle Moraine which begins in Door County, traversing the western portion in a southwesterly direction, thus forming a watershed between the streams running into the Fox and its tributaries and those flowing into Lake Michigan. This range of hills extend in a loop through the south central part of the state, the western arm extending upwards as far as Langlade county. The underlying strata of the county are of rock of a variety which is denoted by geologists as Niagara limestone. Layers of this are exposed along the course of the West Twin River in the townships of Gibson and Cooperstown and several caves are there found. These attracted but little attention until the eighties, when, however, they became widely known as curious formations. The prevailing soil is clay strongly impregnated in places with limestone and with gravel in the northwestern part of the county. Sand is abundant along the river valleys and on the lake shore, the latter being particularly adapted for building purposes. The limestone is of a fine whitish variety and several quarries, notably at Grimms Station, have been opened in order to utilize the product. In some places it is of such a fine-grained quality that in an early day it was mistaken for marble. Thus a discovery of supposed marble upon the Nachtwey farm in the town of Gibson was once much heralded and several years before the Baker marbles were widely known, being named after the discoverer, a resident in the town of Rapids. The stone was remarkably compact and uniform in crystallization. In the early thirties gold deposits were rumored to have been found in what is now Kewaunee County, creating much excitement, it being supposed that this precious metal would be found in that section of the state in considerable amount. Such hopes, however, proved without foundation in fact. As early as 1850 one Joel Smith, brother of P. P. Smith, while at work in the present township of Gibson, discovered specimens of what was believed to be copper quartz, but owing to his subsequent blindness the vein was not located. At intervals of a few years similar discoveries were made, leading finally to the sinking of a shaft on the farm of Adolph Hudson, which, after fruitless endeavors of several months in duration, was abandoned. Finds were later made on the Robinson farm in the same vicinity, while similar discoveries have been made at times in the town of Manitowoc Rapids. The clay in certain parts of the county, notably near the city of Manitowoc, is of a peculiar variety, which can be manufactured into cream colored brick and this industry has been an important one. On several occasions small veins of natural gas have been struck, notably in Newton in 1865 and later in Manitowoc Rapids, not of sufficient magnitude, however, to be of commercial value. A peculiar black sand in the town of Two Creeks was early made use of in the manufacture of matches and large quantities have continued to be exported. With these exceptions the county has been without developed mineral resources.

The surface of the county is gently undulating, being the highest in the northwest and southwest portions. The highest point in the county is in Township 21, Range 21 in the town of Schleswig, which is 359 feet above the level of the lake. The average levels of various of the towns are as follows:—Cooperstown 210 feet, Gibson 95, Mishicott 60, Maple Grove 200, Kossuth 100, Two Rivers 29, Cato 250, Manitowoc Rapids 120, Manitowoc 50, Franklin 300, Meeme 200, Schleswig 290 and Centerville 60. A portion of Eaton and Cato and a large part of Rockland are swampy, but as a whole there is very little waste land. The county is well drained, thus adding greatly to its fertility. The principal stream is the Manitowoc, after which the county was named, which is forty-five miles in length and drains about four hundred square miles. It rises in Calumet County and after a winding course through Rockland, Eaton, Liberty, Cato, Rapids and Manitowoc, it finally empties into Lake Michigan, its descent being 262 feet in the last fifteen miles of its course. Numerous small tributaries swell its flow, notably the north branch which flows into it in the western part of the town of Rapids, after draining a goodly portion of the northern part of county, the North Mud Creek, which joins it in the town of Rockland and which flows through Reedsville, and the South Mud Creek. Good water power was afforded at an early day at eight places along the course, notably at Murphy's mills and at Manitowoc Rapids. The stream was then much higher than at present and was navigable for canoes nearly to Lake Winnebago, as Lapham says in his description of Wisconsin, written in 1844. At about this time a canal was proposed to connect it with Lake Winnebago, which would require, it was estimated, thirty-seven locks but the project never received much attention. High water and floods were often causes of great damage, those of 1881, 1885 and 1888 being particularly destructive to property, including many dams and bridges. At the mouth of the river, where it entered the lake, sand bars formed before improvements began and the lands in the vicinity were very low and marshy, necessitating much filling in improving the village of Manitowoc.

The next largest streams of the county are the Twin Rivers, the Neshoto or West Twin and the Mishicott or East Twin, which unite a few rods from the point, where they enter the lake. The East Twin is the shorter and rises in the town of Montpelier in Kewaunee County, flowing southward after being joined by Mauvais Creek, while the West Twin rises in Brown County and flows through Cooperstown, Gibson and Kossuth southeastward into the lake. Good water power was once utilized on both, notably at Mishicott and Neshoto. The Sheboygan River flows southeastward through the town of Schleswig and receives several tributaries from that portion of the county, among them Meeme Creek. Water power was also early utilized on this stream. Besides these principal rivers there are several creeks, emptying into the lake at points along the shore, among them the Little Manitowoc, whose mouth is in the northwestern part of the city of Manitowoc and whose course is largely marked by marshes and bayous, Silver and Calvin Creeks, three and four miles south of the city respectively, Point Creek, seven miles south and Centerville Creek, running through the village of that name. The southern and western parts of the county are dotted with small lakes. Among the largest are Cedar Lake in the town of Schleswig, English Lake in Newton, named after a surveyor who is said to have fallen in that body of water, Pigeon Lake in Liberty, Silver Lake in Rapids, Long Lake in Rockland and Prairie Lake in Meeme. These, as well as the rivers and creeks, are fed by numerous springs of pure water. In fact the water supply of the county is unvarying in quantity and high in quality. At Manitowoc the nearness of the lake made it unnecessary to dig artesian wells but the domestic wells used before a water works system was installed were very satisfactory and the veins seemed inexhaustible. At Two Rivers, however, it was necessary in one instance to drill 1700 feet before a flow was obtained and in several portions of the county wells for farm purposes have been drilled to a considerable depth.

When the first settlers came to the county they found it an almost impenetrable wilderness. Pine was the prevailing timber, great forests of it growing along the banks of the Manitowoc and in the northern part of the county. Hemlock was also growing in great quantities, particularly in the northeastern part around Two Rivers, while the tamarack filled the swamps in the western portion. The hard varieties, such as the beech, elm and maple were also of abundant growth and the wild crabapple, willow and sumach fringed the banks of the streams. The hand of the lumberman in twenty years devastated this virgin forest but even up to the present day the county has been fairly well wooded, particularly in the northern and western portions. In the past the thick growth of trees offered in many respects an excellent opportunity for the spread of fire and the fear of this danger was not the least of the anxieties of the pioneer. The most destructive of the great forest fires, which Wisconsin has experienced, that in 1871, touched the northern portions of the county and resulted in great loss of property. In other years also, among them 1864 and 1895, considerable damage was the result of these conflagrations. The native vegetation of the county originally was that usually found in the northern states. Wild grape vines clung to the trees, berries were hidden under the pine needles, wild rice grew in the marshes and the open places were carpeted with all the various kinds of grasses. The hand of man here too soon made itself felt and as the years rolled by waving fields of grain and rich meadows spread in extent until Manitowoc's present reputation as an agricultural county was established. Hard wheat was the first chief product of the cultivated soil but the softer varieties and oats, barley and rye soon supplanted it, while hay was always an important crop. Vegetables find the proper qualities in the soil to bring forth abundant crops and the result has been that pease, beans, cabbages and potatoes have been raised in great quantities. Manitowoc County pease, in particular, have, as canned products, gained a wide reputation. Fruits too, principally apples, cherries and plums, are raised to a considerable extent.

In the early days wild animals roamed at will through "the forests primeval." Bears subsisted on nuts and berries and were seen in the county as late as the sixties quite frequently. In 1859 a lynx was shot within a half mile of Manitowoc and deer were numerous even at a later period. The wild ducks and geese visited the wild rice fields in the autumn and the rabbit, gopher and squirrel made their permanent habitation in the trunks of old trees and beneath their roots. Snakes were never very plentiful and those of a harmless variety. In the streams fish were abundant, including bass, pickerel and "bullheads", while in the lake whitefish, trout and herring were caught in quantities, Two Rivers being the center of that industry. In the rivers of the northern part of the county, particularly in Kossuth and Gibson, clams are abundant and several valuable pearls have been found. Crawfish are also numerous at the mouths and along the courses of the streams.

In climate Manitowoc County has much, for which to be thankful. The mitigating influences of the lake have prevented extremes of heat and cold and, although the springs are frequently somewhat raw and inclement, the autumns are most pleasantly prolonged and frosts are often postponed until late October. The county has never been visited by a severe cyclone or destructive winds and has in a remarkable degree escaped floods and drougths. On the whole Nature did much in providing so favored a region for a community to work out the results, of which the account is given in the succeeding pages.

## CHAPTER II.

## THE INDIANS.

How far back the American Indian dates in history is altogether a matter of speculation. And yet Manitowoc like most other American communities is interested in such a discussion, for the very name of the river and county suggest the race which gave them an appelation. Various significations have been given to the word by Indian philologists, but the best seems to be that it is an abbreviation of the form Munedoowk, which in Ojibway and Chippewa means "habitation of the good spirit". It was originally applied to the river and as early as 1844 Lapham in his "Wisconsin" speaks of it as signifying "the river of spirits" and the territorial legislature very wisely applied this aboriginal name to the civil division which it formed in 1836. Whether good or evil spirits were intended was long a subject of controversy but in a letter to the Prairie du Chien Verdict in June 1847, A. Benson, an authority on Indian languages, seems to have settled on the former interpretation and it has since been followed. He also stated that in his opinion the change from the original Ojibway word was due to the misunderstanding of it by the Menomonees and those tribes who later inhabited the region. What legend or story may have been connected with the name is wrapped in mystery but, knowing Indian nature, as modern students do, it seems certain that there must have been one. Other names in the county also afford a field for philological study. Mishicott has been translated as meaning "hairy leg", Meeme as signifying "pigeon" and Neshoto as an Indian name for "twins", a name suggested by the rivers of which it was one.

Whether or not the mound builders existed in the county also gives rise to interesting speculation. Certain mounds and implements have been found at various places in the southern part and in Sheboygan County. These have borne a resemblance to simple breastworks, being about four feet in height and twelve feet in width at the base. Little investigation, however, has been made concerning these primeval inhabitants in this portion of the state. Whatever may be true concerning them, of a tribe of Indians, more ancient than those with whom the first white settlers came in contact, traces have been found. Particularly is this true on the shores of the lake northeast of Two Rivers, where at various times numerous remains have been discovered. In June 1893 mounds were opened which contained six skeletons and many copper implements, all of which were sent to the Smithsonian Institute for preservation. H. C. Hamilton of Two Rivers has been an indefatigable collector of these relics of an earlier race and the size of his gatherings betokens the existence of many an ancient community within the confines of the present county. It has also been said that the Indians, who in the early forties resided near Two Rivers traced their lineage to this more ancient and, it seems, more aristocratic tribe of aborigines. The former, although extremely poverty-stricken, despised the reservation Indians and lived wholly by fishing along the Mishicott and Neshoto Rivers.

Who, if any, of the early French explorers ever touched upon what is now Manitowoc County also lies in the realms of mystery. Many of them coasted the shores of the lake and it may not be impossible that they landed at the mouth of the little river, where so natural a harbor was afforded. Marquette and Joliet, the very first among these adventurers, are said to have skirted the lake from the Illinois line to Green Bay in 1673 and it is not improbable that their voyage was frequently punctuated by landings on Wisconsin soil. However that may be, a century passed before the first specific reference was made to the region. During this time, however, a remarkable shifting of the Indian population of Wisconsin was taking place. The inhabitants of the eastern part in the seventeenth century had been Foxes, Sacs and Mascoutins, but in a report to the secretary of war made by Jedediah Morse in 1822 it is said: "Major Swan informed me on the authority of Col. Bwyer and an old Ottawa chief, living at Mainitouwauk, the river of the bad spirits, that more than a century ago (before 1727) the Fox and Sac Indians, who were then inhabitants of the country on Green Bay and Fox River were conquered and driven away by the Menomonees, aided by the Ottawas and Chippewas, that the Menomonees held the country by conquest and that their title is admitted to be good by the Sacs, Foxes, Chippewas and Ottawas." This authority, nevertheless, did not seem to extend as fully towards the lake as it did westward, for within the present limits of the county there was a conglomeration of tribes, consisting of Ottawas, Menomonees, Winnebagoes, Pottawatamies. All of them with the single exception of the Winnebagoes, were of the Algonquin stock and before 1830 this tribe had disappeared from the county and the other tribes had coalesced to a great extent. The presence of these aborigines in large numbers along the shores had attracted the attention of the hardy French "couriers du bois" and it is by one of these that the first printed reference to any point in Manitowoc County is to be found. One Samuel Robertson in 1779 undertook a voyage on Lake Michigan on the British vessel Felicity and embodied his experiences in a book called "A Voyage On Lake Michigan." On Thursday November 4th of that year, while off the present site of Milwaukee he wrote: "The Indians also told us that they had sent for Monsieur Fay, who is at a place called Twin Rivers, eighteen leagues north of Milwaukee; he had two canoes of goods from the committee, but he said it was against his orders to go among them, and they supposed so as no trader had ever entered at that place." This somewhat obscure reference seems to indicate that there was an understanding between Fay and the British, who were then in authority, as indeed had most of the French traders in both the war of the Revolution and that of 1812. This Monsieur Fay is said to have been located at Twin Rivers at intervals until 1780.

The next heard of Manitowoc was in 1795, when the Northwestern Fur Company sent one Jacques Vieau, sometimes known as Jean Vieau, from Mackinac to establish trading posts at various points on Lake Michigan. Accompanied by his family and a clerk, named Michel de Pelleau, this hardy Frenchman proceeded as far as a point where Two Creeks now stands and there, making a landing and strapping their packs on their backs, the party marched overland in a southwesterly direction to a point, where a little stream, christened Mauvais (Bad) Creek, a tributary of the East Twin, enters that river. On Section 27, of what is now the town of Gibson, a trading post was erected and an agent left in charge, after which Vieau detoured to the lake, skirted the shores until the Manitowoc River was reached and, ascending it to a point near the Rapids, another post was established. Then resuming his journey southward he visited the present sites of both Sheboygan and Milwaukee. The next spring Vieau and his family returned to Mackinac gathering furs and skins enroute. These annual trips were made for many years and Solomon Juneau, the founder of Milwaukee, was one of Vieau's clerks in 1818. The settlement was of an intermittent character, however, and the only important results seems to have been the familiarization of the Indian, by contact, with his white brother. The Indians were numerous in the region and must have afforded a lucrative field for exploitations. Says Colonel Abram Edwards in "Western Reminiscence", in which he described a journey on the lake: "At Twin Rivers and Manitowoc the shore of the lake was lined with Indians---, near Manitowoc many were out in canoes spearing whitefish".

At about this time travel began to utilize old Indian trails in finding a way from Green Bay to the east and in that way many army officers passed through the county. In 1821 the first tragedy enacted in the county took place, in which an American army surgeon was murdered by a savage. Dr. Madison, stationed at Green Bay early in that year received leave of absence to visit his family in Kentucky and taking two soldiers with him started for the south. The story is told by Col. Ebenezer Childs in Volume V of the Wisconsin Historical Collections as follows: "When near Manitowoc and the soldiers a short distance in front on foot, the doctor was shot from his horse, the whole charge lodging in the back of his neck. The soldiers instantly returned and found him badly wounded, whereupon one of them mounted the doctor's horse and returned to Green Bay for help. A number of officers and soldiers started for Manitowoc, but when they arrived the doctor was dead. There were no Indians to be seen and they carried the body to Green Bay for interment. It was some time before the murderer was taken; he was sent to Detroit for trial, together with another Indian, who had killed a Frenchman about the same time. I had to go as a witness; both Indians were found guilty and executed at Detroit." The murderer of Dr. Madison was named Ketaukah; he was a Chippewa and no motive was ever ascribed for the crime.

The next known reference to the region was made in 1825, when Colonel W. G. Hamilton traversed the trail and in a description given of his journey he remarks that there was no settlement between Milwaukee and Manitowoc, but that there was an Indian village at Manitowoc and one at Two Rivers of different tribes, mixed peoples, Chippewas, Ottawas, Menomonees and Pottawatamies. These villages were again mentioned by Morgan L. Martin two years later in descriptions of a journey through the region. These Indians seem to have been well disposed, and traded with the travelers. From 1826 for seven succeeding years two wanderers, Moses Sein and Isaac Haertel made annual visits to the mouth of the Manitowoc to secure furs and peltries in return for the trinkets and bawbles, so fascinating to the Indian eye. Colonel Childs of Green Bay passed through the county in 1827 with a drove of cattle designed for use at that post. Five years later Joshua L. Boyd was licensed by the Indian agent at Green Bay to trade with two tribes residing on the lake and took out an outfit worth $117.89. He was, however, murdered for refusing to give credit to a Chippewa.

Thus matters stood when in 1833 the Pottawatamies and

MICHAEL KELLNER

Menomonees by the Treaty of Chicago deeded away all the lands at the mouths of the various rivers emptying into Lake Michigan. The Manitowoc Indians were represented by Waumegesako, the chief of the mixed tribes at the mouth of the river, of whose connection with the early settlers more will oe said. The Indians, notwithstanding the cession of their land to the settlers remained in considerable numbers about Manitowoc County, fishing in the summer and hunting in the winter. In the early thirties also a few, mainly Chippewas, began the cultivation of the land near Cato Falls, the women raising meager crops of maize. It was over these Indians that chief Waumegesako or Mexico ruled, a man of great intelligence and a sincere friend of the whites. The first permanent settlers saw little of the aborigines but a few years later the latter returned to their haunts and by 1840 were more numerous than the whites. The first Indian scare occurred in 1842, when it was reported by a drunken squaw that the Cato Falls Indians were planning a massacre to take place in two weeks. Immediately preparations were made for defense, the mill hands armed and bullets molded. A Frenchman by the name of Pat Thebieau and E. L. Abbott volunteered to act as scouts but found nothing suspicious. Finally Chief Mexico came into the village of Rapids and reassured the settlers. At this time the Indians had not become the physicial degenerates that whiskey later made them, many of the Pottawatamies being of noble proportions. Mexico was greatly respected by the settlers and received a medal from the government for settling numerous disputes. This medal, which was worth about fifteen dollars, was often pawned by the redskin for necessities but was always scrupulously redeemed. The chief was a signer in the treaties of Butte des Morts in 1827, and Green Bay, entered into the following year. His picture was painted by an Irish artist, George P. Healy, and a copy was presented in 1857 to the Wisconsin Historical Art Gallery. It shows an aged man, clad in the usual garb of a chief, with considerable strength of character evidenced in his tawny face. The old leader died in 1844 and was buried by the settlers with due honors in the town of Rapids, at a point overlooking the river.

The gathering of wild rice was the favorite occupation of the Indians during the forties and early fifties and camps along the rivers were numerous. Then, too, the band of fishers near Two Rivers eked out their precarious existence, under the lead of their chief, Old Katoose. These latter aborigines were often quite lawless, particularly when under the influence of liquor and many were the scares they gave the settlers. In the southwestern part of the county also there was a band of Menomonees, under the leadership of a chief named Solomon, which maintained a planting ground in Schleswig as late as 1859. Another such cemetery was situated in the present town of Gibson on what was later the Smith farm, while others were found near Cato and Two Rivers. Across the line in Calumet County the Indians were very numerous, particularly along the upper course of the Manitowoc. The nearness of the early settlers to these redskins must have added strange color to the pioneer life of the county. The deadly enemies of the Indians, which led to his gradual extermination in Manitowoc County, were three in number, whiskey, cholera and smallpox. The cholera attacked the various tribes in 1850 and drove many of them out of the county, while the indulgence in "fire water," led to a fatal end in many cases. All of the eastern Wisconsin tribes left or were exterminated in the course of time, except the Menomonees, who still have been retained within the borders of the state on a reservation near Shawano. It must be here remembered that the Calumet County Indians were not natives but importations from New York, which was also true of the Oneidas in Brown County.

As late as 1862 Manitowoc in common with other Wisconsin communities suffered from an Indian scare, so long had the redskin been the "bete noir" of pioneer life. It was in the darkest days of the Civil War, when gloomy forebodings were natural and the scare came on the heels of the news of the Indian massacres in Minnesota. It was on the morning of September 2nd, that rumors flew through the county that the Indians were coming. The report seemed to come from the westward and gained credence as it passed from mouth to mouth. At the village of Branch where the fright seems to have progressed so far as to assume the size of a panic it was said that a few miles to the west the redskins were mercilessly robbing, pillaging and murdering. Families gathered together their valuables and made haste towards the county seat. The terror manifested was something most curious and many were seized by it despite their incredulity and their knowledge that there were none but a few peacable Indians in the vicinity. A few men, scoffing at all fears, remained in the little settlements, but all the women and children, even the sick, were transported hurriedly to town. Here, too, panic reigned for the influx of the terror-stricken seemed to have driven the inhabitants into a frenzy. The first to bring the news of the uprising were settlers from the Branch. Although the reports were somewhat discredited, doubt soon turned to belief when a boy rushed to town, reporting that a comrade had been captured a mile from the village. Preparations were then made for defense; some gathered at the Court House, while the women prepared boiling water, with which to overwhelm the invaders; others spoke of boarding vessels and sailing out into the lake, while still others formed companies to spy upon the enemy. It was one of these parties that had frightened the boy, who spread the later alarm, into believing that a comrade had been captured. This party returned, reporting having seen Indians but it was later revealed that the supposed foes were but another band of skulking villagers, searching for the elusive redskins. Reports came from Kellnersville of a terrible massacre at that place. Several hundred men marched from Manitowoc to the scene of carnage but on arriving found it to be a hoax. By this time it was ascertained that the entire scare had been without cause and the settlements soon took up their routine existence, albeit somewhat shamefaced over the affair. This may well form an end to a chapter on Indian life in Manitowoc County, for in a few years there were none of the race left within its confines.

## CHAPTER III.

### EARLY SETTLEMENT.

The beginnings of actual settlement in Manitowoc County date from 1836, but certain events of the year before are of importance as explaining the character of this settlement. Four villages, Manitowcc, Manitowoc Rapids, Two Rivers and Neshoto sprang into existence almost simultaneously and the early history of each is replete with interest. The speculative and expansive tendencies of the year 1835 first brought the unsettled regions of northeastern Wisconsin into prominence. Gold deposits were rumored near Kewaunee and it was even suggested that a metropolis would grow up in the reregion. Three surveyors from Green Bay, Daniel Le Roy, M. L. Martin and P. B. Grignon in 1833 made a cursory examination of the locality. Two years later a land office was opened at that place and A, G. Ellis was deputized to make a survey of the region now included in the county. On the sixth of May President Jackson issued a proclamation for land sales to be held in Green Bay, which signified the opening of all this portion of the state to settlement. The first entries in the territory later composing the county were made by William Jones of Chicago and Louis Fizette on August 3rd. at what is the present site of Manitowoc city and by Francis Leframbois and William Jourdain at the Rapids. Fizette sold to C. P. Arndt, also of Green Bay, soon after.

Said the Green Bay Intelligencer in its issue of April 9th 1835: "The Yankees, anticipating a day of sale have penetrated as far north as the Manitowoc River, thirty-seven miles south of this place, seizing upon all the choice and commanding mill sites and making claims. Exploring parties have also been on the Manitowoc River recently, where it is probable that a saw mill and other improvements will be commenced this coming summer." The speculative mania then became rampant, Arndt selling his recent purchases at $100 an acre, and many who had never visited the region invested heavily. It is from this time that the Jamieson heirs, who laid claim to certain lands in the city and county in 1896, based their title, one Lieut. Jamieson having purchased considerable property at the time. The Green Bay Intelligencer in speaking of this speculative tendency remarked on March 2nd, 1836, "The principal points now sought are at the Manitowoc and Rock Rivers. A year ago Milwaukee was suspected of having some pretensions to its own site but we have done speaking of that place now. The speculators are now past that place. It is old. The rush now is down the lake. Sac Creek (Port Washington), Sheboygan and Manitowoc are at this moment all the rage. Within a month the lands at Manitowoc have risen from $10 to $250 an acre and they are talking of a communication with Fort Winnebago." It was in the spring of this year that an actual beginning was made at settlement in three places.

And first as to the founding of Manitowoc, at the mouth of the river of the same name. The first entry of land in this locality had been made, as said before, in 1835, including all of the land, south of the mouth of the Little Manitowoc for a distance of three miles and west from the lake to the present line separating the towns of Manitowoc and Rapids. Early in 1836 the firm of Jones, King & Co., otherwise known as the Manitowoc Land Company was formed in Chicago. A town plat was made of the proposed city by one Alexander Martin and high hopes were entertained of its future greatness. The two leading members of this firm were brothers, William and Benjamin Jones, and of these the latter is more properly the founder of Manitowoc, since he later took the Wisconsin property as his share, while his brother remained in Chicago, where his holdings made him immensely wealthy. Benjamin Jones was of Massachusetts stock, having been born on July 24 1795, and at the age of sixteen fought in the

war of 1812. Marrying in 1825, after some years in the east he determined to bring his family to Chicago, then but just founded. He arrived at his destination via the Great Lakes on the schooner United States in the fall of 1833 and built a house and store on what is now South Water Street, near Dearborn. Chicago then had 3000 inhabitants and the pioneer supported his large family, which consisted of a wife and twelve children, by keeping a small stock of merchandise. Speculating in land he laid up a comfortable sum and the result was the purchase of Manitowoc land in 1835 and 1836, some two thousand acres in extent. The Jones brothers early in the latter year determined to realize on their investment and accordingly sent up from Chicago a large number of men on a vessel, the party arriving on May 5th. The reception accorded them by the dark pine forests and storm-tossed waves seemed to inspire a sentiment not unlike terror in their souls. By night out of the party but five remained. Some walked to Sheboygan settlement by way of the beach and thus in the course of time found their way back to Chicago, while others struck off on the Indian trail to Green Bay. Three of the men, however, E. L. Abbott, Mark Howard and a third by the name of Farnham, remained at the place all winter, occupying themselves with the construction of a rude log cabin at the foot of what is now Seventh Street and in cutting timber for shipment the next spring. Before the winter was over they had cleared away a large tract of land near the mouth of the river and then waited for their employer, who set out overland from Chicago to visit his new acquisitions in February 1837. The latter part of the journey is described by J. A. Noonan in the Wisconsin Historical Collections as follows: "When I started from Milwaukee to Green Bay I went with the mail carrier, an Indian half-breed named Powell and two or three of the firm of Jones, King & Company, who were going to visit their embryo city, where Manitowoc now stands. The mail carrier as well as the Chicago men were on runners. A gentleman from Buffalo and myself were on horseback. At Sheboygan the only house was a hotel, erected by the company owning the village plat. There was no house between there and Manitowoc and the only buildings in Manitowoc County were a saw mill and two dwellings at Manitowoc Rapids, owned by Jacob Conroe. The road was a trail cut out the width of a wagon track." Upon their arrival Mr. Jones rewarded his faithful workmen by presenting them with $100 apiece besides their wages and assured them that they would be speedily joined by other settlers. Abbott remained in Manitowoc until 1856, marrying Maria Smith, a sister of P. P. Smith, this being the first ceremony performed in the county, but the other two men left soon after.

The new settlers arrived on the schooner Elwellyn on April 17 1837, about forty all told. Among them were Oliver C. Hubbard and D. S. Munger with their families, Moses Hubbard, and others. Included in the party were the four infant sons of O. C. Hubbard, Giles, Harvey, Frank and Erwin. All of the pioneers were hardy persons and soon accustomed themselves to the arduous duties of their new life. They lived at first in the rough log house that the laborers had built the fall before but soon more substantial quarters were secured, the Mungers building a home just south of the present site of the M. E. Church, while the Hubbard family also found permanent quarters. On July 17 the schooner Oregon arrived from Chicago with the family of Benjamin Jones, consisting of his wife, son Alonzo and two daughters, together with Perry P. Smith, a brother-in-law, who had arrived in Chicago from New York State the year before. Mr. Jones soon had a comfortable dwelling ready for his family at the corner of York and Seventh Streets and the little settlement was soon in a prosperous condition. The old boarding house used by the settlers continued to stand as a landmark until 1887, when it was destroyed by fire. By the end of the summer there was a clearing made between Chicago Street and the river and oats had been sown early in the spring, some fifty acres being under cultivation. The first white child born in the county made it appearance at the home of D. S. Munger in September 1837. The infant, who was named Charles, remained in the village until 1846, when with his parents he moved away, being now a resident of Orleans, Indiana. One month

H. F. HUBBARD.

later a daughter was born to B. Jones, who became the wife of Dr. Blake, a prominent surgeon.

Although the Rapids settlement was much larger, the residents at the mouth seemed confident of the future until the effects of the panic of 1837 commenced to be felt. The speculative values immediately disappeared, the mill which B. Jones had built was obliged to suspend and general disaster seemed imminent. One by one the settlers moved away, only the Jones, Hubbard and Munger families remaining. Other places were also affected and Manitowoc gained one inhabitant by the arrival of Peter Johnston, who had lived at Kewaunee, which place was now deserted. In 1838, however, lumber shipments were resumed, schooners being loaded and sent to Chicago. The early forties witnessed little if any growth at Manitowoc. In fact Two Rivers until 1850 seemed to have much more of a future. Mr. Jones left his colony for a year and a half about this time, during which interval P. P. Smith attended to his interests. Increase A. Lapham in his book "Wisconsin," published in 1844 speaks of Manitowoc as a village of twenty or thirty buildings, and mentions it as a depot for lumber sent down from the mills above. However a pier and a lighthouse had been erected and, as he remarks, "The interests and safety of lake navigation require a permanent harbor at this point, which it is hoped will soon be constructed by the general government." After 1845, however, prospects seemed to brighten. Immigration began to be resumed, sturdy New England lumbermen and English settlers coming first. In 1846 Perry Smith brought the first stock of groceries to the little settlement, building a store where the Smalley Manufacturing Company's plant now stands. By this time the German influx had commenced and a large number of that nationality settled in the little village, making it assume more and more importance as the years passed. Said the Green Bay Advocate on August 4th 1847: "Manitowoc has many claims as a lake port but is far too modest in urging them, or perhaps as we suspect, is shrewdly holding back and mustering energy for a prodigious and successful heave upward. Emigration has begun to seek that point and with the fine country, climate and other material advantages, its chances are among the first of the towns on the west shore". But it was still some years before the little town at the mouth of the river gained sufficient importance to become the county seat.

Of the settlements of the county that at Manitowoc Rapids was the earliest in point of time. Here eastern prospectors in 1835 looked over the grounds and the result was the purchase of many hundreds of acres in that year by Jacob W. Conroe and later by his brother John G. Conroe, both of Middlebury, Vermont. The former reached his new holdings by way of Green Bay in the spring of 1836, taking with him about thirty men to build a mill. The lumber for this structure was purchased at twenty dollars a thousand, plus five dollars for freight from Chicago and landed at the mouth of the river. It happened that at Green Bay during the fall Conroe met Captain J. V. Edwards, who had just arrived from New Jersey and was desirous of going to Chicago. When he heard that there was a schooner about to sail for Manitowoc with supplies for Conroe's mills he shipped on board, thinking to get nearer to his destination and upon reaching Manitowoc in November was induced by Mr. Conroe to remain for a time, at least, in his employ. It was Mr. Edwards who built the scows which enabled lumber to be taken from the Rapids out into the bay and to be loaded into vessels for transportation, thus being the first ship builder in the county. Jacob Conroe's brothers, Horace, John and Levi soon joined him in his enterprises as did also Mrs. Conroe, who was the first white woman in the county. The mill was well started by the spring of 1837 and continued to run through the panic period, although it was the only one to do so. Horace Conroe endeavored to cultivate five or six acres about a mile north of the mill during the summer, but gave up in disgust and returned to Vermont a year later. Chief among the lieutenants of the Conroes was Pat Thebieau, a Frenchman, who had been at the Rapids from the very first and continued to reside there until his death in the eighties. Walter McIntosh, Francis Flinn, William McCrady and Joshua Burns came up from

PERRY P. SMITH.

MRS. PERRY P. SMITH.

Sheboygan in 1837 and joined the little colony. Another mill was soon started, it being the enterprise of one J. L. Thayer. On May 1, 1837 a party consisting of Thayer, Pliny Pierce, H. McAllister, Samuel Martin, Joshua Sequoin, William Holbrook, Joseph Sequoin and wife, Frank Pugh, C. Severin. Amos Robier, Deacon Lyman, John B. Oas, B. Doyle, Jessie Burnell and a Mr. Wheat started from Waddington, N. Y. with Manitowoc County as their destination. Reaching Detroit they chartered a boat to carry them and their belongings to Green Bay, from whence they tramped three days along the Indian trail, finally arriving at the Rapids. Pushing up the river they soon after constructed a mill and a log boarding house, calling the settlement Thayersville, the property being owned by the firm of Thayer, Rouse and Thompson. The little settlement numbered about twenty souls. The effects of the panic were very destructive upon the enterprise, however. Thayer became bankrupt and all the settlers gradually disappeared except McAllister and Pierce, who were given lands for their compensation. The former immediately went to farming and became the first actual agriculturist of the county, a fair crop of oats being raised in the fall of 1838. The first wheat ground into flour came from his farm, it being transported to Green Bay for that purpose. Joseph La Counte, who came to the Rapids in 1837 and worked with Thayer, also did some farming, planting potatoes, which, however, proved to be no larger than nuts. Another early settler was E. Lenaville, who resided near Branch. The winter of 1837-1838 was one of great hardship; the flour in the settlement became moldy and the pioneers were obliged to live largely on salt fish with an occasional haunch of venison. In the fall of 1837 Mr. La Counte's family joined him, coming up from Milwaukee on the schooner Jessie Smith and in the next summer Pliny Pierce went back east and brought his wife and children, Alonzo and Jerome, both of whom have since resided in the county. He traded the Thayer lands for a mill site above the Rapids and soon built the Pierce mill. In succeeding years he constructed another mill at Cooperstown, which was later sold to W. H. Bruce of Green Bay, finally becoming the Aldrich mill. Oliver C. Hubbard removed from Manitowoc to Rapids in 1839, where he built a house and soon after engaged in the business of making sash, doors and blinds, using a part of the Conroe mill. In 1847 he built a mill of his own near the Rapids, which he continued to operate until his death in 1855. The mill at Thayersville was soon reopened, John G. Conroe having a large interest, and by him it was run for four or five years, after which it was owned and operated by H. H. Champlin, still later passing into the hands of Wyman Murphy and being known as Murphy mill. In these early years the Rapids was easily the center of industry and life in the county and consequently it was there that the county government had its seat. The Conroes sold out and left the village in 1845. Levi died of consumption at Racine in 1850, while his brother John continued in business in the same city until 1855, when he too died, at the age of forty-five. Said the Racine Advocate: "To the world at large Mr. Conroe was a rough, stern man, but those who knew him best recognized the kind heart beneath that outward garb and the poor and distressed never appealed to him in vain." From this time, although some new blood was received by immigration, the Rapids continued to decline and by 1850 had been distanced by Manitowoc, which three years later became the county seat. Jacob Conroe, the founder of the settlement, returned to Vermont in later years, where he spent the reclining days of his life.

The third settlement to be considered is that at Two Rivers. Here another element, besides lumbering, that of fisheries enters into the story of its foundation. The first entries on the present city site were made by D. Wells, Jr., of Milwaukee, Morgan L. Martin, of Green Bay and S. W. Beal, of Fond du Lac, in September, 1835. In the same year a Frenchman, Oliver Lougrine, who was ordinarily called J. Lonzo, entered 320 acres for settlement. This man, however, did not definitely locate upon the land until late in the next year, when he was employed by Robert M. Eberts, Judge George Lawe and John P. Arndt, of Green Bay, who bought up the site, and erected a mill with which to take advantage of the water power afforded by the Mishicott and Neshoto rivers, the structure being completed in the spring of 1837. Lumber was plenty, the hemlock forests near by affording an almost inexhaustible supply and by the end of the year fully forty people had gathered at the hamlet. It was in the same year that Captain Edwards started a fishery at Two Rivers in a small way, walking to Green Bay to get the twine for his seines. Taking with him a man from the Rapids, his son Henry, then thirteen years old and P. P. Smith, he established himself on the shore and dropped his seines about half way between Manitowoc and Two Rivers. The first haul brought him ten barrels of the finny tribe and this success determined him to follow the business for a livelihood. But others were on the field also during the same year. J. P. Clark, a Detroit fisherman, arrived in Wisconsin at about this time and entered fishing sites at several places along the shore, including Two Rivers and Whitefish Bay. Later he sent twenty men to the former place on the schooner Gazelle and a regular business was begun. Captain Edwards was then taken into the partnership, he remaining at the Little Manitowoc while the Clark camp was fitted out two miles north of Two Rivers. Clark's schooner visited the place monthly, loading a cargo and carrying it to Detroit and returning promptly with supplies. Fishing was carried on entirely by seines, varying in length from forty to one hundred and sixty rods, the nets being set from boats and being hauled in by means of windlasses. The business was a profitable one, since the catches were large, one haul bringing in fish sufficient to fill 175 barrels, holding two hundred pounds apiece, the annual catch at all of the Clark camps being about 2,000 barrels a season. The product sold in Detroit at that time for twelve dollars a barrel. J. P. Clark, himself, moved to Whitefish Bay in 1838 but continued to look after his interests at Two Rivers until four years later when his brother, Isaac C. Clark, carried it on, the pursuit being profitably continued until 1853. J. Lonzo ran the Two Rivers mill until the results of the panic of 1837 compelled it to be shut down. For some time it was idle but in 1843 Andrew J. Vieau took possession of it under the direction of Judge Lawe of Green Bay, who now owned the property. At that time Two Rivers was but a small fishing village of eight or ten houses and about twenty-five inhabitants. Says Mr. Vieau in an article on the subject: "A part of the time I ran the mill myself but leased it for the most part, to Bascom and Wail, in 1844, to Daniel Smith, in 1845, to H. H. Smith of Milwaukee, who finally (1847) bought the plant. I also did some trading with the Indians while at Two Rivers." This H. H. Smith was in reality the founder of Two Rivers and it is from his arrival in 1845 that progress begins. He had been a lumberman on a large scale in western New York, but meeting with reverses he had come to Wisconsin to retrieve his fortunes. For six years he engaged in the lumbering business, at the end of which time he turned towards manufacturing, forming the company of Aldrich, Smith & Co., the predecessors of the present Two Rivers Manufacturing Company.

The fourth settlement in the county was that at Neshoto, eight miles from the mouth of the West Twin river, where there was good water power. An interesting story is connected with its foundation. In April 1837, a Mr. Burnham of Detroit settled on the land without entering it or paying for it at the government office. Lumber was ordered to be shipped on a schooner from Chicago for his mill and in due time arrived. Some of the young men at Manitowoc, desiring to do the pioneer a good turn, trudged to Two Rivers on the beach and from thence up the river to Neshoto to inform Burnham of the schooner's arrival. He received the news stolidly and without a word of thanks,—an ingratitude which prompted the youths to revenge. Knowing him to be a squatter, one of them, Howard, hurried to Green Bay with $350 and had entered in his own name three eighty acre tracts on which the mill site was located. On his way back he met Burnham and obliged the latter to pay $2,000, half in cash and half by a note. before he would part with his rights. The firm of Stringham & Burnham was formed and before winter set in the mill was completed. J. G. Conroe also bought up considerable property in that section of the county.

The Neshoto mill continued to be run by the first owners until 1841, when it was sold to Frederick Borcherdt, the first German settler in the county. He ran the mill for seven years, being in the wilderness with no white neighbors until later in the forties, when he induced some Germans to settle in that portion of the county. Removing to Two Rivers in 1848 he sold the mill to Taylor & Pendleton, who in turn soon transferred their interests to Jones & Cooper. The village of Neshoto was laid out in 1858, at which time great hopes were entertained for its future.

The population of the whole county in 1840 was 240, in 1842 263, in 1845 about 600. By the census of 1840 it was shown that there were but eleven horses and eighty neat cattle in the county and the aggregate of all crops raised was but a few hundred bushels. In fact it was not until 1847 that there were sufficient food stuffs raised in the county to do away with the necessity of sending south or to Green Bay for the winter supply of flour and dairy products. Said the Milwaukee Sentinel in December, 1848, speaking of Manitowoc: "The inhabitants of that region are neither very extensive tillers of the soil or producers of beef and pork. The staple and principal products of that section are pine and hemlock the former of which, when manufactured into boards, constitutes the most important part of lake commerce and city and county enterprise—the lumber trade." The immigration to the county was practically nil up to 1845, when a large number of New England lumbermen arrived, among them Lyman Emerson, H. H. Smith, Daniel Smith and others. Before this little advancement in settlement was made beyond the four places described in the preceding pages. True, in the early forties several taverns were built along the line of the Green Bay road, notably that of Joseph Edwards, built in 1841 near the present site of Cooperstown and that of Joseph Poquin in the present town of Kossuth, established two years later, he being the first settler in that township. In 1844 Daniel Smith founded a settlement at Mishicot, building a lumber mill at that place, where there was then good water power. The mill was operated for some time by Ira P. Smith,

who two years later built another. In 1847 the first settlement within the limits of the town of Cato was made by a man by the name of Burns, who was later arrested and convicted on a charge of counterfeiting. R. M. Brown settled in the same place about the same time but did not remain permanently. In the spring of the next year the first settlement was made in the present town of Gibson by Edward Brown, who died two years later. By this time Cooperstown had also received several settlers, including Joseph Allen, John Arndt and C. King, while Pierce and Bruce built a sawmill there in 1847. The first settlement in the present town of Two Creeks was also made at about this time, P. Rowley establishing himself there in 1842

CHAPTER IV.

## GROWTH AND FOREIGN IMMIGRATION.

From 1847 the growth and settlement of the county, beyond the few lumbering villages, commences and the change to the agricultural stage begins to be apparent. This was due in large part to the German immigration, induced by the political troubles then in progress in that country. As before mentioned Frederick Borcherdt was the first German to settle in the county, coming in the year 1841. Among the other early settlers of Teutonic birth were L. Katzmeyer, Ludwig Alsweide, Nicholaus and Valentine Meyer and Henry Grube, all of whom established themselves in Kossuth before the end of 1846 and George Dusold, a Bavarian, who moved to Manitowoc from Milwaukee in 1846 and was employed at the Rapids for some months as a tanner under G. Musson, at that time county clerk. A year later he moved to Manitowoc and was one of the first German settlers on the south side of the river. It was in that year that the rush of German immigration first began to make itself felt. In 1846 the population of the county had been 629, while in 1847 it was increased to 1285. Among the first Germans to arrive were a group from Holstein, whom F. Borcherdt had induced to settle in Mishicott and Two Rivers. Next came fifteen families of Saxons, who soon after settled in Mishicott. and then a number of Rhenish Prussians, who sought the southern part of the county, principally the township of Newton, some forty-seven families settling there, including F. Truettner, who is said to be the first settler in that town, Frederick Schmitz, C. Schmitz, H. Meyer and others. Some of the Prussians were induced by C. Esslinger, a Bavarian, who had been in America since 1837 and was the Buffalo agent of Jones &

Allen, to take up their abode at the village of Manitowoc and they thus aided to bring that center into prominence. Others went to Kossuth, while many of them moved to Sheboygan county. A large number of these earlier immigrants were Lutherans. At about the same time (1847) many arrived from Lippe-Detmold, being directed from Milwaukee to Manitowoc and Sheboygan counties by Frederick Reiniking and settling in the former district, principally in the towns of Newton and Centerville, the city of Manitowoc and a few in Cooperstown and Kossuth. Many of them were extremely poor and worked in the saw mills. A large part of them were members of the Reformed Church. The first settler in the town of Centerville was W. N. Adams, who had arrived in 1847, but in a few months the land was largely taken up by immigrants from Saxony, some of whom were Lutherans, while others were Roman Catholics. It will be noticed that this early influx of settlement seemed to center in the eastern and southern parts of the county. As time went on, however, the Germans gravitated westward, notably the Pommeranians, who were quite a factor in the early settlement of Cato, Franklin, Maple Grove and Rockland. Mecklenburgers and Hanoverians largely centered in Manitowoc, although many from these regions were to be found scattered in various townships also. Some West Prussians also found their way to Maple Grove, Oldenburgers to Liberty and Two Rivers, Westphalians to Kossuth and Newton, while Bavarians were scattered through the county. In 1854 the colony of Badenese, mentioned elsewhere, settled in Eaton, founding St. Nazians under the leadership of Father Oschwald. A pamphlet on Wisconsin's advantages and those of Manitowoc county in particular, written by Gustav Richter, was printed in 1849 and gained a wide circulation, doubtless being a considerable factor in determining the destination of many immigrants. It will be seen from the above descriptions how heterogeneous was the nature of the early German settlement, every portion of that land being represented, a fact which doubtless had most beneficial influences on later development. The emigration of the fifties and sixties was largely from the northeastern part of that country. This element in the population has always been a strong one in the county, nearly 25 per cent of the inhabitants being of German nationality and an even greater proportion of such parentage.

Another considerable element in immigration, early in evidence was that of the Norwegians. The first Norwegian resident of the county was Soren Ballensted, who came in 1843 and who was followed by his brother Allie a few years later. In 1848 O. Torrison settled at Manitowoc Rapids, acting as a clerk in the mercantile business for some time. In that and the next year following the influx of Norwegians was great, many settling in the town of Liberty and Eaton, being the first to come to that region, while others remained in the village of Manitowoc. The first settlement in Eaton was by a Norwegian, O. Swenson, in 1849 although C. Eaton built a sawmill there soon after. Among the early settlers of Liberty were J. Stephenson, O. K. Gigstad and K. O. Oppen. As a sturdy and law abiding people they had no equal and much of the county's prosperity is due to their efforts. Another element in the immigration of the later forties were the Irish. The present towns of Maple Grove, Rockland, Cato, Meeme, Liberty and Franklin were largely settled by them during that period. Among the early settlers of Maple Grove were T. Morrissey. T. Watt and Ava Smith, the last named being an Englishman and enjoying the distinction of having named the township. He built a small house also in 1848 in what is now the town of Franklin and soon a large number of Irish settlers were grouped there, among them were P. Mullins, J. Doolan, J. Kirby and also William Playfair, a Scotchman. In Rockland D. B. Knapp was the first settler arriving in 1849, closely followed by J. Woodcock, L. Cooney and a large number of English families. At about the same time a large number of English pioneers, including William Eatough, James Robinson, C. Hall and J. Squirrel settled in Kossuth and the northern part of the town of Manitowoc. The northern part of Meeme was almost entirely an Irish community. The town was first settled by H. Edson in May 1847, he having been formerly a resident of Rapids, and among the early

Irish settlers were D. Nagle, Peter and Henry Mulholland J. Doolan and P. O'Shea. Scotch and English were scattered through the count in smaller numbers, most of them arriving between 1848 and 1853. French Canadians also came to the county and settled in and about Two Rivers.

The census of 1850 showed the population to be 3,720 of which 1378 were of German, 246 of Norwegian, 175 of Irish, 129 of British and 165 of Canadian birth, while there were in all 255 foreigners from other European states in the county. Of the native born inhabitants 409 were of Wisconsin and 376 of New York birth while 742 came from other states. The tremendous gain of 200 per cent. in numbers since 1847 shows the extent of immigration and also explains much of the activity of the later years. The division of the population among the then existing townships is also of interest, being as follows:—Cooperstown 84, Centerville 210, Manitowoc 766, Rapids 966, Meeme 210, Newton 522, Two Rivers 924.

It was in 1850 that the first scourge of cholera broke out in the county. The disease had been in evidence in Milwaukee the year before and it was in August of the following year that it appeared in Two Rivers. On Sunday August 5th, the Indians at that place had been having a celebration; the next day many fell sick and six died. Six more succumbed in another twenty-four hours and the bodies were hastily buried, all in one pit. Within a week the little settlement received three distinct shocks and out of three hundred people then living there fifty died while many more were taken ill. H. H. Smith, the father of the village, was himself stricken with the disease and a son died, as well as eight of his mill hands. The last shock occurred on Monday August 13th, when a boat was expected, upon which most of the surviving settlers prepared to embark. Its arrival was, however, delayed three days and as soon as it reached the dock, a stampede occurred, Mr. Smith furnishing the funds for the exodus of many of his employees, most of whom sought refuge at Sheboygan. The disease also spread to Manitowoc, where twenty-two settlers died and two Indians living near the Rapids also succumbed and were left unburied until H. F. Hubbard and Lyman Emerson volunteered to inter the corpses. On September 4, 1850 H. H. Smith had a notice, dated at Two Rivers, placed in the Sheboygan Mercury, which read as follows: "No new cases of cholera have occurred at this place for the last ten days. It may now be considered as healthy and all absent from the place may return with perfect safety." It was, however, several years before the village regained its former position. Four years later another siege of the plague was encountered and this time proved particularly virulent on the north side of the river at Manitowoc. The epidemic lasted four weeks and many died, including Judge Ezekiel Ricker and District Attorney James L. Kyle. The cemetery was then on Park Street and many were the new graves dug during those few terrible days. Doctor Preston was the only physician in the village and his faithful and wearing service during the panic was long remembered. Several also died of the disease in Kossuth and other portions of the county at this time. A village board of health, consisting of D. A. Reed, F. Langenfeld, G. Dusold, K. K. Jones, P. Glover and E. R. Smith, were appointed in July, but were unable with the means at hand to do much in combat of the deadly disease.

The growth of the county in population, so rapid from 1847 to 1850, continued unabated in the succeeding years. By 1855 the county numbered 13,050 inhabitants, a gain of 10,000 in five years. The influx of settlement was mainly made up of Germans, although many of the immigrants were Irish, Norwegian, Scotch and English. Then, too, another element was added by the entrance of the Bohemians on the field. The first of this race to come to the county was Michael Kellner, who purchased a home in the western part of the town of Kossuth in 1846. After working for some time as a tanner in Green Bay, spending an occasional Sunday at home, he built a tannery of his own at what later became Kellnersville, later adding a mill and store to his property. In 1852 fifteen Bohemian families settled there and soon after a Catholic church was started. A few years later another colony of Bohemians was established in the southern part of Kossuth and after a time large numbers of that race found their way to various parts of the county, notably Gibson, Two Creeks, Cooperstown and Manitowoc Rapids. A number of Welsh settlers also established themselves in the southern part of Meeme shortly before 1855. During the early fifties the first inhabitants of the present town of Schleswig made a settlement, among them being D. Able, after whom the town was in its first years of existence named and others. The village of Kiel dates from 1856, at which time the founders, H. F. Belitz and F. R. Gutheil purchased a large part of the present site. Clarks Mills was also established in the early fifties, the village growing up around the mill built there by Ira Clark. To show the rapidity of growth of the county's population it may be remarked that in 1854 three steamers alone brought two hundred immigrants from Buffalo. Accompanying this growth in settlement there was also a remarkable increase in the amount of agricultural products raised in Manitowoc, the wheat crop alone rising from 214 bushels in 1849 to 38415 bushels in 1855.

Village life was also progressing during this period. Manitowoc by 1855 had 2185 inhabitants, of which 1385 were of foreign birth. This was divided as follows: First ward, 1507, Second ward, 678, showing that the north side had by that time lost its earlier ascendency. The depression in the lumber trade, which the market experienced in 1851 and 1852 did not seem to affect local prosperity to any great extent and trade in many commodities showed a rapid increase. Even as late as 1851, however, the commerce of Manitowoc did not equal that of Two Rivers, the exports of the latter place in that year being $112,762 while those from Manitowoc were $72,122, the imports from Two Rivers being $106,721, while those into Manitowoc amounted to $115,010. This fact was largely due to the increasing industrialism at Two Rivers. Cyrus Whitcomb and Rufus Allen had organized the Wisconsin Leather Company in 1850 and an extensive tannery under the management of the former was soon in operation. In lumber also Two River's exportation was almost double that of Manitowoc, while that of shingles was about four times as large. Said J. Gregory in his book, Industrial Resources of

Wisconsin, published in 1853; "The lumber trade of Two Rivers must be considerable, when at a very early season 5,500 logs have been got out, ready to float down the river. When sawed, these will make ten million feet of lumber. Shingles and cedar posts to an enormous amount have been bought for the Chicago market, which depends entirely on other states for its supply of lumber." The population of the town of Two Rivers was 1852 in 1855, double that in 1850, although of course a part of this increase was outside the village, which at this time had not been set off from the town. On the other hand the village of Rapids had ceased to grow, the whole township gaining but 78 inhabitants in the five years elapsing between censuses. Neshoto, however, still retained its importance, the exports in 1854 from that village being 3,500,000 feet of lumber, 50,000 feet of lath, 400,000 feet of pickets, 850 cords shingle bolts, 24,000 railroad ties and 700,000 shingles. Mishicott also thrived, the mills of Messrs. Smith and Sprague doing a prosperous business. Branch was one of the villages that grew rapidly at this period, too, the mills of Charles McAllister and E. Lenaville being thriving institutions. The former was sold to the firm of Lee & Cain in 1854. At about this time mills were built at several other places in the county, and in 1853 the largest of these plants, that of B. Jones & Company, was constructed at Manitowoc, it employing fifty men.

The county cannot be said to have changed from a lumbering to an agricultural community until at least 1865. While of course before this time the farm land had gradually acquired greater and greater extent, the lumbering industry still led in point of financial returns and the county accordingly continued to be regarded as a source of supply. Thus from 1855 to 1860 the number of mills increased largely and many settlements grew up around them. This was true at Reedsville, where Klingholz, Reed and Stupecky built a mill in 1856 and at Cato where Lyon and Chamberlain started a similar enterprise. Other mills were started at Branch by Pierce and Slye, at Meeme by Weeks & Co., while Pierpont, Hall & Company bought up the Taylor and Pendleton interests at Two

Rivers, making them one of the largest lumber dealers in the county. The depression in the lumber trade in 1858 somewhat affected the county, but nevertheless a large increase in the amount of exports was noticeable all through the fifties, the county being the ninth in the state as regards this industry. In 1857 the total exportation of the product was 31,400,-000 feet, valued at $314,000, while as late as 1865 the exports of Two Rivers alone amounted to 12,255,737 feet. The timber supply was being rapidly depleted, however, and thus it was not many years before mill after mill ceased running and as time passed, only a few vestiges of the former industry remained.

Manitowoc County's population in 1860 was 22,412, the gain since 1855 having been somewhat smaller than in the preceding five years. Nearly one thousand of this increase had been in Manitowoc village, which now had a population of 3065, divided between three wards of 1051, 1109 and 905 inhabitants respectively. Two Rivers gained somewhat more slowly, registering 1340 inhabitants in its two wards. Large gains had been made in various of the rural townships also, notwithstanding many had been decreased in size by the setting off of new ones. In ten years also the acreage in improved lands had increased from 1122 to 26,177, while that of unimproved farm land had also risen from 6927 to 40,936, the total valuation reaching $801,102 in 1860 in comparison with $49,500 in 1850. Wheat was the leading product and according to the census of 1860 the total yield was 135,147 bushels, betokening a remarkable agricultural growth. Yet the fact that the county was largely in its original state is proved by the abundance of wild game, bears and deer being shot within a few miles of the lake shore hamlets. Due to the course of the war the increase of population from 1860 to 1865 was small, being but 4330, the inhabitants of the county in the latter year numbering 26,742, the village of Manitowoc including 3398 and that of Two Rivers 1300. But notwithstanding the war material progress here, as elsewhere at the North continued unabated. It wars at this period that the village of Two Creeks was founded due to the establishment of a tannery by G. Pfister & Co., at that place. The village of Kiel also prospered but seemed to be much more tributary to Sheboygan than to Manitowoc markets, due to better transportation facilities. Another Schleswig village, Rockville was also established, a grist mill being located there. In fact the grist mill at this time took the place of the lumber mill in many settlements, several being constructed in Manitowoc, Two Rivers, Mishicott and Rapids. In 1866 the village of Centerville was given birth, largely from the fact of the erection of a brewery by C. Scheibe, and the erection of a pier two years latter. Grimms station also dated from this period as does Tisch Mills. A large number of Bohemians and Norwegians poured into the county in the sixties and in the latter part of the decade the Poles commenced to arrive also, settling most largely in the southwestern part of Manitowoc, the village of Two Rivers and in the towns of Newton and Two Rivers. By 1870 the county's population had reached 33,369, of which 5168 was credited to Manitowoc and 1365 to Two Rivers, the latter place having received hardly any increase in ten years.

By 1875 the population of the county had increased to 38,456, a gain of over five thousand in five years. A large part of this growth was in the urban communities, the population of Manitowoc being 6724, and that of Two Rivers 1951 the increase being largely due to increase in manufacturing and the new railroad facilities offered by the Milwaukee, Lake Shore and Western. The latter also increased the importance of the little hamlets that happened to lie along its line, including Centerville, Newton, Branch. Cato, Grimms, Reedsville, and Pine Grove. Kiel was also given a healthy impetus by the Milwaukee and Northern, which was built at that time. In 1875 fully one-half of the population were foreign born although this percentage declined in later years. Strange to say the years 1875-1880 witnessed a decrease of 1050, the census of the latter year showing a population of 37,506. Most of this falling off was due to the movement westward on the part of the American settlers from various of the rural portions of the county. But the urban centers suffered also, Manitowoc losing 357 inhabitants, although Two Rivers gained a few, her population in 1880 amounting to 2052. Manitowoc suffered because of the removal of the railroad shops. Nevertheless by 1885 she had recovered herself, then having 6881 inhabitants. Two Rivers also gained, registering an increase of 512, while the county's population had increased to 38,692, although the migration westward continued. Many of the farms thus left idle were, however, bought up by foreign immigrants and the sum total of agriculturists was n)t decreased. Between 1885 and 1890 another decrease in the county's population was noticeable, it falling off to 37,831. although the inhabitants of Manitowoc and Two Rivers had increased to 7710 and 2870 respectively. This shows the decline of the agricultural community in a marked way. Nevertheless the amount raised was constantly increasing, while the horticultural and dairy interests became increasingly profitable. By 1895 the county was again seen to be gaining, the population being 40,802, most of this increase taking place in the two cities, Manitowoc having according to this census 9427 inhabitants and Two Rivers 3593. The gain continued in the succeeding five years, the last census of the nineteenth century giving the county's population as 42,261, of which the city of Manitowoc included 11,786 and Two Rivers 3784, while the villages of Kiel and Reedsville numbered 924 and 528 inhabitants respectively. The city of Manitowoc has expanded above all as a commercial and not as a manufacturing center. Two Rivers, on the other hand, has pursued the opposite line of developement, its manufactured products being great in quantity and of wide exportation. A comparative table of the products of the county according to each census will be found in appendix "A". Of the growth of the county's commercial and manufacturing interests the story is told later.

CHAPTER V.

MEANS OF COMMUNICATION.

Before a single white settler had made his habitation within the present confines of the county of Manitowoc it was traversed from north to south by many a pioneer. This was true because of an Indian trail, which existed as early as the twenties from the Milwaukee trading post to Green Bay. Later, when a regular mail carrier was placed on the Green Bay route, at times the Manitowoc road was used and sometimes that west of Lake Winnebago. With the influx of settlement this trail was more and more utilized and naturally it occurred to the settlers that the road should be improved. It was by this way that the Conroes secured their men and supplies from Green Bay. The condition of the thoroughfare in 1837 is described by a traveler in the Collections of the Wisconsin Historical Society as being most crude and unsatisfactory. For military reasons it was deemed advisable for a United States road to be built and reports were ordered from the government engineers as to the practicability of the improvement, upon resolution from Delegate Jones in Congress on December 26, 1836. Captain Cram in his report of January 30, 1840 recommended the continuance of the project, then already begun. He described the trail as the principal mail route east and south from Green Bay and told how the mail was carried on foot three times a week from that place to Milwaukee, a distance of 114 miles, remarking that it took four days to carry it from Green Bay to the southern boundary of the state. Fifteen thousand dollars was appropriated for the project in 1838, but it was not drawn upon until the next year due to difficulty experienced in surveying the route. Said Captain Cram in his report of 1840; "This road has been located nearly all the way through the greater part of its length, construction has commenced and it is expected that the contracts for cutting and clearing the road will be completed by the first of January next (1841)" The original estimated cost of the road entire from Milwaukee to Green Bay was $48,381, that of the section between Sheboygan Falls and Manitowoc Rapids, twenty nine miles in length, including the building of 67 bridges and culverts, being $5941.85, while that of the section between Manitowoc Rapids and Green Bay, thirty-four miles in length and necessitating 34 bridges and culverts was $6774.71. At first there was no settlement between these two points and it was impossible before the road was improved to drive a two-wheeled vehicle north of Milwaukee. When completed the road was the principal means of communication by land to the outside world and upon it all mails were carried. It was not a pretentious highway. being but four rods wide and banked in the middle to the width of but one rod. Due to mismanagement much work was wasted, planks lying on the side of the road rotting, when they should have been used in the road itself. The bridges, too, were not completed as required by the estimates. Settlement gradually spread along the thoroughfare but at first it was slow, as late as 1846 the only stops on the section between Rapids and Green Bay being a little tavern at French Creek and two taverns, kept by Joseph Alle and Clifford King about half way on the route.

This government enterprise, important as it was, could not meet the local needs of the settlers and even before it was built the latter had taken steps towards securing lines of communication. The territorial legislature in December of 1838 passed a bill, whose object it was to lay out and establish a road "from the town of Manitowoc on Lake Michigan to Manitowoc Rapids, thence to Thayer's mills on the best and most direct route", and thence to Clifton on Lake Winnebago, B. Jones, Pliny Pierce and Horace Conroe being chosen commissioners to lay it out. Although a rough trail connected the first two places, the county board also took up the matter at its first meeting, and on March 15, 1839, it appointed John Watson, Horace Conroe and J. G. Conroe commissioners to survey the route. The road was soon built as far as Murphy's Mills above the Rapids, being constructed north of the river, it now being known as the River Road. In the same year a road was being considered by the board, from Manitowoc to Two Rivers, but was not built for some months. At the legislative session of 1839, three territorial roads were mapped out, the first being from the mouth of the Manitowoc River to Green Bay, B. Jones, P. Pierce and J. G. Knapp being chosen commissioners; the second from Manitowoc Rapids to Sheboygan Falls, David Giddings and Charles Cole of Sheboygan and Hiram McAllister of Rapids being appointed commissioners, and the third from Rapids to the Fox River, Horace Conroe being one of the commissioners. The first two were made unnecessary by the U. S. Road soon after built, although the road was not chopped through to Sheboygan until 1843, Joseph La Counte being the contractor. The third project never advanced beyond an incipient stage. In 1839 J. W. Conroe had been appointed county road superintendent, but at the January meeting of the board the county was divided into three districts, the first under S. C. Chase, the second under D. S. Munger and H. McAllister and the third under J. G. Conroe. A few months later it was decided to build a county road from Two Rivers to Neshoto, thence to connect with the United States road, and it was constructed under the guidance of R. M. Eberts, S. C. Chase and A. Richardson. Roads between Manitowoc and Two Rivers and from Manitowoc to the United States road were also built in 1841.

Then followed a long period of inaction, which the stationary condition of the county's population necessitated. It was in 1846 that the next action was taken, which commenced the history of the second important thoroughfare of the county, the Calumet Road. The legislature in February of that year appointed Paul Champlin, E. L. Abbott and P. Pierce to lay out a territorial road from the town of Manitowoc "to intersect at such point or place as such commissioners may select or determine, the U. S. road leading from Green Bay to Fond du Lac". The survey took place in the fall, Perry Smith acting as one of the party. As a public road the project was not pushed, although Stockbridge was fixed as the western terminus. In 1850 the legislature incorporated a company to carry out the project, known as the Calumet Plank Road Company with $100,000 capital, among the incorporators being H. H. Champlin, A. McNulty, O. C. Hubbard and P. Pierce. On Februry 12, 1851, a public meeting was held at the Merchants Exchange Hotel and the next month the stock books were opened for subscriptions. Although a mail carrier was placed on the proposed route during the summer, the work of construction was delayed. It was, however, partially built during that year and A. Baensch, A. McNulty and C. Eaton were chosen commissioners to improve it in 1852. The legislature of the next year amended the charter so as to permit the towns along the route to assist in building the road, and in 1855 the time of completion was extended two years, and S. A. Wood, C. W. Fitch, W. Bach and J. Lueps were added to the list of commissioners. Chilton residents were interested in the project and meetings were held there as well as in Manitowoc during the succeeding years. Finally in 1856 a fresh incorporation took place, K. K. Jones, G. Kremers, T. Clark, H. Berners, and W. Bach representing the county and in a few years the latter assumed charge of the thoroughfare.

Another project was launched February 11, 1847, when the legislature appointed Evander M. Soper, Loyal H. Jones and James D. Doty to lay out a territorial road from Manitowoc to Winnebago Rapids, later known as Menasha. This, too, as a state enterprise, lapsed, and the next year the Neenah and Manitowoc Plankroad Company was organized by Harrison Reed. George W. Lawe, Charles Doty and Cornelius Northrup of Neenah and E. M. Soper of Manitowoc as incorporators. The capital stock was fixed at $200,000, made up of ten dollar shares and a board of directors were to be chosen annually. In that year and again in 1850 Congress was appealed to for aid and books were opened for public subscriptions early in the latter year. By the end of that year five miles of the Manitowoc end had been completed, although the whole distance was forty miles. A state road was also projected to Menasha, via Stockbridge, in 1850 and D. B. Knapp, D. W. Halstead and D. H. Whitney were chosen commissioners but the plan did not materialize sufficiently to militate against the private enterprise. George Reed was made secretary of the latter company and work was pushed late into the winter of 1850-1851. The Evening Wisconsin of June 10, 1852 contained the following item, "G. Reed, Esq., passed through this city Saturday, on his return from the east, where he has successfully negotiated the funds of the Manitowoc and Menasha Plank Road Company. The road will be completed forthwith." It was not, however, although towns which it was purposed to traverse were given authorization to vote aid to the company, and forty men were placed at work, a steam mill being erected to furnish the planks. The project clashed somewhat with the Manitowoc and Mississippi Railroad and George Reed's interest in it was one of the reasons leading to discord in the railway management. Annual elections were held by the road company, H. McAllister being president for some time, but the highway was not pushed much beyond the McAllister farm, near the intersection with the Green Bay road, although the way opened was made a toll road. The thoroughfare, however, was completed during the latter fifties by the county through Branch Cato and Reedsville, touching several important mills, and from time to time commissioners were appointed to see to its maintenance, while later a state road from Maple Grove to Appleton was made to connect with it. In 1862 the legislature reduced the number of directors to three and three years later authority to lease or sell the property of the company was given. Daniel S. Conley purchased its rights in 1866. and maintained the piece of road for many years, but in 1899 the county board bought the thoroughfare for $4,000, this being one of the last toll roads in the county to be purchased.

In the later forties and early fifties other roads were also projected and the county built bridges at Two Rivers, Manitowoc and Manitowoc Rapids. Among the former projects was the territorial road, authorized in 1848 from Port Wash-

HENRY MULHOLLAND, Sr.

ington to Manitowoc, of which E. M. Soper was chosen a commissioner, but it was not built at that time. On February 9, 1850, the Manitowoc and Manitowoc Rapids Plankroad Company was organized with a capital stock of $10,000, the incorporators being Alden Clark, P. Pierce, O. C. Hubbard, T. A. H. Edwards, E. H. Ellis, R. Klingholz, T. A Baker, Martin Heywood, T. Fenton and M. S. Morse. During the next two years this company constructed a plank road on the south side of the river, known as the South River Road, it being completed in the summer of 1852 and thus affording a second means of communication between the two villages. It later became a county road. In the same year, 1850, the Two Rivers and Green Bay Plankroad Company was formed by H. H. Smith, C. P. Daggett, H. C. Hamilton, of Two Rivers, D. Smith of Mishicott and four Green Bay men, with a capital stock of $100,000. This was considered an urgent necessity, although some dispute arose as to where it should connect with the U. S. road. The subscription books for this project were opened July 15, 1851 and by August 1852 nearly $14,000 had been subscribed, but although a mail line was established between the termini, the company was not successful in its projects. In 1850 Assemblyman Malmros had presented pepetitions for a state road between Manitowoc and Two Rivers, but this not being forthcoming, a private corporation was organized two years later and a charter secured. The promoters were C. W. Fitch, J. H. W. Colby, C. Esslinger, J. Edwards, S. A. Wood, R. E. Glover, P. P. Smith, W. Rahr, and P. Glover of Manitowoc and C. Kuehn, H. H. Smith, V. Kaufmann, A. Lamere and H. C. Hamilton of Two Rivers, the capital stock being fixed at $5,000. A toll road was built and maintained, albeit not as well as it might have been, until 1876 when the legislature authorized its purchase by the two towns of Manitowoc and Two Rivers, upon the payment of $800. The inroads made by the lake in the nineties upon this road, where it crossed the Little Manitowoc, occasioned much trouble, the town authorities being obliged to build a breakwater. Four years after the incorporation of the road three of its promotors, P. Glover, H. H. Smith and H. C.

Hamilton joined with Chauncey Gilbert, W. Boot, Alfred Smith, Daniel Smith, L. S. House and R. Klingholz in forming the Two Rivers and Mishicott Plankroad Company with a capital of $10,000, which was maintained as a private enterprise for some years. The year 1852 also witnessed the incorporation of the Manitowoc and Green Bay Plankroad Company by James Bennett, A. W. Preston, A. Baensch, O. Koch, J. E. Platt, G. Othersoll, J. H. Jerome, G. Bennett, J. Spencer, J. C. Leist, H. Riley, J. Praquin, J. Alle and Clifford King of Manitowoc County and H. S. Baird, A. G. Ellis and John Day of Green Bay. The purpose was to connect with the old U. S. road and to repair the latter, and the capital was fixed at $100,000, which led to the construction of the Town Line road. A second corporation of the same name was chartered in 1870, among the promotors being Richard Klingholz of Manitowoc. The charter was repealed, however, three years later, this being the last enterprise of the kind organized in the county.

In 1855 H. F. Belitz of Kiel was one of the commissioners to lay out a state road from the town of Herman, Sheboygan county, to Menasha, touching the southwestern part of this county. At about the same time S. Blake, R. Wheeler, A. Buchanan, Jr., and J. M. Sherwood, were authorized to lay out a state road from Depere to Manitowoc and a similar line of travel from De Pere to Two Rivers was proposed. A year later the North River Road which was extended to Clarks Mills was in need of repair and D. B. Knapp, T. C. Cunningham and C. Gustaveson were chosen by the legislature to superintend the reconstruction. As early as 1851 a memorial had been presented to that body for a state road from Two Rivers to the Door Peninsula and six years later one was authorized to be built to Big Sturgeon Bay, S. B. Sherwood and F. Walsh representing Manitowoc county. In 1859 another route was authorized from Mishicott to Ahnapee, Manitowoc being represented on the board of commissioners by J. N. Struthers and J. Killen. H. Schlichting of Kiel was a commissioner of a state project for connection between Kiel and Fond du Lac at about the same time. During the sixties road building was chiefly directed to schemes in the southwesterly portion of the county. On April 15, 1861 the Chilton and Manitowoc Plankroad Company was organized by Calumet county men with a capital of $200,000 and townships were authorized to aid the project. Immediately after the war a state road was ordered laid out between Kiel and Manitowoc, W. Bach, A. Krieger and P. P. Fuessenich acting as commissioners and another from Manitowoc to Taychedah, via Kiel, H. F. Belitz being one of the incorporators. It was the failure of the latter project that caused the incorporation of a private company in 1870, the Manitowoc and Kiel Plankroad Company by J. Schuette, T. Windiate, R. H. Hoes, H. Berners, C. Gustaveson, S. Samuelson, A. Schad and E. B. Treat, with a capital stock of $30,000. The days of plank roads and private enterprises were soon over, however, and one by one these were incorporated by county or township, both these units now having full charge and maintenance of all the thoroughfares of the county. The Kiel and Sheboygan turnpike was the last to be made free, the event occurring in 1900.

Closely connected with road building as a means of communication was the development of the postal service and mail routes. As was said before the old Green Bay trail was the first mail route in the county. Before 1840 J. G. Conroe and later T. Baker were postmasters at the Rapids, then the only office in the county. their successors being P. Pierce, O. C. Hubbard, J. P. Champlin, E. H. Ellis and E. D. Beardsley, who held office during the forties and fifties. In nine months of 1840 the total income of the Manitowoc postoffice was only $57.56, of which half went as compensation to the postmaster. In 1847 the Manitowoc postoffice was established, J. H. Colby being appointed postmaster. Francis Flinn and Henry Edwards carried the mail from the south during these early days, trudging the weary distance to Green Bay on foot. When night overtook Flinn he would pursue his lonely journey with a lighted lantern swinging from side to side. and once he made the trip from Rapids to Green Bay and return without sleep. He passed away February 22, 1855 at the age of fifty-six years, one of the picturesque figures of pioneer days. For many years there were but three postoffices in the county, Manitowoc, Manitowoc Rapids and Two Rivers. Among the first postmasters in the forties at the last named place were Andrew J. Vieau and H. H. Smith. One Oscar Burdicke carried the mail in 1846 from Manitowoc to Two Rivers, his compensation being the revenue of the route. In 1846 Meeme was added with Henry B. Edson as its first postmaster and later in the year Cooperstown also, A. A. Cooper being the first official at the office, which was at that time in Brown county. With the addition of these two new offices new mail routes were made necessary and were accordingly put in operation. In 1851 routes from Manitowoc to Green Bay via Two Rivers and Mishicott and from Manitowoc to Stockbridge were added, while the next summer daily mails were instituted by boat from Chicago to Manitowoc. At about the same time the government was memorialized to change the Green Bay route back to the original road through Francis Creek and the line was later re-established. The anxiety of the inhabitants for mail facilities was manifested by frequent petitions sent Congress during the next year, including requests for lines from DePere to Manitowoc, by way of Morrison, Brown County, from Chilton to Manitowoc, from Sheboygan to Chilton by way of Schleswig and from Mishicott to Door county. In the course of time all of these lines and many others were established.

J. H. Colby, Manitowoc's first postmaster was succeeded by James L. Kyle, a Whig appointee, the office being located in the store of J. E. Platt at the corner of North Seventh and Commercial streets. James Bennett was Kyle's successor and he in turn gave way to S. A. Wood who surrendered the place in 1857 to A. Wittmann, President Buchanan's appointee. During Wood's administration the office was at the corner of Franklin and Eighth streets, but later was removed to the present site of the Victoria Hotel. From 1854 the establishment of postoffices in the county was rapid. In June of that year P. M. Falrich was appointed the first postmaster at Mishicott; in August the Maple Grove post office was opened with Joseph H. Cheney as postmaster and in October Branch P. O. at McAllister's Mills, W. R. Williams being the first postmaster. In August 1855 Newton P. O. was established, John Meyer being appointed to the place, followed by that at Oslo the same year and in January 1856 by the offices at Eaton, Niles, Francis Creek and Centerville. In the next ten years offices were opened also at Larrabee, Paquette, Clarks Mills, Hika, Kasson, Kiel, Mosfield, Neshoto, Reedsville, Rosecrans and Two Creeks. The postoffice at Oslo was abolished in 1860 but re-established ten years later. Among the early postmasters at Two Rivers were B. J. Van Valkenburgh, C. P. Daggett, P. Phillipps and A. Bemis. William Conine became postmaster in 1870 and remained so until his death in 1885. At Manitowoc Charles Esslinger was appointed in 1861 to succeed Wittmann and held the office twenty-five years. At first the office was at the corner of South Seventh and Franklin Streets but in 1866 a small building was erected on South Eighth street near the bridge for its occupancy, in which it remained until the new brick structure it now occupies was finished in 1891. As to mail facilities many were the complaints in the latter fifties and early sixties. Particularly was this true in the winter, when the stoppage of lake navigation well nigh shut Manitowoc out of the world. Even as late as 1866 but three mails a week were received from Milwaukee, one from Menasha and three from Appleton, stage lines carrying them. A new line was placed in operation to Menasha in 1863 by Thomas Windiate, while Davis and More operated the lake shore stage for many years.

In the latter sixties the postoffices of East Gibson, Mann's Landing, Elk, Nero, Prag and Wayside were established, three of which, Prag, Elk and Mann's Landing were in later years discontinued, as was also Mosfield P. O. In the early seventies the building of the M. L. S. & W. greatly increased mail facilities, the route being at first to Milwaukee via Appleton. The growth of the newer portions of the county also called for the establishment of new offices, including Cato, King's Bridge, Northeim, Kellnersville, Millhome and later Grimms, Greenstreet, Steinthal, Tisch Mills,

Osman, Louis Corners, St. Wendel, School Hill, Timothy, Rangeline, Taus and others, some of which were abolished after a few years of existence. In 1885 under a Democratic administration, A. Piening became postmaster at Manitowoc succeeding Esslinger and U. Niquette succeeded Mr. Conine at Two Rivers. Postmaster Piening in turn gave way to Judge R. D. Smart, a Republican, in 1890, but that gentleman died in June, his wife remaining in charge of the office until 1894. At Two Rivers W. Hurst followed Postmaster Niquette, giving way to George Wehausen in 1894, who in turn resigned in favor of Frank Riley four years later. Free delivery was instituted in Manitowoc on March 15, 1893, three carriers being utilized, the number being later increased by three. Henry Vits became postmaster in 1894 and after four years was succeeded by H. G. Kress. The growth of the local business was very rapid during this later period, having increased from $7809.79 in 1889 to $14,326.92 in 1899. Among the new offices established in the county during this decade were Collins, Eastwin, Zander, Melnik, Stark, Cleveland, Valders, Whitelaw, Wells, Menchalville, Clover, Rief, Quarry and Bleser. On March 15, 1900, the first rural mail delivery in the county was established with John Houghton as carrier, the route being westerly from the city and south of the river. Six other lines were planned and instituted within a few months, three diverging from Manitowoc, one from Kiel, one from Valders and one from Cleveland.

Another means of communication, which is of importance is the telephone and telegraph. Early in the sixties a telegraph line to Green Bay had been proposed and partly established but was later abandoned. In December 1864, however, the poles and wires for a line to Milwaukee were put in by the United States Telegraph Company and the connection was made February 1865. The first message was sent by Editor Crowley of the Pilot to Editor Robinson of the Green Bay Advocate in the following words: "The Pilot's compliments to the Advocate and is happy to be connected by telegraph." To which a reply was made: "Here is to you by telegraph. Let the old Advocate and Pilot have a social bumper together. The world moves." Later telegraph lines followed the extension of the railroads and soon also telephone lines were placed in operation, the first being the Wisconsin Telephone Company. When the Bell patents expired, however, independent companies were possible and in the nineties a system of connections were made, touching nearly every village and hamlet in the county, The Manitowoc and Western Telephone Company, being particularly energetic in this regard.

Allied to the movements, whose object it was to extend means of communication, were those which aimed to reclaim the waste swamp lands in the western part of the county. These lands were largely in the towns ot Eaton, Liberty, Franklin, Rockland and Maple Grove. Much of it was sold in the fifties and made tillable by private enterprise but it was seen that this was not a rapid or a profitable method so the state took a hand. Certain sums were set apart by it from the proceeds of swamp land sales as a drainage fund. In 1859 this fund amounted to $1575 for the county and the average per year was about that sum. The legislature in 1860 passed an act for the disposal of the fund in the repairing of roads and bridges under the direction of the county supervisors. Two years later drainage commissioners were authorized to be appointed for Calumet and Manitowoc counties and the funds to be used for draining certain lands designated. A year later the swamp lands were granted to the county and the supervisors were directed to elect a commissioner to hold office for four years, he, with the Calumet county commissioner, to superintend the expenditure of the drainage fund. In 1865 this act was repealed and a joint board of commissioners from the two counties provided for. Another alteration took place in 1866, the legislature granting fresh lands to the counties, M. Mahoney and J. C. Eggers being selected to represent Manitowoc county and W. Watrous Calumet county. The committee met at Clark's Mills on July 11, but refused to accept the grant from the state, although it was found that about 21,000 acres, worth then only 40 cents an acre, might become areable at a small expense. A year later D. B. Knapp, L. Faulhaber and P. Brennan were created trustees of the land in question, together with O. R. Potter and A. Watrous of Calumet county, by whom the lands were administered until 1870. Mr. Potter was very active in the work and devised extensive plans for the utilization of the swamp along the course of the river. At about this time a dam was placed in the river at Cato and this raised the water so much that much of the reclaimed land was damaged greatly. The farmers under the lead of Captain Potter tore out the dam and this proceeding, oft repeated, finally induced the owners to secure an injunction against them. After some years, in which unsuccessful efforts were made to buy the water power out, a bill passed the legislature authorizing the removal of the obstruction. In 1873 W. Carey succeeded P. Brennan as a trustee from Manitowoc county and T. Kerstens of Calumet and A. Piening of Manitowoc were added. New commissioners were chosen in 1874, those from Manitowoc being J. Behnke, J. Franz and Ira Clark, Behnke being succeeded by J. Halloran three years later and J. Stephenson being added in 1878. In 1883 the trust created in the commissioners was terminated by the legislature and the lands left undisposed of were authorized to be drained and sold, power being given to the commissioners to carry out the provisions of the act. Since this did not prove an altogether successful means of disposing of the subject eight years later a bill was enacted, under which those land owners who might be benefited by the drainage of lands, could borrow money from the trust funds of the state, the act being applied to residents of the towns of Eaton, Cato and Rockland. Finally in 1893 it was provided that whenever twenty-five owners petitioned for the appointment of a drainage commissioner such an officer should be appointed by the circuit judge. This drainage movement meant much in the development of the western part of the county and there are still funds in the state treasury, ready to be devoted to this purpose.

## CHAPTER VI.

### MARINE.

Situated as it is upon the lake, one of the most important phases of Manitowoc county history is that of its harbors, lake commerce and transportation facilities. This is particularly true in regard to the city of Manitowoc, since it may be said in all truth that its position on the lake has enabled the town to become the thriving center it now is, and how important has been the result of this natural and advantageous outlet upon the back country is beyond calculation. The subject of marine history, as taken up in this chapter, naturally subdivides itself in the following subheads:—Harbor development, transportation facilities and shipbuilding and marine disasters. This line of division, then, will be followed.

#### HARBOR DEVELOPMENT.

There are within the county two harbors, those of Manitowoc and Two Rivers. Besides these two other points, Two Creeks and Centerville, capable of limited development, have undergone some improvement under private initiative. Chief among all, of course, in natural advantage is that of Manitowoc, situated, as it is, about eighty miles north of Milwaukee in the recesses of a wide and deep bay, offering safe anchorage without artificial protection and occupying a position where boats from the lower lakes begin to near the shore. Its natural advantages were early recognized and there is no doubt that even in the early thirties schooners sought shelter in the bay. That the reputation of the harbor was good from the first, is attested by an extract from a letter written to the New York Courier and Express in 1865 as follows: "I was told last August on my approach to this place, by an old and experienced navigator of the lakes, Captain Chamberlain of the steamer Lady Elgin, that Manitowoc was the only point on the west side of Lake Michigan, where there was any real safety for vessels in a southwest gale." It is not then remarkable that the efforts of improvement should have begun almost coincident with the first settlement of the county. The message of the first governor of the territory in 1836 suggested "the propriety of asking Congress for an appropriation sufficient to cover the expenses of surveying all the necessary harbors on Lake Michigan and the construction of lighthouses and harbors." In answer to this suggestion the legislature did ask Congress in that year (1836) for an appropriation of $25,000 for Manitowoc and $6,400 for TwinRivers as it was then called. In January 1837 a resolution was presented in Congress by Delegate Tweedy, then representing Wisconsin Territory, requesting the survey of the "Manitowoc, Sheboygan and Ioway rivers" and a Senate resolution to the same effect was offered later. The result was the report of Engineer John M. Berrien submitted to the War Department in October, 1837, and brought before Congress at its December session. Manitowoc was one of the five harbors examined and of it he said: "I have the honor to transmit to you the map and report of the Manitowoc River, together with an estimate for its improvement. The Manitowoc, which ranks next in size to the Milwaukee river upon the western shore of Lake Michigan, has its source within six or seven miles of Lake Winnebago in a low and marshy country. It is occasionally broken by rapids, as it approaches Lake Michigan, but it is supposed to offer by far the most direct and practicable route for communication between the waters of Lakes Michigan and Winnebago. The rapids offer no serious obstacle and above these the stream is represented as deep and sluggish. Its valley is fertile and abounds in valuable timber of all kinds, especially pine. It empties itself into Lake Michigan about twenty-five miles north of the mouth of the Sheboygan and is the first point north of it capable of improvement. A reference to the map will show that it is peculiarly adapted to improvement, compared with mouths of streams generally. Its discharge is direct and but little obstructed by bars. There appears to be no deposit of any amount by the stream; the bar indicated upon the map being formed by the wash of the lake. Should the contemplated improvements upon the river be made, rendering the means of communication with Lake Winnebago, its commercial importance would be much increased, but its value as a refuge for the shipping of the lake is alone sufficient to warrant the improvements. It is proposed in the accompanying plan to carry the piers into the lake to fourteen feet water, where they are strengthened by pier heads. The mode of construction, which experience has proved to be capable of resisting all storms upon the lake is minutely represented by the accompanying drawings. Within the piers the channel is to be dredged to a depth of ten feet. As no work of any extent has yet been made at this point the precise cost of materials is difficult to arrive at, but it is believed that those adopted are sufficiently liberal. Timber of all kinds is found near at hand and in the greatest abundance. I know of no stone quarry in the immediate neighborhood as much search has not yet been made, but I have no doubt that, on a more careful examination, sufficient will be found within a reasonable distance." The specifications accompanying this report went into details as to the mode of piers to be built, the amount of dredging necessary, the cost of labor, etc., the final conclusion being that the entire cost of the improvement at Manitowoc would necessitate the expenditure of $82,979.44, while similar plans proposed for Sheboygan and Kewaunee were even more costly.

No action, however, resulted from these recommendations although memorials and petitions kept pouring in. Delegate G. W. Jones on Dec. 28, 1838 presented a memorial to Congress for the improvement of the Manitowoc, Twin and Sheboygan rivers and on the same day offered a resolution asking for further surveys. The only practical result gained in these years was the erection of a brick lighthouse near the harbor mouth at Manitowoc, constructed in 1840, among the first keepers being Peter Johnson and M. Burlingame. On January 24, 1840, the legislature presented an appeal asking for $30,000 for Manitowoc, saying; "Manitowoc and Sheboygan, situated north of Milwaukee, are each places of considerable importance, possessing a water power which furnishes three or four millions of feet of lumber annually. This lumber is all taken on board of vessels by means of lighters at great risk and expense." The bar at the river mouth gave much difficulty and in 1843 P. P. Smith, then a lad, spent three days in scraping the sand away sufficiently to permit of the entrance of the schooner Solomon Juneau. In 1844 another survey was made but still no action followed. It was March 5th of the same year that Delegate Henry Dodge presented a petition of 76 citizens of the territory of Wisconsin asking Congress for an appropriation for a harbor at the town of "Manitowic on the western shores of Lake Michigan." It was in that year that Racine and Southport (Kenosha) secured their first appropriations. When Delegate Dodge became governor in his first message delivered in 1846 he touched upon Manitowoc's needs as follows: "Estimates have been made under direction of the War Department for the harbors at the mouth of the Manitowoc and Sheboygan Rivers, where towns have been commenced and are increasing in commercial importance, and the country settling rapidly in the interior with enterprising inhabitants, who merit the aid that can be derived from the most secure navigation of the lakes." In December of the same year through Delegate Tweedy, citizens of Wisconsin again prayed for the construction of a harbor at the mouth of the Manitowoc river and in fact an item for the project was included in the harbor bill of that year, which was vetoed.

Private enterprise had, in the failure of government aid, not been absent during this time. In 1843 a bridge pier was extended out into the lake at the foot of what is now Franklin street and was long maintained by the firm of Case & Clark, being sold in April, 1852 to Edwin C. Hubbard, by whom it was used in the forwarding business for many years. Disgust and exasperation at the delay of Congress in improving Wisconsin harbors rapidly increased. Said the engineer's report in 1847, speaking of Manitowoc and Sheboygon: "Nothing has been done at either but to make surveys, plans and estimates. These harbors are extremely essential to the commerce of the lakes as steamboats after leaving the Manitou Islands make for the western shore of the lake but at the present time find no harbor or port of refuge short of Milwaukee, 160 miles distant from the islands by the shortest line." The legislature again memorialized Congress in 1850 and in December of that year the Weekly Herald remarked tersely: "The schooner E. Henderson beat about the bay two days before getting in. She succeeded at last, -- no thanks to Congress." Two years passed, however, without any move being made. By that time citizens were seeing the absolute need of better facilities, and decided to make a start, at least, themselves. Thus at a meeting held in January 1852 the villagers resolved to raise $15,000 by a loan, levying a tax of one per cent to m et the interest. They applied to the legislature for the desired permission, which was granted and by the same act the office of harbor master was created, while the body also memorialized Congress to add $25,000 to the sum to be raised by the locality. The Milwaukee Wisconsin in commenting on the action said: "The commencement of a harbor will be more likely to aid in obtaining an appropriation from the general government, which we trust it may be the good fortune to get this very session." The wish was realized in a limited manner for in that year Congress did grant $8,000, scarcely enough to commence work, although it had as an effect the failure of the village to appropriate the money voted by it. In this year also Two Rivers secured a lighthouse the property being bought of H. H. Smith and he doiug the work of construction. A further survey of Manitowoc harbor was taken in 1852 and under the supervision of Temple Clark, the local agent and U. S. Engineer Graham the work proceeded. Since the plans called for an expenditure of $60,000 it is easily seen that the sum actually expended did not go far, merely paying for the laying of a few cribs and the dredging of a twelve foot channel. In 1853 the legislature had asked for $15,000 in order that the work might be continued but no further aid was forthcoming, notwithstanding frequent efforts to that end. An appropriation of $12,500 failed of passage in 1855; another in 1856 shared the same fate. In February of the same year Senator Dodge asked leave to introduce separate bills for Manitowoc, Sheboygan, Milwaukee, Racine and Kenosha, and such leave being granted, the share of Manitowoc was fixed at $12,500. Senator Seward offered an amendment, striking out that sum and inserting $62,780.92, in order that the entire project might be completed. This was agreed to but the bill in its final form failed to become a law. In 1858 a special appropriation for Manitowoc was introduced by Congressman Billingshurst but it was pigeon-holed. Thus it came to pass that no further action was taken by the government in improving Manitowoc harbor until after the civil war, as that conflict during its progress put a damper on all projects of such a nature.

Manitowoc was made a port of entry in 1854, C. W. Fitch being chosen the first deputy collector and a fog bell was placed at the river mouth during the same year. That fall Col. K. K. Jones began the construction of what was known as the north pier at the foot of Chicago Street. It was 950 feet in length and was built by Capt. Rouse at a cost of $6000. Mr. Jones continued to run the pier until 1861, when he sold it to Peter Johnston. A bridge pier was also built at Two Rivers in 1854. With these limited facilities, two bridge piers, a lighthouse and a shallow channel, citizens of Manitowoc began to wake up to the importance of action and had it not been for the war something might have been done much sooner. The Pilot estimated that the village had lost in the single year, 1860, by not having a harbor, the sum of $150,000. It was this feeling that prompted a harbor meeting, called February 5, 1861. S. A. Wood officiated as president, C. Esslinger was secretary, while remarks were made by H. Berners, P. P. Smith and A. C. Pool. It was decided to appoint a committee, consisting of J. Bennett, H. McAllister, H. Berners. S. A. Wood and H. Mulholland, Sr., to draw up a bill authorizing the county to raise a harbor tax of $30,000. At another meeting held in April much discussion over the proposed bill took place, Assemblyman Joseph Stephenson opposing it strenuously, being ably assisted by Assemblyman Graves of Calumet county, both of whom represented the inland interests. The matter remained in abeyance until January 1864 when another meeting was held to discuss the same project. In Jahuary 1865 the village board petitioned the legislature to allow the town to raise $60,000, the result being that on March 11 the latter body did pass a law authorizing the village to issue $30,000 in bonds at seven per cent., running twenty years, to be paid in taxation. The bond issue was to be voted on at a special election, which was not to take place unless the county, excluding the towns of Two Rivers and Two Creeks voted a like amount for the same purpose. Harbor commissioners were named by this act as follows:—J. Vilas, H. Berners, Jacob Grimm, F. R. Gutheil, Ira P. Smith, Hansen Rand and J. Taugher, representing the various portions of the county, these men being empowered to choose a superintendent of the work. Construction was to cease in case the national government appropriated a sufficient amount to complete the work. The plan came to naught, however, since the village board refused to allow the matter to be voted upon, claiming that taxation and not a bond issue was desired, although for this decision the members were roundly scored. In 1866 the legislature amended the act materially. The town of Manitowoc was by the later law permitted to raise during the years 1867 1868, and 1869, $20,000 annually. The terms were much the same as that of the preceeding act, although in this instance the board of harbor commissioners was to consist of eight members, viz. J. Vilas, T. C. Shove, Charles Luling, Jacob Halverson, John Schuette, H. Berners, W. Rahr and H. Becker. Application was made for government aid and the money was to be expended under the advice of the government engineers. Another act permitted any town by a majority vote to raise not more than $1000 annually for harbor improvement during the same three years, but this was repealed the next year. The town of Kossuth, however, did vote in favor of a $3000 tax in April. The election in the town of Manitowoc was held on February 13, and resulted in an overwhelming majority of 304 out of 392 votes cast, in favor of the proposition.

The government in the meantime had again taken a hand. In 1865 Congress had been memorialized by the state legislature to continue improvement at Manitowoc, "the most accessable and surest harbor on the coast." In 1866 an extensive harbor bill had been prepared and was passed, one of the items being $52,000 for Manitowoc. Col. Sitgreaves arrived in the city in April to survey the harbor and the government soon advised the citizens to utilize the $20,000, raised by taxation in the construction of a dredge and in preparing the channel, the harbormasters acting on the suggestion. The dredge was built and in the spring of 1867 the government began to get the material ready for the work, the actual construction being begun in June at the north side of the river entrance. The original plan of Major Wheeler, prepared in 1866, was to extend two parallel piers to twelve foot water and this was made possible by liberal appropriations in 1867, 1868 and 1869, it being completed in 1871. The legislature repealed further authorization of special village taxes in 1867 but from that time much money was nevertheless spent in dredging, in 1867 47,070 cubic yards being excavated, in 1869 20,000, in 1870 19,000, in 1871 18,000, in 1872 41,490, in 1873 33,665 and in 1874 32,700. Docks were also put in along the lower river frontage at a cost to the abutting property holders and to the city of $50,000, an amendment to the village charter in 1868 having given the latter power to enforce docking and dredging. The new piers were so far advanced by 1871 that the old bridge piers were abondoned and dismantled. In this period great gratitude was felt by the citizens towards Senator S. O. Howe and Congressman Philetus H. Sawyer for their championship of the harbor and their assistance in securing appropriations .J. D. Markham went to Washington in 1868 also to assist in interesting the national authorities in Manitowoc, while the harbor commissioners as a whole were most active in their co-operation until 1870, when they were dissolved as a corporate body and their powers transferred to the board of aldermen. The first city chart-

EDWARD SALOMON

er conferred extensive harbor powers upon the latter body, provided for a harbor master and through a later amendment permitted of municipal dredging projects.

In 1872 the channel had reached a depth of thirteen feet and Engineer Houston, then in charge, estimated the cost of an eighteen foot channel at over $75,000. It was in this year also that a breakwater was suggested as a means of deadening the effects of the swell up river. From 1870 to 1880 the government appropriated $100,500 and cribs were sunk at the rate of four or five a year until in 1879 the north pier was 1620 feet long and the south pier, commenced eleven years before, was 1550 feet in length. From 1879 to 1881 one hundred feet were added and the plan to make the depth 13 feet with 18 feet at the entrance was carried out. A change in the project occurred in 1881, it being decided to extend the piers to 18½ feet water and to dredge the harbor to a depth, varying from 14 to 18 feet, thus making the total estimated cost of improving the harbor $308,000 of which $247,000 had already been expended. H. Truman went to Washington, at this time to present the city's case but the appropriation secured was not as large as expected and therefore the city in 1882 dredged about 9000 cubic yards outside the harbor at its own expense, in order to facilitate the work, a favor which was later reciprocated by the government engineers. An effort was made by Mayor John Schuette to induce the government to dredge a 15 foot channel up as far as the bridge at Eighth Street but this the latter refused to undertake. It however, recognized the importance of the harbor, the engineers calling it in 1885 "one of the most important harbors north of Milwaukee". In 1885 the north pier was completed according to the original plan of the engineers, although much of it was rebuilt in years following while the south pier was completed in 1887. The continued extension of the shore line, due to accretions made necessary further extensions in succeeding years. From 1880 to 1890 $59,000 was appropriated by the government for the harbor and it was the general comment of the engineers that the work accomplished had been successful in character. In 1890 a new project was recommended in the construction of an extension breakwater, running northwest and southeast near the north pier entrance. An interior harbor of refuge was also considered by the engineers but only the former scheme was deemed advisable. J. D. Markham was again sent to Washington and secured Congressman Brickner's aid but no appropriation sufficiently large was secured that year. In 1892 and 1894, largely through the efforts of Congressman Wells the necessary $40,000 was procured and the construction took place in 1895, the Wisconsin Dredge and Dock Company doing the work.

In May 1895 the city council by ordinance fixed the dock lines above the Main Street bridge, an action made necessary by the new railroad improvements and in February of the following year a meeting of citizens was called to discuss dredging along the upper course of the river. Joseph Vilas presided and among those present were President Abbott, General Manager Whitcomb, Vice president Greenleaf and Attorneys Gill and Abbott of the Wisconsin Central and Land Commissioner Thayer of the C. & N. W. A commitee was chosen, composed of Mayor Torrison, G. G. Sedgwick and A. J. Schmitz, to present the matter to Congress and if possible to secure aid. They were successful, an appropriation of $44,440 being made, with which the government extended the south pier 500 feet to the twenty foot contour and dredged a twenty foot channel from the harbor line outward. In May the War Department granted the C. & N. W. the right to remove 320 feet of the south pier for their car ferry slip and in turn the company built 2000 lineal feet of protection piling along the lake front. Dredging in 1896 was the order of the day. The city in June appropriated $25,000 for this purpose and with this sum excavated 273,400 cubic yards, thus affording a twenty foot channel from the inner end of the harbor pier up river 5500 feet. A turning basin was constructed in the upper course of the river and in 1896 the removal of 200,000 cubic yards of earth was authorized. The Manitowoc

Terminal Company also did a large amount of dredging and the channel resulting was one of the deepest on Lake Michigan, that of South Chicago alone approaching it. In 1899 a survey was ordered to inquire into the advisability of extendding the breakwater and the building of an inner harbor of refuge. The former project was reported by the engineers to be possible by the expenditure of $37,000 but the latter was deemed by them impracticable. The Congressional River and Harbor Committee inspected the harbor in August 1900 while on a tour of the Great Lakes, being entertained by the city. A year later up-river dredging again came up for discussion, it being urged that the boats, which for many winters had made it a practice to lay up in the harbor and which brought large sums into circulation, could be better accomodated. A mass meeting was held, plans drawn up for the dredging of the river to a twenty foot depth around the so-called Lueps Peninsula and the contract for a part of the work let in the autumn. On the whole the citizens of Manitowoc have not been slow in realizing that it is the harbor, in which lie hopes of future commercial ascendancy and a spirit of liberality has always characterized them when called upon for financial aid, sums aggregating over $100,000 having been expended by the municipality since 1866.

A summary of government appropriations follows:

| YEAR | SUM | YEAR | SUM |
| --- | --- | --- | --- |
| 1852 | $ 8.000 | 1880 | $ 7,000 |
| 1866 | 52,000 | 1881 | 4,000 |
| 1867 | 45,000 | 1882 | 10,000 |
| 1868 | 17,500 | 1884 | 15,000 |
| 1869 | 17,820 | 1886 | 15,000 |
| 1870 | 20,000 | 1888 | 8,000 |
| 1871 | 11,000 | 1890 | 8,000 |
| 1873 | 20,000 | 1892 | 28,000 |
| 1874 | 10,000 | 1894 | 20,000 |
| 1875 | 10,000 | 1896 | 44,440 |
| 1876 | 8,000 | 1899 | 3,300 |
| 1878 | 15,000 | 1901 | 45,000 |
| 1879 | 6,500 | | |
| | | Total | $448,560 |

from Two Rivers soon after the war closed, also made efforts at improvement. In 1867 the Packard pier was constructed and in 1870 the government made a survey, which was backed up the next year by a legislative memorial to Congress. The first sum appropriated, in 1871, was $25,000 and the original project was to build two parallel piers. 260 feet apart, extending to the 18 foot curve and to dredge a channel, crossing the outer sand bars, the total cost of which was estimated at $265,588. Appropriations were made from year to year and the work continued under difficulties, much trouble being experienced with shifting sands. This fact made sand-proof revetments necessary, greatly increasing the expense, and the piers also changed the shore line. In 1874 the Two Rivers lighthouse was built and private parties did considerable docking. A volunteer life saving service was established, the station becoming a permanent one with a paid force in 1878. Captain Scove first commanded the station, being succeeded by Capt. Pilon in 1880. By the latter year there had been expended about $132,000 on the harbor, but the results on account of the shifting sands, were rather unsatisfactory, a ten foot channel being with difficulty maintained. In 1882 this too was also obliterated, trade fell off and Henry Mann offered to pay the expenses of running the U. S. Dredge in order to better matters. Later in the year the city and government co-operated with each other, removing 47,000 cubic yards of earth at a cost of about $4,000. Since the lake commerce of the port remained, the appropriations made became nominal, being sufficient only for maintenance. The pier extension was completed in 1884. since which time portions of them have become dilapidated. In 1894 a great assistance was rendered navigators by the erection by the government of the World's Fair steel tower, 110 feet high, at Two Rivers Point, a few miles north of the city and the placing on it of a strong beacon light, which can be seen for a distance of 20 miles. A survey for extended improvements was made in 1900 at Two Rivers. but the report of the engineers was not favorable, the eleven foot channel being deemed sufficient for the needs of the port. The river divides at the mouth into two branches, neither of which have been dredged for any great distance. The sums appropriated by the U. S. government from time to time are as follows,

| YEAR | SUM | YEAR | STM |
|------|-----|------|-----|
| 1871 | $25,000 | 1882 | $15,000 |
| 1872 | 25,000 | 1884 | 8,000 |
| 1873 | 25,000 | 1888 | 2,500 |
| 1874 | 15.000 | 1890 | 3,000 |
| 1875 | 15,000 | 1892 | 3,000 |
| 1876 | 5,000 | 1894 | 3,000 |
| 1878 | 10,000 | 1896 | 5,000 |
| 1879 | 20,000 | 1899 | 8,000 |
| 1881 | 15,000 | | |
| | | Total | $222,500 |

The village of Centerville in 1887 and the years immediately succeeding had high hopes of securing a harbor. The sum of $4,000 was raised for docking, half of the amount at a public meeting, but despite all exertions government aid was not forthcoming and the project was soon given up. In 1866 two small piers had been authorized to be built at the place and these proved sufficient for all needs. Similar structures were maintained by the firm of G. Pfister & Co. at Two Creeks.

TRANSPORTATION FACILITIES AND SHIPBUILDING.

The harbors at Manitowoc and Two Rivers were of course only a means towards an end. Of themselves they were of little value but the commerce and better transportation facilities that they brought about were of vast importance to the welfare of the two cities. The first intercourse with the outside world was necessarily by the arrival of some trading schooner and it was only natural that these should play an important part in the early life of the community. It was by this means that the earliest settlers reached their new homes, and the arrival of one of these "hookers" was a great event. In the latter thirties only an occasional schooner would drop anchor in the bay. By 1840, however, many of the little traders had regular routes, the schooner Milwaukee, Captain Andros, trading between the city after which it was named and Manitowoc, and the schooner Liberty, Captain Guyles, making voyages to Two Rivers. In the next year more vessels visited both places, averaging perhaps two or three a week, chief among them being the schooner Columbia, Captain Morgan, which traded at Manitowoc, and the Ocean, Captain Guyles, at Two Rivers. In 1842 still more called at the two villages, including the Gazelle, Milwaukee, Savannah, Jessie Smith, Wave, Meeme and Mechanic. In the shipping lists of 1845 are noticeable frequently the names of the schooners Solomon Juneau, Captain Quin; Eagle, Capt. Pach; Baltimore, Capt. Cotton; D. Whitney, Capt. Fleming; and the E. Henderson, Capt. Henderson. As the years passed it became possible for a steamer to stop off the mouth of the river at Manitowoc in calm weather on its way from Buffalo or Chicago, if there were any passengers or freight for the place. But for a long time the sailing vessel was the chief means of communication. That it was utilized needs no further proof than a reference to the marine lists appearing in the Milwaukee papers of the time. Four schooners clearing in one day for Two Rivers was not an unusual occurrence, these little craft bringing lumber down and carrying produce back on the return voyage. It was a strange fact that, whereas up to 1846 Manitowoc led as a trading center, in that year and for two or three succeeding, Two Rivers ranked highest in the amount of tonnage, although when steamboat connections were made the number of schooners trading at both places fell off. The first attempts to run the former style of craft regularly to Manitowoc were made in the season of 1848, when the propeller Rossiter made trips from Chicago as far north as Manitowoc, stopping at Milwaukee and other intermediate points. The round trip occupied about nine or ten days, including stops and after one summer the line was discontinued. A year before the first schooner built in the county was constructed by Capt. Joseph Edwards, christened the Citizen and being a craft of sixty tons burden.

Five years elapsed before another was built, but thereafter shipbuilding became one of the principal industries of the county.

By 1850 a regular steamer line was again in operation, this time one of greater permanence. The craft was the Champion, Captain Howe, of 270 tons and it left Manitowoc for Milwaukee Tuesday, Thursday and Saturday mornings at seven o'clock, stopping at Sheboygan enroute and connecting with the Buffalo boats at its southern terminus. These also began to stop at Manitowoc in case they had any very large number of emigrants desirous of being landed, the flood of travel having by this time turned Wisconsinward. The Lady of the Lake, which was at that time plying between Green Bay and Chicago also stopped at Manitowoc, P. P. Smith being the local agent. The steamer Detroit, somewhat larger than the Champion, was placed on the Manitowoc line by the Ward Company, who owned the steamers, in 1851 and was in turn succeeded by the steamer Arctic, a craft of 857 tons, two years later. By this time commercial activity in Manitowoc had been greatly increased. Said Philo White in a communication to Congress in 1850 upon Wisconsin lake towns: "Manitowoc is vieing with her neighboring ports in the enterprise of her citizens, in the onward march of her improvements and in the rapid development of her material resources. She exported in the items of lumber and fish to the value of $72,726 during the last season and her imports were $117,826. There are five schooners owned there. Two Rivers has also asserted her claim to be inscribed in the list of lake ports by contributing to swell the aggregate of lake commerce. As long ago as 1847 she exported lumber and fish to the value of $53,747 in that year alone." Shipbuilding began in 1852 to take on an important aspect, three or four schooners being constructed in that year and double the number the next. Said the Weekly Herald: It is perhaps no breach of modesty to say that Manitowoc is capable of furnishing more and better lake schooners than any town of its size west of Buffalo. And while our hand is in we might as well add that Two Rivers and this place can furnish employment for double our fleet. With unabated energy the construction of little schooners progressed at both ports down to the opening of the Civil War, the largest built up to that time being the Mary Stockton, constructed by Bates & Son in 1853, which had a capacity of 275 tons. Other shipbuilders of the day were Joseph Edwards, J. Hughes, E. Sorenson, G. S. Rand of Manitowoc and James Harbridge of Two Rivers. It was the last named who built the schooners Gertrude and Joseph Vilas.

Steam, however, in the meantime was being felt as a factor in local transportation. In 1854 facilities were greatly increased. The Read line of Buffalo steamers established a Manitowoc agency and the Collingwood line of steamers also touched at Manitowoc, the Lady Elgin stopping at the harbor quite frequently. The steamer Queen City, for which K. K. Jones was the local agent, left Manitowoc for Sault Ste Marie on Wednesdays and for Chicago on Saturdays, while the Fashion stopped enroute from Milwaukee to Green Bay. The next year (1855) Manitowoc was visited regularly by the Buffalo liners, Lady Elgin, Niagara and Keystone State, while the little steamer Lady of Sheboygan plied between that city and Manitowoc. The Superior, Captain Tomkins. made tri-weekly trips to Chicago and also touched at Two Rivers. She was, however, burned the following year on Lake Superior. The report for the year shows that 82 steamers and 102 sailing vessels called at Manitowoc and 74 steamers and 41 sail vessels at Two Rivers. The year 1856 witnessed the inauguration of the Goodrich Line, which has played such an important part in Manitowoc life ever since. The line had been organized the preceding year and the steamer Huron, of 348 tons, placed upon a route including Milwaukee, Sheboygan, Manitowoc and Two Rivers, daily trips being instituted. Said the Herald in November: "We hope that Captain Goodrich's experience will induce him to try the route another season and that his efforts to accommodate our business community will be duly appreciated." K. K. Jones was the Manitowoc agent of the line and Pierpont, Hall & Co. the Two Rivers representatives. Besides the Goodrich line Manitowoc was also touched by the Collingwood line, including the Niagara which burned off Port Washington in September 1856 and was succeeded by the Planet, the Queen City, Buckeye State and Keystone State and by the Ward steamer Cleveland built in 1852, which ran to Green Bay ports. During the next year facilities remained the same, the Arctic, Captain Dougall taking the place of the Cleveland in September In 1858 the Ward line ran both the Cleveland and the Traveler on the Manitowoc route, the former making tri-weekly trips, while the Arctic still called en route to Green Bay. The Collingwood liners, five in number also continued to stop during this and the two succeeding seasons, furnishing means of transportation east once a week.

In 1858 and 1859 Captain Goodrich put the propeller Ogontz on a line running from Green Bay to Chicago, Capt. Flood commanding. During the latter year and 1860, however, the best facilities were offered by the Wards, the Gazelle, Capt. Butlin making daily trips to Manitowoc and Two Rivers, but this line finally withdrew, leaving Captain Goodrich a clear field. By that time the latter had disposed of the hull of the Ogontz to Racine parties and had purchased the Wabash Valley, but as he sold her to the Milwaukee and Grand Haven Transportation Co., he was compelled to have built at Newport, Michigan, the Comet, a steamer of 385 tons placing her in command of Captain Pabst, the later well known Milwaukeean. She remained in possession of the line until 1870, being transferred to the Grand Haven route. It was on this craft that so many Manitowoc soldiers were carried away from their homes during the earlier years of the civil strife. The energetic captain soon purchased the steamers Lady Franklin and Sea Bird, which were placed on the Green Bay and Lake Superior routes respectively, the former being sold to Chicago parties after two years. In 1860 Manitowoc first began to furnish craft for this line, contracts being let to Bates & Son for the building of the propellars Sunbeam and Union. The latter was launched in April

1861 and was fitted out at a total cost of $25,000, having the engines of the old Ogontz put in her. The Sunbeam costing $40,000, was launched in June and was placed on the Manitowoc route the next season but foundered on Lake Superior a year later. An attempt had been made to fit her out with the so-called Whittaker side-wheel apparatus, but it proved a failure. The Union was sold in the latter sixties to parties who ran her on Green Bay. During the war Captain Goodrich bought the Ward Steamer Planet, 1164 tons, and the May Queen. The former was placed in the Lake Superior trade, calling at Manitowoc, but was later dismantled and sold to the Peshtigo Lumber Co. The May Queen ran on what was known as the west shore route, touching Manitowoc, Two Rivers, Sheboygan and Milwaukee and sank off Sheboygan on September 17, 1865, the hull being later destroyed by fire.

Commercial interests during the war remained largely at a stand still, in Manitowoc at least. However, the first direct grain shipment east was made May 31, 1861, on the schooner Joseph Vilas, Captain Albrecht. The cargo of 8000 bushels was made up by Platt & Vilas, O. Torrison, J. Bennett and S. Goodnow, and the event marked a stage in the development of Manitowoc county, viz: the change from a lumbering to an agricultural community. That Manitowoc was recognized as having an interest in eastern shipping was witnessed by the appointment of Joseph Vilas in 1863 as a Wisconsin delegate to the Canal Enlargement Convention, held in that year. Shipbuilding too had languished during the war, a few schooners alone being constructed. At the end of that struggle, however, a great impetus was given to the industry, in which Manitowoc shared. A new and energetic firm had been established under the management of G. S. Rand, and he soon secured contracts of importance. The Orion, a 600 ton sidewheeler, was his first work of magnitude being launched December 6, 1865, and the engine of the steamer Michigan, purchased by the Goodrich line the year before, being placed in the craft. The boat continued to make trips on the west shore and later on the Grand Haven route until 1871, when she was dismantled and became a lumber barge. In 1866 the Goodrich interests were incorporated as the Milwaukee, Sturgeon Bay and Green Bay Transportation Company, but the name was changed two years later to that of the Goodrich Transportation Company, with Albert E. Goodrich, W. J. Whalling, G. Hurson, A. Conro and S. A. Hasbrouck as incorporators and Manitowoc as the home port. In 1866 the line purchased the propellors G. J. Truesdell and Ottowa, and on November 15 there was launched the second steamer from the Rand yards, the Northwest. The launching was a great event for the village, a thousand persons witnessing it. The steamer used the Planets engines, was 250 feet long, 33 feet beam and had a measurement of 1200 tons. She was placed on the west shore run in May of the year under the command of Captain Williams and was considered one of the finest boats on the lakes, a deserved tribute to Manitowoc industry. Among the other shipbuilders of the time were E. W. Packard and Jasper Hanson, who later associated with himself H. Scove, the firm some years afterwards removing to Two Rivers. Small schooners were also constructed in the later sixties at Neshoto and Mishicott.

Captain Goodrich kept the propeller Truesdell for about thirteen years, running it on the Green Bay route but the Ottawa, after being on the same run for two years, was sold to shipowners in Detroit and the magnificent Northwest, too, after a short service on the Manitowoc route was purchased by the Detroit and Cleveland Navigation Company. On August 17, 1867 builder Rand launched the sidewheeler Manitowoc and the event was a memorable one, the city presenting the craft with a set of colors. The Manitowoc was 218 feet long, 33 feet beam and measured 569 tons, being fitted out with the May Queen's engines. She ran from Chicago to Manitowoc for five seasons and was then displaced by a better craft, being turned into a barge. In this year (1867) the Goodrich line had a rival in the shape of the steamer Hippocampus, which ran tri-weekly from Milwaukee but the venture did not prove very successful and the line was soon discontinued. That year the Goodrich company bought their present dock property and J. W. Thombs was installed as local agent, a position he held until 1891. The company also commenced to lay up its vessels at Manitowoc in the winter season. Then not only did the city have a reputation arising from its shipbuilding but also as a shipowning center, the Manitowoc fleet consisting of 37 craft, including 7 Goodrich boats, 1 tug, 9 barques, 1 scow and 17 schooners. By the sad loss of the Seabird, chronicled later in these pages, Captain Goodrich was sadly crippled and so purchased the Alpena in Detroit for $80,000. The craft was rebuilt in 1876 and was owned by the line until the time of her sinking four years later off Grand Haven. In 1869 the sidewheelers Sheboygan and Corona were launched for the line from the Rand yards. The former was particularly admired at the time, her upperworks being constructed in Detroit at a great expense. The engines for the craft were second-hand, coming from the old City of Cleveland. Both were for years on the west shore, the former being rebuilt in 1896. She is still a staunch craft in active service, while the Corona was sold in 1892 to Buffalo parties to be used as an excursion boat and burned in the Niagara River soon after.

To such an extent had lake interests at Manitowoc grown by 1870 that the subject of securing a dry dock was much under discussion. A company was formed, with Jonah Richards as president, C. H. Walker secretary and George Cooper treasurer, which met the following January to organize. The company was a stock corporation and many citizens subscribed for shares to aid the project which was soon after happily consummated, G. S. Rand being chosen superintendent. The docks were maintained by the company until 1887 when H. Burger purchased them, lengthening them some years later. Mr. Rand in May, 1870 turned out another Goodrich steamer, the side wheeler Muskegon, built for the Orion's machinery and in 1872 added the propellers Oconto and Menominee to his list. The steamer Muskegon was regularly run until 1897, when she was wrecked while undergoing repairs in a Milwaukee drydock, being later abandoned. The Oconto was disposed of by sale, while the Menominee after running for twenty-three years was rebuilt and lengthened fifteen feet, taking the name of the Iowa. After 1870 a great increase in the number of schooners built was noticeable and new firms of builders came into the field. Hanson & Scove, P. Larson, J. Butler, S. Jorgenson,—all did much in the line of construction and in 1873 the firm of Rand & Burger was formed, whose name was widely known on the Great Lakes. Besides the Goodrich work, they undertook the construction of many tugs, lumber barges and vessels of all kinds and descriptions and the employment thus afforded to labor was both steady and lucrative. Next to the Goodrich interests as owners, Jonah Richards ranked next, his fleet being widely known on the lakes.

In 1873 Rand & Burger launched the Goodrich propeller DePere which continued in service until its sale, it later becoming the Barry liner, State of Michigan, sinking off Grand Haven in the fall of 1901. In 1874 the side-wheeler Chicago came out, taking the Manitowoc's cabin and engines and under the command of Captain Sweeney was for many years a familiar sight in the harbor. The boat is still in active service. Three years later Manitowoc secured new connections, the boats of the Lake Michigan and Lake Superior Transportation Company stopping at the Truman & Morse docks. The line was composed of the steamers Peerless, Fremont, Hurd and Duluth and ceased calling at Manitowoc in the early eighties. As early as this hopes were also entertained for connection with Michigan via Flint & Pere Marquette steamers but they remained ungratified for many years. Outside of the building of steamers after 1880 the business of construction manifested a rapid decline, due largely to the supplanting of the sail by steam and thus Rand & Burger, which became Burger & Burger by the death of Mr. Rand in 1885, soon had the field to themselves. Manitowoc also lost the Richards fleet of eight craft by the death of the owner in 1881 and the Goodrich fleet, too, changed its hailing port to Kenosha soon after, owing to some misunderstanding as to local taxation. The propeller Ludington, launched by Burger & Burger in 1880 was the only Goodrich steamer to be built at Manitowoc for nineteen years and was a very staunch and well-modeled craft, being rebuilt and refitted as the Georgia in the winter of 1897-1898. In 1881 the Goodrich company turned for its craft to another source, having the steamers Michigan, Wisconsin and City of Milwaukee built at Wyandotte, Mich., but possession of the last two was not retained for long and the Michigan sank off Grand Haven. Captain Goodrich, whose name was linked with the progress of Manitowoc as a marine center passed away at his Chicago home in 1888, having for forty years been one of the notable figures of the Great Lakes. In the years succeeding the company was ably conducted by the captain's successors and in 1888 the work of construction of a new and costly fleet was begun. The first steamer to be built was the City of Racine, which was launched at the Burger yards in the presence of three thousand people in 1889. Ninety persons from Racine were present and Captain Butlin was the recipient of a set of colors from them. The craft was 217 by 35 feet and proved a most profitable investment, being placed on the Chicago-Grand Haven route. The second steamer of the fleet appeared in 1890, being christened the Indiana and was the last large steamer to be built at Manitowoc. The company a year later had the palatial Virginia and Atlanta constructed in Wyandotte, Mich., and in 1898 added by purchase, the whaleback Christopher Columbus. In 1896 the company constructed repair shops at Manitowoc and has since continued to enlarge its machinery and supply shops, used in refitting the boats during the winter season, thus giving employment to much high-priced labor. In the later nineties the steamers Atlanta, Sheboygan, Chicago and Georgia have made regular runs on the west shore, stopping regularly at Manitowoc and during much of the time at Two Rivers also and both the freight and passenger business has been large. Henry Pates succeeded Mr. Thombs as local agent until 1895, when C. F. Canright was chosen to fill the now important position, and upon his decease George Houghton was appointed agent.

The shipbuilding industry at Manitowoc manifested a steady increase during the nineties. Although the work was largely in repairs, Burger & Burger have built during that period the steamers Petoskey, Fanny Hart and numerous smaller craft. As early as August 1887 there were rumors current of the establishment of a steamer line to Ludington. A petition was numerously signed in the city asking for such connections to the east and forwarded to the F. & P. M. officials in January of the following year. The latter visited the city in June and seemed favorably impressed with the facilities offered but no definite action followed until 1890, when the line was established, F. P. Gaines being appointed local agent. It was thought that a new line might lead to more liberal harbor appropriations and great satisfaction was felt upon the arrival of the first through shipment on the steamer F. & P. M. No. 1, on January 10, 1890, the event being the occasion of the booming of cannon. Said the Pilot: "For over thirty years Manitowoc has been looking for this consummation." At first a round trip was made every two days but as business grew a second and in February a third and fourth boat were placed on the line. At about the same time the C. & N. W. built a large warehouse on the south side of the river entrance for this new line and flour from the west soon filled the building to its utmost capacity, coming in at the rate of over one hundred carloads a day. The route was essentially a winter one and during the summer of the three succeeding years the large steamers were withdrawn and the propellor R. T. Stewart placed on the line. In the spring of 1893 regular trips on the route were discontinued and for several years trans-lake shipments were few. An experiment was made in the summer of 1893 in bringing pulp wood rafts from Canada to Manitowoc, thence to be shipped to the paper mills of the Fox River valley, but the attempt did not prove successful and was given up as impracticable. In December of the same year the first whaleback to enter the harbor, the Pathfinder, unloaded coal at the C. & N. W. Docks.

After a period of depression, as far as harbor interests

were concerned, a reawakening took place with the entrance of the Wisconsin Central. Buffalo grain steamers of a size never before entering Manitowoc began in the summer of 1896 to visit the port, the deep water then attained by dredging making it possible for them to unload at the Central freight docks, built that spring above the Main street bridge. The first of this class to arrive were the Wetmore and Globe and in 1896 the Great Lakes Steamship Line was regularly scheduled on the Manitowoc-Buffalo route, consisting of the steamers Olympia, J. W. Moore, Globe, Charlemagne Tower and Pascadena. To accommodate this new class of transportation it became necessary for the Northern Grain Company, a Chicago corporation, to build two mammoth elevators, A and B, the former being constructed in the Wisconsin Central yards in 1896 and the latter on the south side of the river near the C. & N. W. depot in 1898. The grain capacity of these two structures is very high and they were built at an approximate cost of $600,000. The first shipment of grain from the elevator system took place on May 1, 1897, the steamer Moore taking a cargo of 50,000 bushels. Although the Great Lakes Line was discontinued in the fall of 1898 steamers of other lines and of a large capacity have continued to transport cargoes of grain to Buffalo and the business seems likely to have a great future. A profitable feature of these new facilities for Manitowoc has been the fact that many of the large liners have made it a practice to lay up for the winter in the upper harbor, on account of the cheap and spacious accommodations offered. A large amount of money has thus been put in circulation through the purchase of necessary supplies, repairs, etc. In 1902 the Barry line of steamers commenced to touch at Manitowoc, running the Empire State and Badger State on the west shore route.

A few words in regard to the growth of the carferry system. This novel method of transporting freight without breaking bulk was initiated by the Ann Arbor line between Kewaunee and Frankfort in the early nineties. The steamers Nos. 1 and 2 commenced calling at Manitowoc in 1896

J. D. MARKHAM

and have continued to make the port more and more regularly as local business warranted, connecting with both railroads. Slips were built to accommodate the craft at the C. & N. W. and Wisconsin Central yards and in the winter of 1895 the F. & P. M., which by this time had resumed the Manitowoc route, had built for their use at West Bay City, Mich., the carferry Pere Marquette, later known as Number 16, the largest in the world. It was launched May 19, 1896 and was fitted to accommodate 32 cars and 156 passengers, being 263 by 56 feet in dimensions. Its first arrival at Manitowoc took place on the morning of February 16th of the next year and from that time it ran regularly between Manitowoc and Ludington, often making two round trips in a day. During 1897 the Big Four carferries called for some months at Manitowoc, the other terminus being Benton Harbor, but the distance was too great and the plan was given up. In 1900 the F. & P. M. was obliged to construct another carferry, the No. 17, in order to accommodate increasing business. It was of the same dimensions as the older craft and made its first appearance in Manitowoc on August 25, 1901. Another carferry the No. 18 was added to the line in 1902. This mode of transportation has been successful beyond all hopes and has raised Manitowoc to a high position as a center of through shipment.

A revolution in the ship building industry at Manitowoc occurred in the summer of 1902 when the Manitowoc Dry Dock Company was incorporated with the following officers: President—Elias Grinnell; Vice-President—T. J. Prindeville; Secretary and Treasurer—S. E. Gier; General Manager— Charles C. West. Steel repair outfits were installed and the Burger yards purchased and refitted. The company soon sought contracts for building steel vessels and much is expected of the new departure.

As tending to show the growth in commerce a table, tabulating the clearances and tonnage of the craft at both Manitowoc and Two Rivers is given under the head Appendix B. A list of the craft built at Manitowoc, with their tonnage, is also appended.

## MARINE DISASTERS.

In concluding the record of the marine history of the county, some space should be devoted to disasters, both those that have taken place in the vicinity and those in which Manitowoc was a particular sufferer. The first loss of importance on the lake in the neighborhood of Manitowoc was the burning of the steamer Phoenix on November 21, 1847. The craft had arrived at Manitowoc on the morning of the 20th and had on board two hundred passengers and a large crew, the former being bound for Milwaukee. Only about thirty were Americans, the rest being immigrants from Holland. The boat laid at the south pier all day awaiting calm weather and left late at night. At about four in the morning, while eight miles from Sheboygan and four from land, fire was discovered and in a few moments the craft was all ablaze. The flames were discernable in Sheboygan and the propellor Delaware, that happened to be in port, started to the rescue, as did also a schooner and thus about one-quarter of the number on board were saved, the rest perishing by water or the flames. The captain was ill with a broken leg at the time but was safely conveyed to the rescuing boat. The disaster caused widespread sympathy in the lake towns and was long remembered. On the same day the schooner H. Merrill went ashore at Manitowoc and a Mr. Woodward, who was on board, was drowned. Two years later the brig Ontario was beached on Two Rivers point but got off after some difficulty. In a storm on November 27, 1850, the schooner Jeanette was driven high and dry on the beach near Manitowoc, and other vessels, among them the Gleaner, had narrow escapes from the breakers. A series of years then passed without any accident in the vicinity. In a gale in November, 1885, the brig J. Irwin was lost off Two Rivers and the schooner Amelia off Manitowoc. Three years later the schooner Andromeda was lost about forty miles northeast of the latter port. In the loss of the Goodrich steamer Lady Elgin off Waukegan on September 8, 1860, only one man from the county, Fred Haeffner, of Two Rivers, lost his life. Seven years then passed without any notable wreck, but then came a series of them. On November 24,

1867 the barque Tubalcain went down off Two Rivers with 18,000 bushels of wheat on board, the loss amounting to $20,000 and in December the propellar Adriatic went ashore near Manitowoc. Then came what, for Manitowoc, was perhaps the greatest marine disaster ever experienced, viz., the burning of the Seabird. The terrible accident occurred eight miles from Waukegan on the morning of Thursday, April 9, 1868. The steamer was one that Captain Goodrich had purchased from the Ward line and was nine years old at the time. The crew and passengers numbered thirty-five and a majority of them were from Manitowoc and Sheboygan, en-route to Chicago. It is thought that the fire originated from coals, scattered from the stoves, which the porter was engaged in cleaning. When the blaze was first discovered the boat was imprudently headed for the shore and the wind which was northeast, sent the flames forward and soon reached the machinery. The engines became so heated that they stopped and the four small boats, capable of holding ten persons, could not be lowered, while it was too late to receive any assistance from the shore. The terrible news of the disaster was soon abroad and the wires conveyed it to Manitowoc, the whole village being thrown into consternation by the tidings. R. D. Smart was dispatched at the head of a party to search for bodies along the shore, but very few traces of the accident were ever found. Only three persons escaped, two Sheboygan men and James H. Leonard of Manitowoc. The loss to the north side was particularly heavy. Among those from Manitowoc who lost their lives were George W. Emery, a prominent merchant, Captains N. T. Nelson and John Sorenson, vessel owners, James A. Hodges, clerk of the craft, Charles Reicher, foreman of the Goodrich repair shops, Joseph Dawcett, a grocer, Miss Theresa Olson, a seamstress, James Leykom, August Wilde, Richard Flossbach, William Barter, John Melke, Casper Kleiner, John Fuchs, Herman Jaccby, P. C. Danahy, Amos Meyer, Henry Meinam besides Martin Rogezginter and Wenzel Hartichek with their wives and children, these latter being on their way to Nebraska as colonists. Capt. Nelson was on his way to purchase a tug in Chicago, while Capt. Sorenson and Mr. Emery were also on business trips. The terrible happening left an impress on the people of the village, that was deeply felt, particularly by those whose friends had been thus wrested from them. In September of the same year the steamer Richard Roe sunk near the Manitowoc harbor pier and on October 30th the schooner James Nevagle went down off Two Rivers. Capt. Joseph Gagnon and nine others of the volunteer life saving crew then in existence made a heroic rescue of the crew of the doomed vessel. On board the Nevagle were 15.000 bushels of wheat en-route to Oswego, N. Y. from Milwaukee, all of which was lost. In December, 1871, the schooner Industry sunk about midway between Two Rivers and her destination, Manitowoc, a cargo of produce being lost.

The year 1875 witnessed the loss of the schooner Cornelia D. Windiate, which in December went down between Manitowoc and Milwaukee with her crew of nine men and a cargo of 21,000 bushels of wheat. She was built by Windiate and Butler in 1873 at a cost of $20,000 and had a capacity of 332 tons, being one of the finest schooners on the lake. On November 8, 1877, the Canadian schooner Magellan, bound from Chicago to Toronto, with 20,000 bushels of wheat on board, was lost off Two Rivers. Nine sailors were drowned, the bodies being washed ashore some days after the occurence. The schooner Joseph Duval shared the same fate at the same place in July, 1880, while en route from Kewaunee to Chicago with 140 cords of bark, seven were drowned and the vessel which had been built by Rand & Burger in 1875 at a cost of $7,000 proved a total loss. In a terrible storm on October 16, of the same year the Goodrich steamer Alpena went down on the east shore, carrying seventy-five passengeas and a crew of twenty-six to a watery grave. Arthur Haines, the clerk and William Shepard, the steward, were both Manitowoc young men and their death cast a gloom over the city. In the succeeding March the treacherous Two Rivers Point claimed the barge Grace Patterson, the crew, however, being saved. On December 3rd a terrible storm was the cause of the wreck

of the Goodrich steamer DePere, between Manitowoc and
Two Rivers and the schooner Oliver Cutler near the latter
place. The DePere was in a perilous position for months
and it was thought that she would be a total loss, but by well-
directed efforts she was saved from destruction the following
spring and rebuilt.

Another terrible disaster, long to be remembered, occurred
off Two Rivers Point on October 28, 1887 in the loss of the
screw steamer Vernon. The Vernon was owned by the Northern Michigan Transportation Company and was enroute from
Charlevoix, Mich., to Chicago with from thirty to fifty persons on board, only one of whom, Alfred Stone, a fireman,
survived. He was insane for the remainder of his life, having
suffered terribly, so the true story of the accident was never
known. It is supposed that the accident occurred by some
mishap in the stearing gear while the steamer was trying to
make Manitowoc and that the boat was swamped in the
trough of a tremendous wave. A schooner passed through
the wreckage and saw some persons clinging to boards but
was unable to give assistance. Fishing tugs picked up nineteen bodies during the succeeding days, besides much wreckage. An inquest was held before Justice Walsh at Two Rivers and nine of the bodies were interred in potter's field at that
city, others being identified by friends. Several relics from
the disaster were preserved, being on exhibition at the Teren's
Museum at Mishicott. The Vernon cost originally $75,000
and was commanded by Captain Thorpe at the time of the
disaster. An accident occurred at nearly the identical spot
on November 15, 1890, when the steambarge Nevada, foundered, the crew being picked up by the steamer Manchester.
The craft was eight years old and was valued at $50,000.
The steamer Wetmore suffered a similar fate off Centerville
in November 1894 and in 1898 the schooner L. B. Shepard
went ashore off Two Rivers after being waterlogged, the loss
being $3500. A more recent marine disaster was the sinking
of the scow Silver Lake by collision with the carferry Pere
Marquette a few miles east of Manitowoc in March 1900.
The collision took place in a fog and the crew of the scow,

whose home was in Racine, lost their lives. On the whole Manitowoc has borne her share of the sorrow that always comes at frequent intervals to a people dwelling near waters, upon which they seek a livelihood.

## CHAPTER VII.

### RAILROADS.

Few chapters in the history of Manitowoc county present such a series of failures, disappointments and blighted hopes as that concerning its railroads. For twenty years a continuity of misfortunes of various natures postponed the consummation of the desires of the people and it was not until the county seat had become an incorporated city that the first whistle of the locomotive was heard. Fate also remained unkind after this first success and it was only in the year 1895, the date of the construction of the Wisconsin Central, that the city took the place as a railroad center that it should have attained forty years before. Situated as it is on the lake, in an almost direct line from the great wheat-growing region of the northwest to the markets of the east, it certainly possessed from the beginning elements of natural strength that should have told earlier for advancement.

With the rapid development of Wisconsin in the latter forties and the early fifties came the desire for better transportation facilities. Internal improvement is and always has been the summum bonum, towards which all new regions strive and the virgin Badger State was no exception. In this desire Manitowoc shared from the first. Diverted from the earlier and more chimerical schemes of canal and river systems the minds of the progressive turned toward the rails and the iron horse as their hope of future advancement. Capital was however, scarce and schemes of great trunk lines offering hypothetical returns were numerous, few of which saw a practical fruition. The Milwaukee and Mississippi, later a part of the St. Paul system, was the only remarkable instance of the latter class. In 1851, however, the legislature granted two charters that touched Manitowoc's interests vitally. The first was that to the Chicago, Milwaukee and Green Bay Railroad Company, granted on March 13th, of which, among others, George Reed and K. K. Jones of Manitowoc, and E. Fox Cooke, of Sheboygan, were incorporators, the balance being Wisconsin and eastern capitalists. It was the plan of this company to co-operate with the road also contemplated between Chicago and Milwaukee and to extend the latter northward to Manitowoc at least. There it was calculated that the road should connect with the Manitowoc an Mississippi Railroad, the charter for which was granted on March 15th, two days later. The incorporators of this project were nine in number, viz;— George Reed, H. McAllister, Peleg Glover, Gustavus Richter and C. E. Esslinger, of Manitowoc, Charles Doty, Curtis Reed and J. Keyes of Winnebago County and T. Conkey, J. Hanchett and Oscar Clark of Outagamie County. The capital stock was fixed at $1,500,000 in shares of $100, two thousand of which were required to organize. Five per cent of the shares was required to be paid in at the time of the subscription and twenty per cent. was fixed as the maximum call, sixty days being the length of notice and each share carrying with it a vote. Three years was granted for the commencement of the road and ten years for completion, ten miles to be completed before opening it to traffic. The usual provisions as to reasonable rates, reference of disputes to commissioners, fixing of termini, eminent domain and annual reports were also made. Its original western terminus was designated as LaCrosse but greater latitude of choice was afforded by a charter amendment passed in 1854. This, then, was the form of organization which for so many years engrossed the attention of Manitowoc citizens. With the line from Milwaukee connecting with this transstate route it was thought that a system would be secured that would mean much to the future of the region traversed.

In the meantime those in favor of the two lines were cooperating, largely through the efforts of Mr. Reed. In 1852 Congressman Doty presented a bill to Congress for a land grant to the Manitowoc and Mississippi, which although it came to naught, betokened the spirit of the times. George Reed throughout the year agitated the question of improvement through the columns of the public press and laid particular stress on the Milwaukee road. The year 1852, however, passed without definite action. On January 1853 a grand mass-meeting was held in Milwaukee to push the project of a northern extension, to which representatives from the northern counties were invited. Letters were read from Manitowoc and Sheboygan promising that each would take $75,000 in the stock of the road, besides furnishing depots and water supplies. From Manitowoc there were present C. W. Fitch, B. F. White, Benjamin Jones, J. Medbury and J. M. Sherwood, the last named being one of the vice-presidents of the meeting, while Ezekiel Ricker was chosen as the county representative to act on a steering committe in the state legislature. George Reed was one of those who were present also and in an address he mentioned the Manitowoc and Mississippi as a connection westward. But the lake shore region was not alone in desiring the road. There were delegates from Fond du Lac and Oshkosh present also, who urged their interests and, being more influential, in the end they won. The section of the road from Chicago to Milwaukee was built during 1853 and 1854 and another element was presented in the fact that a railroad had already been chartered under the name of the Fox River, Milwaukee & Fond du Lac Company, which would contest the ground with the Chicago, Milwaukee & Green Bay, should the latter take the more westerly route. The natural result was a combination of the two schemes, which was successfully accomplished, thus forming a powerful check to any hope for the lake shore counties.

On the other hand interest in the Manitowoc & Mississippi remained unabated. Its charter was amended in 1853 so as to permit it to borrow money and to receive land grants and in

April an act was passed allowing towns and counties along its route to hold elections to decide upon the question of granting aid to the project. The latter was largely the result of Mr. Reed's efforts, he having suggested to the village authorities that they ought to apply for such an act from the legislature and he also proposed that the village issue $50,000 in coupon bonds, to be sold in sums not less than $500, running twenty years at 7 per cent., payable semi-annually. The first directors were chosen in October of this year, consisting of George Reed, C. Klingholz, C. Esslinger, Curtis Reed, B. Jones, S. A. Wood, H. A. Palmer, E. D. Smith and N. P. Clinton. But this action did not mean the actual commencement of construction for dallying with the Chicago, Milwaukee & Green Bay continued and other schemes arose as well. Chief among the latter projects was the charter granted to the Michigan and Wisconsin Terminal Company on February 28, 1853. Among the Manitowoc men figuring as stockholders of this road were P. P. Smith, C. E. Esslinger, P. Glover and George Reed and there were besides fourteen outsiders interested in the plan. The capital was fixed at six millions, at $100 a share, business to be commenced only when $200,000 had been subscribed and 5 per cent. paid in, a condition precedent which of course was never met. The proposed route was from Manitowoc to the northern part of the state, east of the Lake of the Desert, having its terminus at Keeweenaw Point in Houghton Co., Mich., and branches to the mouth of the Ontonagon River and Iron Bay on Lake Superior, practically the route of the present Superior Division of the St. Paul system. Fifteen years were given for its completion and subscription books were opened in July at Manitowoc, Menasha and other places. Congressional aid was confidently expected but the company never got beyond an incipient stage. Yet it was in the charter of this road that the legislature made its first attempt to regulate rates in Wisconsin. Another road on paper that came to nothing in that year was the Two Rivers and Green Bay Railroad Comp... to which a charter was granted on April 2nd. Its ... as fixed at $800,000 and the applicants for the charter were H. H. Smith, J. Medbury, W. Aldrich, Horace Hamilton, W. B. Medbury, Lemuel House, C. Kuehn and S. A. Alden,—all of Two Rivers, D. Smith of Mishicot, E. Ricker of Manitowoc and H. S. Baird, T. O. Howe, later a U. S. Senator, and J. S. Fiske of Green Bay. The incorporation shows an evident desire on the part of Two Rivers for railroad connections independent of her southern neighbor, as it was totally unconnected with the other plans.

In the meanwhile matters had been progressing with the other projects. In December 1853 the village of Manitowoc granted the right of way to the M. & M. on Quay, Commercial and Water Streets. On April 11th of the year following it was decided to vote upon the question of extending village aid in the shape of $150,000 in 7 per cent. bonds. The result was 92 votes in the affirmative and only 6 in the negative, while Menasha on May 31st voted a similar amount by 41 majority. All then seemed bright and a ratification meeting was called at Franklin Hall in Manitowoc, on June 3rd, at which C. Esslinger acted as chairman and S. W. Smith as secretary, the following resolutions being passed.

Resolved, That the projected railroad connecting Manitowoc and Menasha is of the first importance to the interests of the two places.

Resolved, That this meeting hails with pleasure the triumph of true friends of Menasha in securing for the proposition of the M. & M. R. R. Co., a majority at the recent election and respond to the greetings of Menasha with our warmest congratulations.

Resolved, That the citizens of Menasha have evinced a praiseworthy regard for the interests of the village by the endorsement of an enterprise of importance.

Resolved, That Manitowoc extends to Menasha the right hand of fellowship with the earnest hope that the union cemented between the two places by iron bands may be accomplished at an early day and be as lasting as the eternal hills.

Definite plans were now under way, President Reed making every effort to push matters. It was even rumored in the early part of 1854 that the road would be completed in a year. On April 7th Mr. Reed made an exhibit of his plan to the village trustees, which resulted in a vote of confidence by that body and was one of the instrumental causes in the favorable popular vote on the bond issue four days later. According to his estimates the cost of the road as far as Menasha would be $924,326, an average of $22,008 for each of the forty two miles, including an equipment consisting of five locomotives, three baggage, eight passenger and fifty freight cars. These figures were on the basis of estimates furnished by C. R. Alton, the consulting engineer. Mr. Reed made his report to the directors in October 1854 in its final form, in which he gave an extended account of the road's past and present. By this time the survey had been completed to Lake Winnebago and, although the total distance to the Mississippi was 284 miles, it was thought best to attempt this first portion only. In speaking of the advantages the road had there were mentioned the Fox River Valley Region thus made tributary, the opening of fourteen rich counties with a population of 17,672 by means of the intersecting plankroads, the connection with the Chicago, Milwaukee and Green Bay at Manitowoc and with the Pere Marquette line then being proposed in Michigan by means of a boat line and finally with two proposed roads from Menasha to Newport and Ripon. The resources of the road were stated as follows:—

Subscriptions paid in 5 per cent. installment...... $100,000
Menasha and Manitowoc Village Bonds........... 300,000
Bonds of County to be secured by First Mortgage.. 420,000
Additional Stock required...................... 120,000

940,000
Entire Cost................................... 924,000

Balance ...................................... 15,674

Of the $120,000 it was thought $100,000 might easily be disposed of in Germany through Charles Klingholz, the company's agent, then in Europe. The first year's receipts, estimated at $262,520 would also, it was expected, assist in making up any discrepancy. This was the roseate hue that the project assumed in the latter part of 1854. But troubles soon commenced. As was said in January 1855: "The basis of the road is stock subscriptions amounting to $100,000, $300,000 in bonds not yet issued and negotiated and a first mortgage on the road amounting to $420,000, which is yet to find a market." Confidence in President Reed was not as great as it might have been and even as early as March 1855 he offered to vacate the position if any one else willing to undertake the work would assume his duties. Hopes in the extension of the Chicago, Milwaukee & Green Bay had not, however, ceased and on March 3rd a meeting was held at which D. H. Van Valkenburgh acted as chairman. Mr. Reed addressed the meeting, stating that its object was to complete the road to Milwaukee and Chief Engineer Alton of the road was also present. A committee of fifteen was appointed to push the matter, consisting of O. H. Platt, P. P. Smith, F. Borcherdt, J. Lueps, S. A. Wood, E. D. Beardsley, H. F. Hubbard, D. H. Van Valkenburgh, B Jones, G. L. Lee, F. Salomon and C. Klingholz. On March 14th a county convention to discuss the building of the road was called and F. Borcherdt was chosen chairman, H. C. Hamilton of Two Rivers acting as secretary. Vice presidents were chosen as follows: Manitowoc, H. Rand; Rapids, G. Clawson; Mishicott, D. Smith; Two Rivers, C. Kuehn; Kossuth, J. Edwards; Newton, William Griebling; Maple Grove, J. Sharp. Resolutions were adopted as follows, pledging the meeting to the support of a loan:—

WHEREAS, We deem the extension of the Lake Shore Railroad to some point within the county a measure of vital importance to the agricultural and manufacturing interests of the northern portion of the state and especially of Manitowoc County, whereby our pupulation is to be increased, the value of our property advanced, our resources developed and the facilities of a cheap and easy inter-communication at all seasons of the year with other portions of the state and the Union afforded us, and whereas we are informed that the Lake Shore R. R. Co. proposes to extend their road to some point within the county immediately, provided they receive from the county sufficient aid and encouragement to enable them to do so, therefore

Be it Resolved, That for the purpose of enabling and inducing the Lake Shore R. R. to complete their road to some point within the county it is expedient that the county of Manitowoc loan its credit to said company for the sum of $300,000, if such sum be found necessary to accomplish the work proposed, provided said company give satisfactory security for the payment of the interest and principal of said loan as the same may fall due. Resolved that a committee of one from each town in the county be appointed to correspond with the Lake Shore Company and obtain from them a definite proposition as to the amount they will need the credit of the county for and the security they will return for the same.

The committee of correspondence was accordingly appointed but all energy was wasted for by this time the road in question, which later became the nucleus of the Northwestern system had already decided to extend northward through the Fox River Valley region.

However as the summer wore on the matters of the Manitowoc & Mississippi advanced. The contract was let to A. P. Graham & Co., an eastern firm, but they lacking confidence in the ability of the owners to compensate them assigned it to N. P. Moulton & Co. in July. Ground was broken by the latter firm on June 10, 1855, but the year dragged on without any continuance of the work. New directors were elected as usual in July, S. A. Wood and J. E. Platt representing the village interests and George Reed being re-elected president, Jacob Lueps, treasurer and George L. Lee, secretary. On October 8th a mass meeting was held in the village for the purpose of raising the deficiency in the stock subscriptions. Among the speakers were A. W. Buel, recently arrived from Detroit, President Reed and Secretary Lee, but the only result was the appointment of a committee to secure the subscriptions. In the succeeding March Secretary Lee resigned and A. Ten Eyck was elected to fill the vacancy. In May the contract with N. P. Moulton & Co., was rescinded, since it

GEORGE REED.

was seen that they were too timid to continue the work and on the 14th of the month Barker & Hoes secured the job, guaranteeing to complete the construction by October of the year 1857. Time wore on and on July 7th the date for holding the annual director's meeting arrived. Dissentions had been growing and it was soon seen that a faction, headed by Benjamin Jones, who was a surety for the contractors, was clearly opposed to the Reed management. This faction was at first successful, scoring a point in having a motion passed that only full paid stock should be represented. This permitted them to control the meeting and Charles Cain, a Milwaukee mill owner, was chosen president, S. A. Wood, vice president, C. Esslinger, treasurer and A. Ten Eyck, secretary; while the board of directors comprised C. Cain, B. Jones, J. E. Platt, S. A. Wood, E. D. Beardsley, M. Fellows, all of Manitowoc and C. Doty and J. Turner of Menasha. It was decided to put forth a grand effort to complete the road by November as far as Branch Mills. But the Reed partisans, consisting of George and Curtis Reed, C. Klingholz and H. L. Palmer, who had been summarily ejected from the directorship, would not down and bolted, forming an organization of their own with George Reed as president. Feeling grew high, the Manitowoc press vituperating Mr. Reed and his friends for opposing the progress of the road. J. Lueps, however, with great skill secured a vote of confidence from the village trustees in the Reed management, much to the chagrin of many of the latter's constituents, since popular sympathy in Manitowoc seemed to be with the Cain faction. In fact the representatives from the second ward, I. Parrish and H. Rand, were the objects of a public remonstrance, signed very numerously, appearing in the weekly Herald on August 9th, to which they also replied in justification. The vote of confidence had its effect nevertheless and a temporary compromise was effected by which the Cain directors gave way to the Reed management.

Though work was resumed and continued throughout that fall and the following spring, by May 1, 1857, one year after the contract had been let, Barker & Hoes had only completed one third of the grading on the eastern end and no

JOSEPH VILAS, SR.

depot grounds had been fixed. It was in the spring of that year also that the legislature chartered the Manitowoc and Fond du Lac Railroad Company, another scheme that came to nothing. The projectors were C. Kuehn, W. H. Glover, W. Bach, N. Wollmer, B. Jones, C. W. Fitch, T. Clark, C. H. Walker, all of Manitowoc and several Fond du Lac parties. No steps toward further organization were taken however. As to the Manitowoc and Mississippi, confidence began to disappear and the Green Bay Advocate said in April: "It is our honest conviction that the M. & M. railroad when completed to Menasha, will not pay for the oil necessary to lubricate its car wheels." Manitowoc parties, who acted as guarantors of the contractors, became exercised at the progress and a final coup was decided upon, by which it was planned to grant the first allotment of shares to the contractors in order to facilitate matters. This was done partially by giving them six hundred $100 shares against the protest of President Reed at a meeting held on June 17th. The contractors thereby gained a control that Mr. Reed and his friends claimed they had not earned. The Reed partisans thus ousted, held a directors' meeting on July 1st and organization was effected as follows: President, George Reed; Vice-President, Jacob Lueps; Secretary, R. Klingholz; Treasurer, N. Wollmer; Stock Agent, Jacob Lueps; Directors, G. Reed, N. Wollmer, Curtis Reed, B. J. Sweet, J. Lueps, R. Klingholz, A. Baensch and C. H. Walker. The Cain organization met five days later and, the Barker & Hoes shares being in the majority, put in C. Cain as president, W. Bach as vice-president, and S. A. Wood as secretary, B. Jones, J. E. Platt and S. A. Wood representing Manitowoc on the board of directors. Thus it came about that two organizations were in existence aiming to build the same road and at sword's point with each other. Work consequently came to a standstill, the Cain organization hindering in every way Hewitt & Co., who had been hired by George Reed to commence the Menasha end of the road. Taunts and recriminations flew fast through the summer of 1857 and when Jacob Lueps who was in Germany for the purpose of selling the bonds of the road, heard of the turn affairs had taken he refused to continue his agency and soon after returned home. To add to the company's distress the panic of 1857 came on, business was at a standstill and the road was advertised for sale for the non-payment of $3,130 interest due on the first mortgage and Menasha bonds, the former of which had been issued to Azariah Flagg and James Horner, New York capitalists. President Reed opposed this sale, but his opponents had the books and refused to show them up. Suits were commenced by the Cain organization against their opponents for the proceeds of what bonds had been sold and also for other stock. The two Menasha members of the organization, Messrs. Doty and Turner, became frightened and placed themselves in the hands of D. F. Pulling, Cain's attorney, with instructions to get what settlement could be effected. It was decided to postpone the sale finally but this was not the end of complications.

The Menasha residents, having so much at stake, became restive and at a public meeting called there on January 9, 1858 it was decided to appoint an investigating committee, since certain charges were made against Reed's management. The committee appointed reported in a few weeks, completely exonerating Reed from all charges and expressing it as their opinion that he could prosecute the work better than anyone else. It also censured the action of Doty and Turner as also that of the Cain supporters at Manitowoc. It was claimed that all members of the latter had "axes to grind" in wishing the railroad project harm and that the members of the Cain board had no confidence in each other or in their ability to build a road. The financial condition of the project, it was reported, was good and all would be well if dissensions could be hushed. The statement made was as follows:

ASSETS:
Cash Subscriptions .................................... $ 31,700
First Mortgage Bonds ................................. 426,000
Manitowoc and Menasha Village Bonds ........... 274,000
Grading, Bridging, Ties, etc ......................... 360,000
Due from Contractors Overdrawn .................. 52,000
Farm Mortgages. Interest on Same ................ 6,800
Lueps' Subscription conditional on Reed's Management 50,000
    Total ............................................. $1,200,500

## LIABILITIES.

| | |
|---|---|
| First Mortgage Bonds in hands of Contractors | $ 89,000 |
| Interest on Bonds | 4,000 |
| Miscellaneous | 7,500 |
| Taxes | 500 |
| Full Paid Stock | 140,000 |
| Total | $ 241,000 |

At this time the road had been graded as far as Reedsville and iron had been ordered for the first twenty miles. It was then that George Reed made the following proposition to the committee:

"Gentlemen:—In answer to your inquiry as to what we will undertake to do towards carrying forward the work of the M. & M. we will state that if the authorities of the villages of Menasha and Manitowoc within thirty days will treat with and recognize the "Reed organization" so called in contra-distinction to the "Cain organization" and agree to carry out in good faith the contract as representatives of the company and if the village of Menasha and the stockholders of Menasha will sustain Hewitt & Co. in their contract with the company in prosecution of the work between Menasha and Spring Creek, we will agree to have the whole line of the first division of the railroad prepared and completed, ready for the iron rail, as early as the first of July next, and also if we can command the securities of the company, will agree to have the iron purchased and the track laid by the first of October, or as soon thereafter as possible." Yours Respectfully, George Reed, J. Lueps, C. Klingholz, C. Reed."

This offer was, on the recommendation of the committee, accepted by the village trustees of Menasha at their meeting on Jan. 29th. Finally, however, since no progress was being made during the spring President Reed resigned and, authorized by a special act of the legislature, the stockholders met on July 5, 1858, and elected a new management, in which both factions were recognized as follows: President, Jacob Lueps; vice-president, B. S. Heath, of Menasha; treasurer, H. Rahr; secretary, S. A. Wood; chief engineer, F. Salomon;

directors, J. Lueps, J. M. Sherwood, R. Klingholz, Gerard Kremers, S. A. Wood, J. E. Platt, of Manitowoc and B. S. Heath and S. M. Bronson of Menasha. Prospects seemed bright again and steps were taken toward immediate completion, it being hoped that the road might be in running order by the next July. The governor appointed as a board of inspectors Dr. M. F. Davis, F. S. Lovell and Judge Howe in order to settle all disputes, but the spirit had departed from the enterprise and work was not resumed because of lack of funds. On April 21. 1859, the interest on the old issue of bonds and also on another issue, made in 1858, remaining unpaid the road was advertised for sale and bought in by Jacob Lueps and B. Jones for $100,000. In July P. Latimer, a New York capitalist, appeared upon the scene and made a proposition to Lueps and his associates that he would build the road, shipping the iron within fifteen months, if the village would issue its full amount of bonds Besides the bonds of the two villages, still unissued amounting to $274,000 he also asked $450,000 in first mortgage security and $242,000 in second mortgage bonds, a total of $977,000. A meeting of citizens was held to discuss the proposition on August 10, S. A. Wood acting as chairman and F. Borcherdt as secretary. While the village did not desire to go ahead and build the road itself, it did not favor Mr. Latimer's proposition and the majority report of the committee on resolutions was adopted as follows:—"Resolved, That the board of trustees of this village be advised by this meeting not to issue any of the bonds of the village to the M. and M. Railroad Co. upon the contract signed with P. Latimer, submitted to this meeting under date of July 30 and to no other person or company until sufficient guaranties are given by them that the principal and interest of such bonds will be punctually paid and not until such contract in all its bearings and provisions be submitted to the people of this village in meeting assembled." G. L. Lee and J. D. Markham signed this report while Temple Clark offered a minority report, favoring Latimer.

J. E. Platt went east in September to confer with capitalists and reported on his return to the village trustees that they had advised the formation of a new company and an issue of bonds. Contractor Barker at about the same time offered to build and equip the road for $874,000, but the resolutions passed by both the Menasha and Manitowoc trustees, favoring the issue of $75,000 in bonds by each village were not a sufficient encouragement. During the fall and succeeding months J. Lewis, a financial agent from Toronto looked over the road as did also a Mr. Grant, but no offer of completion resulted. The Menasha people in the meanwhile blamed the Manitowoc stockholders for blocking Mr. Reed's projects, he, it was claimed, being the only one capable of completing the road. In May and June of 1860 two Canadian capitalists, Messrs. James Beachell, of Toronto and R. Bell, of Ottawa, inspected the road, becoming favorably impressed. They might have come to a definite proposition had it not been for an injunction, which had been pending since March 24, secured by George and Curtis Reed and aimed at any purchasers of the road. It seems that certain legal requirements as to the publication of notice of the sale had not been met and Judge Whiton sustained the restraining order. The Reeds refused to settle the matter and feeling against them was again very high on the part of those who desired to transfer the property. It was proposed in June that there should be an election and re-organization but the fears then entertained on the part of the Menasha people that the destination of the road might be changed to Appleton interfered with such an arrangement. N ) officers had been elected since 1858 and in the threatening days, so full of political excitement, in the latter part of 1860, further interest in railroad matters seemed to lapse, although feeble attempts were made at reorganization the succeeding spring. The Reed organization continued to hold adjourned meetings, lacking a quorum, throughout the war, thus leading an anomalous existence, with headquarters in Menasha.

After the issue of the war had been decided attention was again turned towards railroad matters. A proposal was made in January 1864 that all stockholders place their shares on a common basis to be disposed of to some eastern men with capital enough to construct the road. Mr. Reed also had proposals to make at about this time, he having effected an understanding with Jacob Lueps, the purchaser of the rights of way. Two years passed, the Reed organization still maintaining its legal existence. Then on April 4, 1866, the charter of the M. & M. was consolidated, the new incorporators being George Reed and Jos. Vilas of Manitowoc; Henry Hewitt, R. M. Scott and Curtis Reed of Menasha. George Reed was chosen president and Joseph Vilas vice-president and on March 1st an act was passed providing that whenever the company should deposit in the First National bank $100,000 and release the village from the $37,000 in bonds then due the clerk of the village should deposit $100,000 of the village bonds subject to exchange for stock in the company. Two years more passed without definite action when, on March 6, 1868, the Manitowoc and Minnesota company was organized to succeed to the corporate rights of the old M. & M. The promoters were Henry Hewitt, Curtis Reed, R. Klingholz, I. S. Buck and George Reed and the capital stock was fixed at ten millions. It was given the power to enforce the bonds of its predecessors and the first directors were to be elected in May 1869. It was expected that the aid of such capitalists as Hiram Barnard and S. J. Tilden of New York could be enlisted and it was planned to include Appleton on the route and to reach the Mississippi. Judge Reed thought to take advantage of an old grant of a right of way to Lake Superior via Stevens Point, a distance of about three hundred miles in all,—eventually the line of the Wisconsin Central. Eastern connections with the F. & P. M., which had been urged as early as 1857, were again proposed also. In September the village board put the question of advancing $100,000 in village bonds to aid the project and the election held on the 22nd resulted as follows: For proposition, 304; against, 80, a majority of 224. The usual delay resulted, however, and by this time attention was turning in another direction.

It seems that a grant had been made to a company known as the Milwaukee and Lake Superior railroad in 1856, its rights being extended ten years in 1866. Capitalists had taken up this project, which had been allowed to lapse so long and on March 5, 1869 it was given permission by the legislature to build its road through Cedarburg, Grafton, Port Washington, Sheboygan, Manitowoc and Green Bay to some point on Lake Superior. F. W. Horn, the president of the road, visited Manitowoc in October 1869 in its interest and a railroad meeting was held on November 13. Captain Guyles acted as chairman, F. Borcherdt as secretary and among the speakers were J. D. Markham, E. B. Treat, C. E. Esslinger, S. A. Wood and D. Smoke. Committees were appointed and soon Joseph Vilas, always a master organizer, was attracted towards the new plan as a most practicable project. Mr. Reed, however, did not remain inactive and in December asked further aid for his road to pay the expense of a survey and other preliminaries. A vote on the question of advancing it was taken, resulting in 103 for and 188 against the proposition and it was thus seen that Manitowoc was not favorable to his plans. The railroad committee, appointed in November, went to Appleton and found the people there very enthusiastic over the prospects of a new outlet. Another meeting was called for January 29th, 1870 at Klingholz Hall. Captain Guyles again acted as chairman and the principal business was the receipt of a letter from Milwaukee, asking what assistance Manitowoc would give. A second committee was accordingly appointed, consisting of S. A. Wood, C. E. Esslinger, J. Lueps and J. D. Markham to go to Madison and assist in securing a charter. The struggle was a hard one, the opponents of the project being the Milwaukee & Northern and the Wisconsin Central, the latter of which was now being built with George Reed as one of its principal promoters. The committee representing Manitowoc worked hard and long but their efforts at first met with disappointment for on March 2nd the assembly by a vote of 43 to 41 voted against the charter. A few days later, however, an amendment was assented to changing the name from that of the Milwaukee, Manitowoc, Mississippi & Minnesota company, which had been proposed, to the Milwaukee, Manitowoc & Green Bay and, as such, articles of incorporation were granted to it on March

10th. The capital stock was fixed at five millions, with authority granted to double the amount and the incorporators were Joseph Vilas, Charles Cain, I. M. Bean, D. Taylor, F. Hilger, J. W. Vail, S. W. Cozzens, Levi Blossom, R. C. Merrington, W. S. Chandler and Jacob Lueps, most of them outside capitalists. Authority was given to towns, villages and counties along its route to grant aid also. In the same month organization was effected by the election of the following officers:—President, Charles Cain; vice-president, S. W. Cozzens; secretary Joseph Vilas; treasurer, R. O. C. Merrington. Thus all the elements, it will be seen, that were present in the older railroad efforts in the county were in the new organization, minus Mr. Reed, who opposed this new project strenuously in the legislature and outside it.

A large mass meeting was held on March 23rd at which it was decided without a dissenting vote to submit to the citizens the question whether or not the county should subscribe $250,000. In the meantime a meeting was held of the directors of the old Appleton & New London Railroad company, which had existed for some years on paper and Joseph Vilas was elected president, so that the management of the two roads became almost identical. The charter of this latter road had been so amended that it might connect with the other at some point on Lake Michigan and from 1870 on it and the Milwaukee, Manitowoc & Green Bay were one project. The vote in Manitowoc county was taken on April 12th. Manitowoc city and town voted in favor of the bond issue almost unanimously, 1,493 ballots being so cast and majorities favorable were secured also in the towns of Rapids, Kossuth, Cato, Newton, Franklin and Rockland, amounting to 2,544 while an aggregate majority of 1,921 against the issue was the result in Two Rivers, Mishicot, Gibson, Meeme, Maple Grove, Liberty, Cooperstown, Centreville, Two Creeks and Schleswig. The aid voted was divided, $150,000 to the Appleton and New London and $100,000 to the Milwaukee, Manitowoc & Green Bay and the result of the total vote was 597 majority for the latter and 661 for the former proposition. In the words of the local press: "Now one more railroad company has got all it has asked for from the county and we are waiting for them to fulfill their part of the contract." Brown county also signified a willingness to aid the project, if assurances would be given that the road would touch that section.

Work began on the road north of Milwaukee in May and on June 4th Port Washington voted to take $30,000 of stock in the Milwaukee, Manitowoc & Green Bay by 210 majority. Directors were elected in July and the following officers also chosen:—President, Joseph Vilas; vice-president, C. Cozzens, of New York; secretary, R. Merrington; treasurer, C. C. Barnes. During 1870 and 1871 the Milwaukee & Northern Railroad company was also pushed and the town of Schleswig by a large majority granted $15,000 in aid to the road. Joseph Vilas, president of the other road, was in the meanwhile making frequent trips to New York, interesting capital there and getting matters in final shape for the construction. It was his persistent efforts more than anything else that brought about a successful consummation of the plans so soon. Other projects were still considered, however, and in January 1871 George Reed called a meeting at the courthouse in the interests of the old Manitowoc & Minnesota, promising to build the road to Menasha in a year, providing the city would get the right of way ready for the rails. Another meeting was held by O. H. Waldo and other promoters of a scheme to build a road from Milwaukee to Manitowoc via Cedarburg and Sheboygan Falls but neither this nor the former proposition were favorably received, the Manitowoc and Minnesota a few months later becoming consolidated with the Wisconsin Central and George Reed being elected president of both corporations. Thereafter his interest in Manitowoc railroad projects was at an end. For twenty years had he been identified with them and there are those who believe that had he been allowed to proceed unhampered at the first the Manitowoc & Mississippi might have been built and in active operation before the Civil war.

In the meanwhile work was being pushed on the Appleton & New London, between Appleton and Manitowoc, the part first to be built. President Vilas in April, 1871, purchased 1500 tons of iron rails, a locomotive and several platform cars, the rails arriving May 30. In the early dawn of Sunday morning, June 22, the first locomotive, named the Benjamin Jones, after the city's founder, was brought into the harbor on board the two-masted schooner Mediterranean, having been shipped on the craft at Buffalo. All day a stream of visitors gazed upon this herald of a new day and hopes for the future seemed now near realization. The lofty railroad bridge near Branch Mills was constructed in this month and in July at a meeting of the stockholders all was reported as prosperous. Joseph Vilas was re-elected president, Henry Mann chosen vice-president, C. Luling, secretary, C. C. Barnes, treasurer and eleven directors, two from Milwaukee, one from Port Washington, three from Sheboygan, besides Jacob Lueps, J. D. Markham, M. Fellows, C. H. Walker and Joseph Vilas, were elected. It had now been definitely settled that Appleton was to be upon the route and upon the advice of Hiram Barnard, the New York capitalist, that city extended considerable aid. The satisfaction expressed by the rapidity of the work on the Appleton division was augmented, when in September news reached the city that work north of Milwaukee would be pushed immediately. In June the company asked for further aid, $75,000 of the city of Manitowoc and $25,000 from Two Rivers. The latter was to be in consideration of an agreement to build a branch to that city along the line granted the year before (on March 24, 1871) by the legislature to the Manitowoc & Big Sturgeon R. R. Co., the incorporators of which were J. Vilas, John Schuette and C. C. Barnes of Manitowoc; H. H. Smith of Two Rivers and W. Wyatt of Kenosha. Meetings were held to discuss this new proposal and sentiment seemed to be so in favor of the extra aid that an election was held on June 7th, resulting as follows in Manitowoc:

| Wards. | For | Against |
|---|---|---|
| I. | 152 | 77 |
| II. | 99 | 17 |
| III. | 232 | 39 |
| IV. | 125 | 54 |
| Total, | 578 | 187 |

In Two Rivers the vote was taken on the 24th of July and resulted in 299 votes being cast in favor of the proposition as against 96 against it, a result which met with enthusiastic acclaim. Sheboygan city also voted $50,000 and the county $80,000 in aid of the project, the sum total of the amounts voted by the lake shore counties to the road being $480,000. In the fall of 1872 the road from Manitowoc to Appleton was opened for business. Work was also progressing north of Milwaukee, being completed as far as Sheboygan by the time winter set in, under the able management of engineer H. G. H. Reed, in charge of the construction. The panic of 1873 did not interrupt the work, due to the efforts of President Vilas, and on September 22nd of that year the road was formally opened to Milwaukee, the Two Rivers branch being completed the following year. During 1872 and 1873 the officers remained unchanged with the exception of the addition of Charles Luling, who acquired interests in the project at about this time. The name Milwaukee Lake Shore & Western was assumed in 1873 as the designation of the consolidated system. Trouble soon arose, however, the road being unable to meet its obligations held by eastern capitalists and early in 1874 it became necessary to turn it over to the bondholders. Directors Fellows, Lueps, Markham, Elwell and Colzhausen stepped out and L. Wells, W. H Guion, S. S. Sands and S. H. Knox of New York City; I. O. Horning, of Philadelphia and R. Bard of Baltimore, who had bought the bonds, filled the places vacated. On May 6th a re-organization was effected, F. W. Rhinelander of New York succeeding Mr. Vilas as president and Henry Mann of Milwaukee being chosen vice-president. Old obligations were then settled, claims adjusted and the road extended westward from Appleton from year to year until the Lake Shore system became one of the best equipped of the smaller roads of the state. Joseph Vilas and Charles Luling were at this time and for many succeeding years the only Manitowoc men interested in the road, being directors.

It can scarcely be said that Manitowoc received all the benefit it had expected from railway connections. The much hoped for eastern lake route did not materialize and, although the division railroad shops were located at Manitowoc at first, even these were removed to Kaukauna in 1883 much to the chagrin and detriment of the city. In 1884 rumors to the effect that the Two Rivers branch would be extended to Kewarnee were rife and again in 1887 the Milwaukee and Northern contemplated an extension from Kiel to Kewaunee, public meetings to consider the project being held in the country towns but no action resulted from either project. In the meanwhile the city and county were beginning to realize that the money subscribed for stock in the railroad companies had, by the reorganization of the M. L. S. & W., become a debt and nothing more. The county board in January, 1884 appointed a committee, consisting of Supervisors Stoker, Schmitz and McCarty, to investigate the matter and see if any relief was possible. At that time $216,000 of the county subscription was still unpaid and all the money advanced by the cities of Manitowoc and Two Rivers was owing. An attempt had been made in earlier years to come to some agreement, notable in the efforts being John Carey, but the cities had been backward in co-operating, wishing to ascertain what were the company's motives. Two lawyers were consulted by the committee and gave their opinions, Michael Kirwan holding that the county had no redress and was bound to pay the bonds while F. W. Cotzhausen of Milwaukee maintained an exactly contrary position. It was finally referred to Attorney Joshua Stark of Milwaukee, who upheld Judge Kirwan's opinion. The county bonds became due on July 1, 1890, being held in New York, Sheboygan, Manitowoc and elsewhere, selling in 1888 at a premium of five per cent. In that year another committee, consisting of J. P. Nolan, of Maple Grove; J. Murphy of Cato and F. Schuette of Manitowoc, was chosen by the board to ascertain the best method of paying off the debt. Discussion continued at intervals until the November session in 1889 when the proposition of County Treasurer Gielow was adopted, by which the bonds were to be refunded and an arrangement made to pay $18,000 annually for fifteen years. The town of Schleswig was meeting with similar questions with regard to its Milwaukee & Northern bonds and made a settlement somewhat similar, agreeing to pay $1000 for thirteen years. During the twenty years these bonds had run Schleswig had paid $24,000 in interest, nearly twice the amount of the original aid extended. The bonds of the cities of Manitowoc and Two Rivers became due in 1892 and the former refunded the $35,000 then remaining due in twenty year bonds, Two Rivers making a similar arrangement. On several occasions talk arose of possible connections between the M. L. S. & W. and the Wisconsin Central but nothing definite came of it. In 1889 the former asked the city council of Manitowoc for a franchise granting the right of way on Franklin and Quay streets from their depot to the lake front, promising the city much benefit from proposed improvements at the latter point. Much opposition arose, however, and General Manager Whitcomb and Mr. Thayer representing the road were called upon to address the council upon the matter. The right of way was finally granted after the imposition of some conditions as to the use of the same. Damage suits were then brought by abutting property holders, which dragged on for many years, the attorneys for the plaintiffs, Sedgwick, Sedgwick & Schmidt, finally securing a decision in the fall of 1901. The railroad company had bought the Hinckley and Allen property, consisting of nineteen acres, on the lake shore for $13,000 but year after year passed without any of the promised improvements being made with the exception of the building of a warehouse for the transferring of freight to the F. & P. M. liners. In 1891 steps were taken looking toward the incorporation of the M. L. S. & W. into the Chicago & Northwestern system. By this time no Manitowoc capital was invested in the former road and the change, perfected August 19, 1893, would have been immaterial had it not injured the city's facilities by the fact that many of the through trains were thereafter run over the Wisconsin instead of the Ashland division, as the Lake Shore was now called. About the time of the change a depot was built, which filled a long felt need, the new structure being a neat and commodious one, costing $15,000. Although the C. & N. W. continued through shipments across the lake in 1892 business fell off and the panic of the next year still further depressed trade. The Kewaunee short line, established at about the same time was also a disturbing factor affecting local business. It was at this unpropitious time that the Northwestern asked for the vacation of the lake front street ends on the south side, thus raising a question that vexed the city fathers all during the summer of 1893. Upon showing that it was purchasing the right of way for a proposed belt line around the southern limits of the city the company was unanimously granted the privilege after much opposition. The belt line was, not, however, completed until five years later.

And now in the time of deepest industrial depression, when Manitowoc seemed to have little future before her there came to a head as magnificent a scheme of transportation as the city had ever hoped for. The old desire to be located on a through line to the east, which had been entertained as early as the fifties, was finally obtained and that through the medium of the Wisconsin Central, by the strange irony of Fate, the successor to the very privileges granted to the Manitowoc & Mississippi. The earliest rumor of an extension of the Central eastward from Menasha gained currency through the columns of the Milwaukee and Menasha papers in January, 1894, although it later came to light that had it not been for the panic the road would have been built in 1892. In December 1894 the Superior & Southeastern filed articles of incorporation, of which Ex-State Treasurer Hunner was one of the projectors, with Manitowoc or Sheboygan as its projected terminus. The plan although it did not go beyond the stage of incorporation preceded by a few weeks certain peculiar actions that continued to mystify citizens for three months. Options were taken on city property just above and north of the Main street bridge, surveyors were seen in the neighboring country and wild rumors were afloat. Some thought that the land was being secured by the C. & N. W., others that the Inter-Ocean Transportation company was seeking property and still others attributed the actions to the Wisconsin Central but the result was that the price of lots went up and

Manitowoc experienced something of a real estate boom. Zander & Co., planing mill proprietors, and others sold their property on what was known as "the flats" and condemnation proceedings were filed on March 20th by a corporation calling itself the Manitowoc Terminal company against many of the neighboring tracts. The true facts of the case did not come out until April 18, when in a special edition of the Manitowoc Pilot the whole matter became public information. It seems that the Wisconsin Central had been responsible for the activity and that as channels of action there were two corporations, the Manitowoc Terminal company and the Milwaukee & Lake Winnebago Railway company. The former secured quietly all of what was known as "Shipyard Point" and "Lueps' Island" while the latter had been obtaining a right of way westward to Hilbert Junction. Continuous dockage and acres of track space were thus afforded and it was announced that the depots would be placed near the Main street bridge. The vastness of the project was early understood; in the language of a newspaper of the time: "It is self evident that these lines are not to be built to secure local business but have in view eastern connections." But most remarkable of all the company asked no bonus, merely requesting the vacation of the streets on the "flats." Fear that it might be the C. & N. W. in disguise was quieted by the arrival on May 8, of E. H. Abbott, president of the Central; General Manager Whitcomb, Chief Engineer Tweedy and P. S. Abbott. The project by this time had become widely advertised and Manitowoc received much notice. Attorney Gill appeared before the council upon the question of the vacation of the streets on May 13th and President Greenleaf of the Manitowoc Terminal company communicated with that body concerning necessary co-operation by the city in dredging the river soon after.

The contracts for the grading of the new road were let to Evans & Richards of Minneapolis in a month and the work was completed by May 1, 1896. Sub-contractors took the job of digging the deep cuts, one of which required the excavation of 158,000 cubic yards of earth. A commencement at the grading of the terminals was made in November 1895 and dredging continued during the fall and succeeding spring. Railroad officials were frequent visitors during the spring months in order that they might keep in touch with the work being done. At last the rails were laid and the first train crossed the new jack knife bridge, which had been erected near the ship yards, at 3:10 p m. on June 24, 1896, the last spike of the road being driven by Captain Carle of the Manitowoc police force. W. Vandegrift of Appleton was chosen local agent and the road was formally opened on July 2nd. The train bearing the officials arrived in charge of Conductor Scott and Engineer Nolan on the morning of that day and speeches were made upon the depot platform by Mayor Torrison, President Abbott, Joseph Vilas and H. G. Kress. Freight sheds were soon constructed and a passenger service of two trains daily in each direction established. Little villages, such as Potters; Valders, Madsen and Collins sprang up along the route forming centers of shipment for farming communities. Extensive yards were established north of the Manitowoc river and it was not many months before they were filled with cars enroute to the east. All this railroad activity led to increased marine facilities, the establishment of elevators and also of carferry routes, referred to in the preceding pages.

The energy displayed by the Central in opening terminals at Manitowoc seemed to have an inspiring effect on the Chicago & Northwestern as well. Early in 1895 rumors were abroad that the latter would utilize the carferry system and build slips on its lake front property. It was finally decided by that company to improve its facilities and in May 1896 a slip 450 by 110 feet was constructed. Coal docks with a capacity of 250,000 tons were also added, being managed and operated by eastern firms, until sold to the Reiss Company in 1899. With all these improvements business naturally increased at a rapid rate until in 1900 that done through the local office of the Northwestern was greater than at any point on the system outside of Chicago and Milwaukee.

What the future has for Manitowoc in the way of railroad development it would be difficult to tell. It is well

THOMAS WINDIATE

known that some corporation has purchased the right of way over the submerged property from the north side of the river entrance to the mouth of the Little Manitowoc and it may be that some day another belt line may be added or indeed facilities may be increased in a different way. Rumors have been prevalent in years past of the entrance of the Illinois Central, the Chicago, Milwaukee & St. Paul and other lines, but definite results have not been forthcoming. Nevertheless the city need have no fear of the future when it is considered how much money is invested in terminal facilities. In truth it seems as if the dreams of the village founders were at last approaching consummation.

Manitowoc has been somewhat tardy in securing street railway facilities. In September 1887 a franchise was asked for by P. S. Tillson and Henry Schmidt, of Manitowoc and H. Saemann of Sheboygan. The matter was not pushed, however, and it was not until the summer of 1900 that it was revived. At this time Thomas Higgins of Menasha and Henry Higgins of Marinette, both street car promoters, asked for a franchise under the name of the Manitowoc & Northern Traction Company, proposing to run an interurban system between Manitowoc and Two Rivers with possible later extensions to Kewaunee and other northern points. After some discussion and competition by other promoters the Higgins brothers were granted a thirty-five year franchise by the city council of Manitowoc on October 13th and by that of Two Rivers soon after. Construction was begun the following June and the road was opened for traffic in the spring of 1902. Some activity was also manifested throughout 1900 and 1901 by a traction company, which proposed to extend a line northward from Sheboygan through Manitowoc county to Green Bay. Votes favorable to the project were taken in several of the townships but no definite action followed.

## CHAPTER VIII.

### MILITARY.

The American always rejoices in the annals of his military achievements. That the valor of the nation has stood the test of many a conflict is sufficient cause for such a feeling. Such a pride loses nothing of its essence but is in fact enhanced when history is narrowed down and brought home to any community. Thus the part played by Manitowoc county in military affairs of over a half a century is of interest, the more so since all of the actors were known as neighbors and many of them linger still in the form of sad memories in the minds of the older generation.

When Wisconsin was organized as a territory the old southern militia system, wherein every able bodied citizen within certain age limits was enrolled, was adopted. Of course in such a newly settled region it was impossible to mobilize the force or to hold any drills but the system existed on paper nevertheless. As early as the later thirties Manitowoc county was assigned as a part of the Second regiment, remaining so for some years. Reorganization took place in 1839 and in 1842 the county regiment system was adopted, whereby each county was made a unit of military organization, Manitowoc being a part of the First Bat., Second Reg., First division. According to the records on February 17, 1842 Company E was constituted as follows:—Captain, Pliny Pierce; first lieutenant, Alfred Wood; second lieutenant, P. P. Smith. In 1847 T. A. H. Edwards was made colonel of the Manitowoc county militia, C. H. Champlin, lieutenant-colonel and A. D. Soper major. Then came the Mexican war, causing a general reorganization in military circles.

Manitowoc county was too far in the wilderness to take a part in this struggle, although a few of the later settlers, notably S. W. Smith, had served in it. The Wisconsin militia regiments were brigaded at about this time and in 1848 Daniel Bolles was made colonel of the county regiment. Such appointments continued during the fifties, among those holding military commissions being J. M. Sherwood, W. Lozier, S. W. Smith and Temple Clark, the latter becoming particularly prominent as major-general of a district composing Manitowoc, Calumet, Brown and Kewaunee counties, known as the Eighth division. Reverend M. Hoyt was division chaplain in the later fifties, Colonel A. Wittman, quartermaster, Dr. White of Two Rivers surgeon and H. C. Hamilton of the same place aide to General Clark. In the first brigade were Manitowoc and Calumet counties under command of Brigadier-General S. W. Smith, F. Borcherdt acting as aide and Dr. A. W. Preston as surgeon. Manitowoc county composed the Thirteenth regiment under Colonel F. Salomon, Lieutenant-Colonel W. Aldrich and Major C. Bates. Under this system, which obtained until 1861, there were about 2,600 enrolled militia in the county.

An end was put to this more or less amateur soldiering by the approach of the dark clouds that portended serious civil struggle. The crash came suddenly and in the county as in fact throughout the whole north it was almost stunning in its effect. Busied with plans of material development the settlers along the lake shore had not realized the imminence of war until Sumter was fired upon. But then like thousands of other communities enthusiasm and interest was at a high pitch. Six days after the first gun had been fired the first war meeting was called at Manitowoc in the courthouse. It was convened by President Collins of the village; J. F. Guyles was chosen chairman and E. D. Beardsley and S. W. Smith secretaries. Speeches were made by Temple Clark, Henry Baetz, B. Anderson and Dr. Preston and then the committee on resolutions, consisting of C. C. Barnes, J. D. Markham and Jere Crowley, brought in a report. Some disagreement arose, Mr. Crowley not signing the report favored by the other two members, he being at the time a sympathizer with the south. Inflammatory speeches followed by C. C. Barnes and W. M. Nichols but Mr. Crowley, when called upon, refused to express his opinions, introducing instead a Mr. Wright of New York, who happened to be in the village. The latter was a strong Secessionist and made bold to say that he would fly the Palmetto flag from his sailboat, which was in the harbor, but the crowd would have none of him and he was hissed to his seat. Resolutions were then offered by P. P. Smith favoring Lincoln and recommending the raising of a company. These were passed after a wordy battle and volunteers were called for. The meeting was one of the largest ever held in the village. Similar gatherings were held in Two Rivers and interest was high there also, it being stated on April 24th that "the volunteers from Two Rivers will more than fill a company." Two days before forty men had enlisted at Manitowoc and this number was increased by fourteen the next day. Judge Thayer of the circuit court was at the time holding a term at Manitowoc and in his charge to the grand jury referred feelingly to the stirring times. On the evening of the 22nd another rousing meeting was held, a procession being formed to escort Judge Thayer to the courthouse, where he addressed the citizens. J. F. Guyles acted as chairman and S. W. Smith and Otto Troemmel as secretaries while among the speakers were Reverend Engle, J. A. Bentley, J. D. Markham, C. C. Barnes, Temple Clark, C. C. Esslinger and A. Wittmann. The company then mobilizing was soon denominated the Manitowoc County Guards and on April 25th it elected officers as follows:—Captain, Temple Clark; first lieutenant, Horace Walker; second lieutenant, Peter Scherflus, after which Banker M. V. Adams made a patriotic speech. Three Mishicot young men. Lafayette Smith, James W. Langworthy and Horace Price, together with D. A. Shove and G. E. Waldo of Manitowoc. did not await the calling out of the Manitowoc Guards and accordingly went to Milwaukee and joined the First Regiment, being the first from the county to enlist and see active service.

C. ESSLINGER

All through the county by this time the people were aroused. At Branch Mills a flag raising afforded the occasion of expressing enthusiasm and a similar occurrence took place at the Second ward school in the village of Manitowoc. In the meanwhile interest centered in Captain Clark's company, the support given to it being unanimous. A private subscription was raised amounting to $1800 to form a soldiers' fund as a further inducement to enlistment. In the list were $100 gifts from C. C. Barnes, W. Goodenow, Platt & Vilas, J. Lueps and B. Jones & Co. and $50 donations from T. C. Shove, W. Murphy, T. & J. Robinson, M. Fellows, J. Bennett, Collins & Co., Louis Sherman, J. A. Koehler, T. Windiate, S. Hill, J. Richards, McDonald & Bros., Beer & Kern, C. Esslinger, J. S. Guyles, A. Wittman, J. D. Markham, T. G. Olmstead, H. Berner, J. Roeffs, E. Haywood, W. Hand, G. Glover, H. Baetz, W. H. Nichols, R. Klingholz and O. Torrison. Said the Weekly Herald: "If every man in the company wants the Herald for his parents, wife or sweetheart while he is fighting he shall have it." On May 1st 1861 Captain Temple Clark issued the following proclamation to citizens: "The company of volunteers from this county has been accepted by the governor and the officers commissioned. The company will be clothed and equipped at the expense of the state as soon as they are assigned to a regiment and ordered to rendezvous; in the meantime they will be kept under constant drill and such of them as do not belong in the village will be boarded at the expense of the state. One of the most necessary articles for the equipment of the soldier is the blanket. The enormous demand for these renders it impossible for the state to procure them in sufficient quantities to furnish all the volunteers in the state unless aided by private contributions of this article and we are obliged to make a call upon all our patriotic citizens to contribute from their private stores as many blankets as they can spare towards supplying this necessary want of our company. Respectfully Yours, Temple Clark."

The result was the formation among the ladies of the village of societies for the preparation of necessaries for the soldiers. The Guards in the meantime were fearful lest the war might be brought to a sudden termination and thus they be deprived of an opportunity to show their valor. At last after several weeks of weary waiting Captain Clark received orders on May 21st to fill his company to a full quota of 100 men and to be ready to march upon a moment's notice. Six days later a third mass meeting was held and stirring addresses made, patriotism being foremost in all minds. Still no word came for the company to move. On June 12th Colonel Emery arrived and mustered the company into the state service. During the same week a beautiful ceremony took place in the presentation of a flag to the company made by the ladies of the village, the presentation address being made by Mrs. Collins and the captain replying in a few feeling words. The flag was captured at Cold Harbor but was later retaken and after an exhibition at the Centennial was placed in the Capitol at Madison.

Then came the command to mobilize at Madison and on Sunday evening, June 23rd, 1861, the Manitowoc County Guards embarked on the Goodrich liner Comet and were carried southward. The largest crowd ever assembled in the village was present at the pier and the scenes enacted were of a nature never to be forgotten as partings were said, in many instances for the last time. Upon arrival at Camp Randall in Madison drilling was the order of the day and on July 13 the men were mustered into the United States service as Company A, Fifth Wisconsin infantry. Said the Madison Journal of the company: "They are strong, hardy men from the lumbering districts, who have been well drilled in machinery but have not been exercised in the manual of arms." This paper also described graphically the surroundings of the company's quarters. White pebbles had been utilized to make inscriptions giving the name of the organization and in front of the captain's tent were the words: "Captain Clark, God Bless Him," while three flags floated above this portion of the camp. The record of the Fifth during the war was a noble one. After the battle of Bull Run the regiment with others was hurried to the front and the first engagement in which it participated was that at Lee's Mills, Va., on April 16, 1862. Captain Clark was transferred in a short time, being promoted for bravery at Corinth and occupying a position on the staff of General Rosecrans. Thus the command early devolved upon Captain Walker, who through the troublous Virginia campaigns under McClellan, McDowell, Burnsides and Meade, led his men until at Rappahannock on November 7, 1863 he was struck down by a bullet. The company, however, continued its career until July 1864 when it was mustered out, its three years of service being at an end. Many of the members re-enlisted in other regiments while the remainder returned home. During its service twenty-three men on the muster roll were killed outright, ten were reported missing and twenty-seven were seriously wounded. Thus it happened that out of the 106 men that left Manitowoc on that June evening only 36 returned. Among these names later well known were those of J. S. Anderson, W. Rickaby, F. Stirn, J. Mill, J. Gilbert, D. Buboltz, F. W. Borcherdt, J. L. Cox, J. Enert, A. B. Gibson, J, R. Leykom, G. B. Engle and J. H. Leonard.

The first company sent to the war had not left the village before it became evident that the struggle was to be a long one and that the nation's resources would be taxed to the utmost. In the early part of May the German residents of the village organized the "Home Guards," Frederick Becker being chosen captain and Colonel Baetz assisting in the recruiting. It was soon announced that the Guards were to form a part of the Ninth Wisconsin. This was not, however, the only organization for which recruiting was in progress during the fall of 1861. In August F. Borcherdt was authorized to raise a company but did not succeed and another attempt was made a month later by Jere Crowley to get together an Irish company, the Meagher Guards, which was similarly unsuccessful. D. A. Shove and G. E. Waldo in the meantime had returned from their three months service with the First Wisconsin and plunged actively into the work of enlisting a company for the Fourteenth and soon Colonel K. K. Jones commenced similar efforts among the Norwegian residents of the county, intending to make his command a part of the Fifteenth Wisconsin which was being raised exclusively among those of that nationality. Other agencies were active also. The county board assembled and appropriated $1,500 for the relief of indigent soldiers' families while in Two Rivers the Ladies Relief Association was formed, the officers being:—President, Mrs. Van Valkenburgh; vice president, Mrs. Joseph Mann; treasurer, Mrs. J. Burns and secretary, Mrs. Alanson Hill. Kindred organizations were formed at Manitowoc and Cato.

Captain Becker's company left the city on October 2nd for Milwaukee and Manitowoc was honored in the choice of one of its citizens, Frederick Salomon, as colonel of the regiment, the Ninth, of which the company was a part, it becoming Co. B. Colonel, afterward General Salomon rose higher perhaps than any other Manitowoc man and the village always delighted to honor him. On the day before his departure he was presented by the German citizens with a beautiful charger which he used throughout the war. There were many men outside of Co. B from Manitowoc county in the Ninth; several from the town of Schleswig were in Co. A while Co. K was made up entirely from men from that and surrounding townships under the command of Captain H. F. Belitz and in Co. I there were several soldiers from the towns of Newton and Manitowoc. The regiment was mustered into service at Camp Sigel at Milwaukee October 18th and left for the west the succeeding January, being a part of the Army of the Frontier, serving in Kansas, Missouri and Nebraska until mustered out in January 1866. During the first year the officers of Co. B were:—Captain, Frederick Becker; first lieutenant, A. F. Dumke and second lieutenant, Gerbert Guetzloe, of Newton. In May 1862 Captain Becker resigned and returned home to engage in business, thus causing changes among his subordinates, Hugo Koch becoming second lieutenant. Captain Belitz resigned his command at about the same time while several months later C. H. Schmidt became a captain of Co. I of the same regiment. The men in this organization although not in many battles saw much hard service, such as scouting, guarding trains, etc. After their gallant colonel had been promoted to a generalship in September 1863 he visited his old home and was given an ovation by his townsmen, a public meeting being called at which many complimentary addresses were made. About twenty-five of the Ninth returned to Manitowoc in December 1864 upon the expiration of their service but many re-enlisted for the two succeeding years.

Later in 1861 two more companies left Manitowoc. The part played by the men from the county in the Fourteenth regiment was a large one. It was Company E of this organization that was commanded by George E. Waldo and D. E. Shove, who were made captain and first lieutenant respectively, while Daniel Ramsdell was commissioned as second lieutenant. The regiment gathered at Camp Hamilton, Fond du Lac, under Colonel Wood and was mustered in January 30, 1862, leaving for St. Louis three months later. There were a few men from Manitowoc in Co. F also, James La Counte acting as first lieutenant for the fi st two years of the service. The regiment after reaching the south was soon plunged into the baptism of fire. At one of the first battles in which it participated, that at Shiloh, the gallant Captain Waldo was struck down, being brought home a corpse. He was a young man of great popularity, a testimonial of which had been presented to him in the shape of a sword before he left the village, and the feeling of loss occasioned by his death was a personal one to every resident. Joseph Smith succeeded him as captain of Co. E and remained such until the end of the war. In the same year B. F. Goodenow became first lieutenant, while among the Manitowoc men to occupy offices in the regiment were W. F. Eldridge, sergeant-major; John M. Read, sergeant-major and adjutant-major, Rev. G. B. Engle of St. James, who in 1864 became chaplain and Dr. S. E. Zeilley, who was the surgeon of the regiment. The regiment saw several years of hard service, fighting at Vicksburg, Champion Hills and in many other battles. Their service expired in January 1864 but a majority, after enjoying a furlough, re-enlisted. The men in Company E returned home in October,

1865 and their duties done, were soon engaged in their various occupations. The Fourteenth formed a regimental association in 1880 and has held frequent reunions. The other company to leave in 1861 was Co. F of the Fifteenth Wisconsin, known as the Norwegian regiment. The men took their departure for the rendezvous at Madison on the 10th of December, and K. K. Jones was given a commission as lieutenant colonel of the regiment, Hans Heg being the colonel. An interesting fact in this regard was that Colonel Jones during the war carried the sword that his father, William Jones, one of the promoters of the Manitowoc Land company in 1835, carried in the war of 1812. Company F was wholly from Manitowoc county, being commanded by Captain Charles Gustaveson of the town of Rapids, a former soldier in the Norwegian army, while the second lieutenant was also a Manitowoc county man, Svend Samuelson of Eaton. The regiment was mustered in at Camp Randall on Feb. 14, 1862 and a month later was transferred to St. Louis. It served faithfully for three years, being engaged at Stone River, in the various battles before Atlanta and remaining in Tennessee until December 1864, when the men were mustered out. A few soldiers from the county went into the Sixteenth regiment and fully half a company in the Nineteenth was also made up of Manitowoc men, W. W. Bates, the shipbuilder, being captain of Co. K, serving ably throughout the Atlanta campaign.

The next full company to be sent forth was Co. K of the Twenty-First Wisconsin, the recruiting for it commencing in the spring of 1862, with headquarters at C. H. Walker's office. By this time it was seen that there were serious difficulties in the way of subduing the foe and volunteers were not as numerous as in the earlier days of the war. A draft was rumored as the summer dragged on and Manitowoc county's quota was fixed at 839 under the call of President Lincoln issued in August. The draft was then definitely ordered and on August 15th and 19th meetings were held to secure volunteers in order that the quota might be met without resorting to such severe measures. Speeches were made by Colonel

Sweet of the newly authorized Twenty-First, P. P. Smith, Judge Taylor and G. N. Woodin. Enthusiasm was high and J. E. Platt offered $50 and forty acres of land to the first recruit. Michael McGuire, a clerk, secured the prize but relinquished it to a second, who in turn gave it to a third. Thus the company was filled with sturdy young men, leaving seven days later on the steamer Comet. In the meantime the draft had been postponed although Joseph Vilas had been chosen commissioner of the county to supervise the drawing while Dr. A. Schenke was appointed examining surgeon. Company K was officered as follows:—Captain, C. H. Walker; first lieutenant, Wyman Murphy; second lieutenant, Joseph La Counte and it was mustered in at Oshkosh on Sept. 5, 1862. Five days later, under command of Colonel Sweet, the regiment left for the south and within a month it had participated in its first battle, that of Perryville. Here Colonel Sweet was wounded and Colonel Harrison C. Hobart succeeded him. After Perryville the regiment went south and participated in the Atlanta campaign, in the march to the sea and in further arduous service, being mustered out on June 17, 1865. Among the officers which the county furnished the regiment were Quartermasters H. C. Hamilton and B. J. Van Valkenburgh, Quartermaster-Sergeant G. T. Burns and Lieut. F. W. Borcherdt of Company D. Mr. Hamilton died of typhoid fever in April 1863 and his body was brought home to Two Rivers and buried with military honors. He was thirty-six years old and had always been prominent in the village of his abode, having served in the county board, the assembly and as first president of the village. Captain Walker was promoted to the position of major in 1864 and was succeeded as captain by Lieut. La Counte. The Twenty-First regiment, organized as an association in 1868, being one of the first to do so but no regular reunions were held until beginning with 1887. Among the officers of the association hailing from Manitowoc have been J. F. Reardon and F. C. Ostenfeldt and in June 1896 the reunion was held in the city, a program of much interest being carried out.

During the summer of 1862 Messrs. Pizzala and Baetz

were also busy recruiting at Manitowoc for the Twenty-Sixth, otherwise known as the Sigel Regiment, headquarters being stationed at Klingholz Hall. Company F was raised in the county and was officered as follows:—Captain, Henry Baetz; first lieutenant, Charles Pizzala; second lieutenant, A. Waller, of Milwaukee. Captain Baetz was later promoted to the position of major and after a period of faithful service the second commander, Capt. Pizzala was killed in May 1863. The regiment was mustered in at Milwaukee in September 1862 and saw much service, fighting at Gettysburg, Mission Ridge, Resaca, Atlanta and participating in the march to the sea. It was mustered out in June 1865. Among the other Manitowoc men serving as officers of this organization were W. H. Hempschemeyer, who became captain of Co. I, and Lieutenant N. Wollmer, who was killed before Atlanta, his burial occurring at Manitowoc on August 30, 1864. The funeral was a military one since many soldiers were home on a furlough, including General Salomon, Colonel Olmstead, Major Baetz, Captains Goodwin, Rankin and Dumke and Lieutenants Murphy, Wimpf and Markham, all of whom acted as an escort. Mr. Wollmer was an early settler and was engaged in the banking business before the war.

Recruiting went on for the Twenty-Seventh as well as for the Twenty-Sixth in the summer of 1862. Manitowoc county responded nobly, furnishing all of the members of Co. K and half of Co. D. The recruiting was under the supervision of T. G. Olmstead, who became lieutenant-colonel of the regiment, Joseph Rankin, who was commissioned captain of Co. D and Peter Mulholland, who later became captain of Co. K but who at first was a first lieutenant in the other company. The men left the village on Sept. 18, 1862, Captain Rankin being presented with a sword by his fellow citizens on the occasion of the departure. The regiment was mustered in at Camp Sigel in March of the next year and under Colonel Krez participated in the Vicksburg campaign, later being active in Arkansas and finally being mustered out in September 1865, the survivors arriving in Manitowoc on the 28th of that month. Among the men from the county who served as

WILLIAM BACH

officers in this regiment were Surgeons Saltzmann and Hutchinson, Lieutenants T. McMillan, N. Hanson and M. McGuire. During 1864 considerable recruiting was done for the Twenty-Seventh in the county and on October 27th of that year a number of new men were sent to the front to join that organization. The Thirty-Second Wisconsin was organized at about the same time as the last mentioned regiment, being mustred in on September 25, 1862. It drew about onehalf of one company, G, from Manitowoc, among the officers being Lieuts. Oscar B. Smith and H. H. Markham. The regiment saw hard service with General Sherman around Atlanta and then remained in Mississippi until mustered out in June 1864. This was the last regular organization to which the county made contribution of her sons for some months.

The first draft, as was said before, had been postponed owing to inaccuracies and general unpreparedness. The return as made by Commissioner Vilas in September 1862 was as follows:—

| Town | Enrolled | Exempt | Subject to Draft |
| --- | --- | --- | --- |
| Franklin | 160 | 108 | 52 |
| Two Creeks | 36 | 8 | 28 |
| Rapids | 200 | 77 | 120 |
| Manitowoc | 526 | 298 | 228 |
| Meeme | 167 | 34 | 133 |
| Schleswig | 147 | 6 | 141 |
| Centerville | 167 | 24 | 143 |
| Newton | 218 | 92 | 126 |
| Maple Grove | 113 | 46 | 67 |
| Two Rivers | 351 | 132 | 219 |
| Kossuth | 250 | 86 | 164 |
| Mishicott | 187 | 30 | 157 |
| Cooperstown | 195 | 55 | 140 |
| Rockland | 88 | 20 | 68 |
| Cato | 158 | 46 | 112 |
| Gibson | 160 | 21 | 139 |
| Liberty | 214 | 72 | 142 |
| Eaton | 131 | 14 | 117 |
| Totals | 3471 | 1169 | 2302 |
| Total to be drafted | | 397. | |

The town of Manitowoc had filled its quota so it became unnecessary to consider that in the estimates. A volunteer fund of $1613 had been raised early in the year and this was used to buy the services of substitutes. After a final examination held in December on January 2, 1863 the draft was carried out at the Court House under the direction of Capt. Weischner, U. S. A. The result was not satisfactory as many drawn were exempt and only about one hundred and twenty recruits were in reality secured and of these many failed to report. One hundred of the men drafted resolved to test the legality of the action, it being doubted by lawyers of ability, and Attorneys Nichols, Pierpont, Reed, Woodin and Bach were retained by them. These gentlemen secured the able assistance of E. G. Ryan, later chief justice and the case came before the supreme court in the January term under habeas corpus proceedings, the claim being made that the draft was void as outside any legal authority. The court, however, sustained the United States and decided the draft to be proper. The case is known as In Re Greiner and is found in the 16th Wisconsin at page 423.

Hardly had the excitement aroused by the first draft passed away when a second one was ordered. Citizens of Manitowoc met on July 21st and formed a draft club, of which Joseph Vilas was chosen president and treasurer and H. F. Hubbard secretary. Each member paid in fifty dollars, and received $300 if drafted, with which he might purchase a substitute, if he so desired. This second draft took place at Green Bay on November 23rd and was attended by the Manitowoc County Board. The county's quota was 388 men, not all of which was raised however, although under J. F. Guyles, who had been chosen provost marshal of the county, an efficient police system was organized. This having passed, another draft was announced to take place at Green Bay on Jan. 25th. At its December session the county board by resolution instructed J. Pellet. J. Carey and A. Wittmann to represent Manitowoc interests at the the proceeding and these gentlemen accordingly attended. The quota of the county at this draft was 232 men, which also was not even approximately reached. In the meantime the practice of raising bounty funds increased. The town of Manitowoc voted $100 per recruit on Feb. 1 1864, while at about the same time Two Rivers raised $5000 for the same purpose, Mishicott $3000, while Manitowoc Rapids offered $125 and Cato $100 per recruit. These grants were later legalized by the state legislature. In August 1864 the quota for the next draft, which was announced for the next month, was published as follows: —Two Creeks 13, Cooperstown 53, Maple Grove 34, Kossuth 60, Mishicot 34, Gibson 38, Franklin 36, Two Rivers 54, Manitowoc 61, Rockland 18, Centerville 33, Meeme 39, Schleswig 12, Eaton 32, Newton 34, Cato 25, Liberty 48 and Rapids 45. Excitement was intense and at an election held in Manitowco on the 26th a proposition to vote a village bounty of $200 per recruit was defeated by 93 majority. Superhuman efforts were made, however, both there and at Two Rivers so that before the 28th of September, the date of the draft, the quotas of these towns were filled. In the former place this result was accomplished largely by a second draft club, which was formed with G. N. Woodin as president and A. Wit'mann as secretary, each member being required to pay in twenty dollars. In the rest of the county the draft bore most heavily, there being no means of obviating its hardships. Feeling ran so high in Two Creeks that a recruiting officer barely escaped being mobbed. The draft took place at Green Bay as usual and there were present A. Wittmann and the county board. The drawing did not fill the quota and a supplementary draft took place on December 22nd for all towns except Manitowoc, Two Rivers and Centerville, which had furnished the required number. By this time the list of those not exempt had been exhausted in Eaton and Franklin and the same condition was rapidly approaching in the other towns, only two or three dozen eligible men remaining in each. Then followed the announcement of what proved to be the final draft. The town of Manitowoc upon hearing the news voted at a special election held January 2, 1865 the sum of $12,000 as bounty money, paying $300 per recruit, one of the largest local bounties in the state. The bounty club was also reorganized. In February a mass meeting was held to raise still more money and Joseph Vilas, J. D. Markham, T. C. Shove, S. A. Wood and E. K. Rand succeeded in doing so, earning the gratitude of their fellow citizens. The first named was presented with a valuable tobacco box by his admirers after the war closed in appreciation of the services rendered during these troublous times.

The quota for the last draft was finally announced as follows:—Manitowoc 59, Rapids 35, Meeme 11, Cato 20, Rockland 15, Centreville 25, Liberty 24, Newton 10, Schleswig 12, Two Creeks 4, Mishicot 8, Gibson 28, Cooperstown 37, Maple Grove 10, Kossuth 6 and Two Rivers 54, that of Franklin and Eaton having already been exhausted. The war, however, came to a close before it was necessary to rendezvous those drawn and in April 1865 Captain F. Borcherdt, then marshal of the county, received orders to arrest no more deserters.

During the last two years of the war there were organized several companies in the county that took the field for their country. In 1864 recruiting went on actively for the Forty-Fifth regiment of which in October Henry F. Belitz of Kiel was chosen colonel. Company B came largely from the towns of Centerville and Newton, being commanded by Capt. Jacob Leiser, while many were in Co. D also. Among the other Manitowoc county men acting as officers in the regiment were Captains C. H. Schmidt of Co. E, Reinhard Schlichting of Co. A, Bernard Schlichting of Co. C and Lieuts. C. Kerten of Co. C, Charles White of Co. D and Peter Ruppenthal of Co. A. The regiment was sent to Nashville in the fall and was disbanded in July 1865. In February of the latter year the Forty-Eighth regiment rendezvoused at Milwaukee, in it being Co. D, Captain A. Wittmann, containing men from Two Rivers and other parts of the county. The regiment was dispatched to Kansas and served in garrison and scout duties until February 1866, when it was mustered out. A few recruits from the county were also enlisted in the Fifty-Second regiment, Captain S. W. Smith commanding Co. D. This regiment got as far as St. Louis but was there returned and soon after disbanded.

MANITOWOC RIVER ABOVE BEND 1896

Thus was the bloody struggle brought to a close. Manitowoc county had furnished nine full companies and parts of three others, about twelve hundred men in all besides those who enlisted independently in various organizations or as engineers, cavalrymen or artillerymen. All through 1865 and even in the spring of the next year the blue-coated veterans came straggling home and warm was their welcome. A festival had taken place in the Windiate House in February 1864 in honor of the return of the three year men and similar functions followed in 1865, among them a grand reunion given by the Ladies Soldiers' Aid society held in February, one half of the proceeds of which went for the support of indigent soldiers' families and the other half to the State Soldiers' Home. A similar affair was held at Two Rivers a month or so later, five hundred dollars being realized. In fact the work of the women, who strove to be of service at home, was as heroic as that of the men in the field. During the war twenty-two large boxes of supplies were forwarded by the Manitowoc Ladies society and five by the organization in Two Rivers.

Then came the sad and sudden death of Lincoln. Meetings of the returned soldiery were held immediately for the arrangement of a fitting commemoration of his life and on April 29th one of the most imposing ceremonies that the village ever witnessed took place. A procession one mile long was formed in the following order, marching through the main streets:—I. Manitowoc Brass band; II. Committees; III. Company of returned soldiers under Captain Goodwin; IV. Hearse and Urn; V. Village officials; VI. Masons; VII. Odd Fellows; VIII. Sons of Herman; IX. Good Templars; X. Torrent Engine Company, No. 1, Hook and Ladder Company, Bucket Co.; XI. School children and ladies. At Union Park Reverend Smith delivered a funeral oration and the assemblage then broke up. Thus did Manitowoc honor the memory of the immortal president. Soon after the draft club made its final report, the total receipts since its formation having been $16,558, of which a balance of $2038 remained in the treasury. It was first proposed to put this money in the harbor fund but it was later decided to divide it pro rata among the membership. Naturally the returned soldiers kept up the associations that had so long held them together, the result being the formation in Manitowoc of a post in July 1868. C. H. Walker was chosen commander, W. I. Gilbert senior vice commander, John M. Read post adjutant and A. J. Patchen quartermaster. This organization, however, dissolved in the course of time and it was not until April 22, 1881, that Horace M. Walker Post No. 18 of the Wisconsin G. A. R. was formed. Since that time it has led an active existence with a large membership and good equipment. Among the post commanders have been J. S. Anderson, E. R. Smith, Frank Stirn, Richard McGuire, F. Ostenfeldt, H. Hentscher, C. E. Spindler, J. F. Reardon, H. Schmidt and J. D. Schuette. Gen. Lytle Post No. 190 was formed at Kiel on Dec. 27, 1884 and Joseph Rankin Post No. 129 at Two Rivers June 16 1886. The commanders of the former have been P. Mattes, F. Krieger, P. Jergenheimer, L. Gutheil, C. Beck and C Peschke; those of the latter W. F. Nash, W. Henry, W. Wagner and Louis Hartung. Several local members have held important positions in the state organization.

Naturally military affairs after the war were given little attention for some time. In the summer of 1868, however, the Manitowoc Volunteer Militia company was formed with over sixty members. On August 9th Frederick Becker was chosen captain, W. H. Hempschemeyer first lieutenant and Henry Schweitzer second lieutenant. It was made part of the state militia as Company A Second regiment, remaining so designated until 1894, when it became an independent organization. The twenty-fifth anniversary of the company was celebrated with great festivities on July 10, 1893, speeches and parades making up the program. The captains of the company from its formation were F. Becker, A. C. Becker, Emil Schmidt and Henry Schweitzer. Reorganization took place in the nineties and many of the company went into the new Rahr Guards, of which Captain Joseph Willinger has been for some time the commander. An independent company was formed in the seventies among the Polish residents of Northeim, being known as the Pulaski Guards, that formed a brilliant feature on several public occasions but they disbanded after a short existence. On December 29, 1881 a new company was organized at Manitowoc under the name of the Rankin Guards. The first officers were:—Captain W. H. Hempschemeyer, first lieutenant, Ole Benson; second lieutenant, Emil Baensch. The company soon became incorporated into the state militia as Company H, Second regiment, and the rivalry between the two organizations in the city was a healthy one. An event of interest was the encampment at the County Fair Grounds in August 1886 of the members of the Second Regiment, ten companies being present. Captain Hempschemeyer was succeeded in command of Company H by Emil Baensch, he by William Kunz and he by William F. Brandt. In the nineties William Abel was chosen captain and remained such during the Spanish-American war. That struggle, suddenly thrust upon the nation for the sake of humanity, called forth a burst of patriotism among young and old. Manitowoc was not behind other communities in this respect and the company of soldiers already in existence in the city was recruited and frequently drilled as the war clouds grew thicker. Finally late in April came the orders to mobilize the state troops at Camp Harvey, Milwaukee, and on the 28th Company H left the city amidst demonstrations of patriotism almost unprecedented. Mustered in at Milwaukee, one hundred and nine strong on May 5th the troops were transported to Chickamauga Park, where they remained a month, later being transferred to Charleston, S. C. Here Captain Abel became seriously ill and command devolved largely upon Lieuts. Knudson and Stahl. The company, embarking on the transport Grand Duchess, arrived in Ponce, Porto Rico July 28 and spent a month and a half in arduous service on that isle. Peace, however, was soon at hand and the Manitowoc guardsmen were with the remainder of the regiment returned, to the United States, reaching Milwaukee September 17th. The next morning they were the recipients of an ovation on the part of their fellow citizens, being tendered a banquet at the Turner Hall and participating in a a lengthy parade. All but four of the company returned, Herbert Coville, F. C. Schwalbe, F. Engel and William Hein giving up their lives for their country. The progress of the war was watched with great interest by the residents of the county and its happy termination hailed with joy. Many young men from the county served in various organizations aside from Company H throughout the struggle and later several were with the troops in the Philippines, fighting the insurgents. The Spanish-American War veterans formed Camp Henry W. Lawton on Feb. 10, 1900, with a membership of forty, the officers being:—Commander, Ernst Heide; vice commanders, M. Jergenson and C. Richards; adjutant, J. C. Jirikowic: quartermaster, Wm. Abel; chaplain, H. C. Berndt; officer of the day, H. Woerfel; officer of the guard, C. Schumacher. The first reunion of the camps of the northeastern part of the state occurred at Manitowoc in July of the following year. In the spring of 1900 a military company, the Twin City Rifles, was organized at Two Rivers, making its first public appearance on Memorial day.

Linked inseparably with military heroism is patriotism and it is well that certain days such as the Fourth of July and Memorial day have been set aside for the proper commemoration of the past. These have been observed regularly in the county, the Fourth particularly, from the earliest days. The manner in which that holiday has been celebrated as the years have passed is most interesting. In antebellum days speeches, banquets, balls and parades were the order of the hour. The feature of the Fourth in 1854 was an excursion to Two Rivers, while two years later a grand celebration was held at Clarks Mills, Judge Lee delivering an address. The program in 1859 was the first elaborate one given in the county. It opened with a federal salute and at noon a procession was formed which, marshalled by W. H. McDonald, I. P. Smith, G. S. Glover, J. P. Barnes and A. L. Pierce, moved to Union Park. In line were the fire companies, the agricultural societies, school children and citizens and when the park was reached a bounteous banquet was spread by the ladies of the Social Circle. The toasts responded to were varied and instructive, being as follows:— "Ladies of Manitowoc," "The Day We Celebrate," "The Teachers of Our Village," "Our National Anniversary," "Italy," "Ladies Social Circle," "Manitowoc and Mississippi Railroad," "The Press and the Union" and "Written on a Shingle -Manitowoc Currency, May it Never Fail." Celebrations were usually held at Union Park during this early period, although later Washington Park was the scene of festivities. In 1861 on account of the war feeling was high and at a celebration at Cato an aged resident was hissed from the platform for supposed Secession utterances. Because of the close of the war an outburst of enthusiasm took place on the Fourth in 1865 and Manitowoc was no exception to the rule. The county board appropriated $300 and with this sum a banquet was tendered the returned veterans. The feast was held at the National Hotel and was presided over by Joseph Vilas, toasts being responded to as follows:—"The President," C. E. Esslinger; "Memory of Lincoln," J. D. Markham; "Officers and Soldiers," C. H. Walker; "The Day We Celebrate," H. Sibree; "The County Board," Jason Pellett; "Memory of the Fallen," G. N. Woodin; "The Press," C. H. Schmidt; "The Clergy," Rev. L. N. Freeman and "The Bar," E. B. Treat. At Two Rivers a magnificent liberty pole was raised and a lengthy parade formed, after which Rev. Herman Bartels delivered an oration. In the years succeeding parades were an annual feature and among the orators were Rev. W. J. Stoutenburgh, J. B. Sherwood, B. R. Anderson, C. E. Esslinger, A. Wittmann and R. D. Smart. In 1872 the new railway was utilized and an excursion to Kaukauna successfully enjoyed. Then came the elaborate celebration of the Centennial Fourth. A monster parade in three divisions was the feature of the day, John Bibinger, G. F. Barker and P. J. Pierce acting as marshals. In line were two veterans of the War of 1812, B. Jones and F. C. Kapple, the Pulaski Guards of Northeim, numerous symbolic floats, fraternal organizations and the fire departments. Exercises were held in Union Park, C. Esslinger acting as orator of the day and Reverend C. B. Stevens as chaplain. In the evening a public display of fireworks witnessed by hundreds crowned the glorious day. Two Rivers also commemorated the occasion fittingly. During the succeeding few years the celebrations were very quiet and each community in the county held its own instead of centralizing at the county seat. In 1883 the celebration at Manitowoc assumed considerable magnitude and again in 1891, in the latter year the city entertaining many visitors from neighboring towns, a magnificent parade and a $1300 display of fireworks being features. Exercises were held in Washington park and Judge Emil Baensch delivered the oration. Since that year, however, no great effort has been made to celebrate the day in a public manner.

Memorial day has also, since its institution, been observed with proper ceremonies in the county. In Manitowoc after 1883 the practice arose of securing outside orators of repute to address the citizens and among the number who have done so have been General F. C. Winckler, Colonel Watrous, Senator Spooner, Senator Quarles, Congressman Esch, Eugene S. Elliott, President S. Plantz of Lawrence University, Reverend Walter E. Cole, Reverend G. W. Ide and Reverend Fraser. Along the line of patriotic movements should be noticed the imposing statue placed in 1900 in the public square at Two Rivers in honor of the soldier dead.

## CHAPTER IX.

### POLITICS.

When the territory of Michigan was organized it included what is now the state of Wisconsin. In the thirties this latter section of the western country was divided into counties and the whole northeastern part was known as Brown county, what is now Manitowoc being embraced within its confines. On December 7 1836, however, soon after Wisconsin became a separate territory Manitowoc county was constituted, although not at first including the present towns of Gibson, Cooperstown, Two Creeks or township 21 of the township of Mishicot, this territory remaining as part of the original county of Brown until February 1850, when it was annexed. The county seat of Manitowoc was fixed at Manitowoc Rapids but no definite county government was established until two years later. In January 1838 an act was passed to the effect "that the county, contained within the boundary lines of Manitowoc County be and hereby is set off as a separate town by the name of Conroe and the polls of election shall be opened at Conroe's Mills." Finally in December the counties of Manitowoc and Sheboygan were organized by the legislature "for all purposes of county government," the first election for town and county officers being fixed to take place on the first Monday in March, 1839 and it was further provided that the county commissioners of Brown county were to canvass the vote and issue certificates of election. It remained dependent on the latter county judicially, however, until 1848. Thus Manitowoc became a political unit, enabling a study of its political complexity as the varying local, state and national issues evolved and disappeared. And first as to its attitude on national questions from the time of its organization until the present day.

### NATIONAL POLITICS.

At the outset it should be noted that Manitowoc county as a whole has always under normal conditions been a Democratic stronghold. The majority of that party has not been so great as to make changes in political complexion impossible when particular issues came to the front but the above statement is borne out by a careful investigation of the votes for presidential and congressional candidates. The first opportunity for a division on national questions was that offered by the election of a delegate to congress from Wisconsin Territory in 1839. Forty votes were cast in the county, of which J. B. Doty, the Democratic candidate, received twenty-nine, while Bennett, the chief opponent, received but nine. In 1841 a delegate was again to be chosen; the total vote was increased by six, Henry Dodge, the Democratic candidate receiving twenty-seven as compared with nineteen for J. E. Arnold, the representative of the Whigs. In 1843 Dodge again carried the county receiving twenty-nine votes as against three for the Whig candidate, W. Hickok. M. L. Martin, also a Democrat, in 1845 received forty majority and in 1847 M. W. Strong, Democrat, received sixty-seven votes to sixty-four received by J. H. Tweedy, Whig, showing a closer division than had existed theretofore. In fact from 1846 to 1852, by which time many German Democrats had immigrated to the county, the balance between the Democrats and Whigs was about even. A year after this last vote for delegate Wisconsin became a state and Manitowoc was placed in the Third Congressional district. The presidential election then came on, the first in which Wisconsin votes could be cast and that Manitowoc was relied on for a Democratic majority is evinced by the following from the Green Bay Advocate: "Well, as what is wanted is to carry the state for Cass and Butler if the 'old North county' can't bring it up we will call in the aid of our sisters, Manitowoc and Calumet —and if all these don't do we will finally give up all claims." The result in the county was as follows:---Cass, Democrat, 159; Taylor, Whig, 77; Van Buren, Free Soil, 30; while the congressional vote was, Doty, Dem., 169; Howe, Whig, 67; Judd, Free Soil, 30. Two years later Mr. Doty ran for congress again, receiving 420 votes, while 165 went to Harrison C. Hobart, the independent candidate, thus showing a great increase in the Democratic vote, despite a disaffection led against Mr. Doty by George Reed and others.

The presidential election of 1852 then approached. Pierce and King the regular Democratic nominees received a majority of over five hundred above all others, the vote being as follows: Pierce, 874; Scott, Whig, 209; Hale, Free Soil, 9. The congressional fight resulted similarly, James B. Macy, Democrat, receiving 843 votes and J. M. Shafter, Whig, 243. In 1854, however, the Democrats of Wisconsin suffered a schism and as a result in the Third district two candidates were placed in the field, Turner the straight and Macy the bolting nominee, while Charles Billingshurst received the united support of the then new Republican party. The result was a victory for the last named all along the line, the vote in the county being: Billingshurst 750, Turner, 374, Macy 125. This defection from the Democratic ranks was due largely to the question of free soil in Kansas and Nebraska and was not of a continuous character for in 1856 the Democrats appeared stronger than ever. In the meantime the county had greatly increased in population and the presidential campaign took on almost modern form. In August a Republican rally was arranged for in order to make a demonstration against slavery extension, the call being signed by C. Roeser, C. Esslinger, J. Bennett, |N. Preston and others, several of whom had formerly been Democrats. An organization was formed with P. P. Smith as president and J. Bennett as treasurer and a similar movement headed by R. Klingholz and H. Baetz took place among the German Republicans, while other clubs were formed at Rapids and Two Rivers, A. C. Pierce and H. Billings being presidents of the respective organizations. The Democrats were equally active and the result was that in Manitowoc two monster demonstrations were held by the two parties on October 11th. People from the rural districts came in with ox teams and a hickory pole was raised with great acclaim by the Democrats, a Buchanan flag being hoisted upon it. A parade was then formed, led by the Sheboygan and Schmitz bands and containing fully fifty wagons full of voters and their families, who proceeded to the Franklin House, where from the balcony Colonel E. Fox Cooke of Sheboygan addressed them upon the issues of the day. The Republican demonstration was led by Colonel K. K. Jones, one of the features of the parade being thirty-two ladies on horseback while many of the sterner sex rode in the rear decked out in all the finery of feathers and plumes. Finally the campaign came to an end, Buchanan carrying the county, his vote being 1907 to Fremont's 1177, Hobart's majority over Billingshurst being about the same for congress. Mr. Billingshurst carried the district however, and was returned to Washington, where he continued to represent his constituents ably. In 1858 Manitowoc county came forward with its first candidate for congressional honors, William Aldrich of Two Rivers being prominently before the Republican convention of the district, but he received but six votes for the honor. Representative Billingshurst was renominated and Charles Larrabee chosen by the Democrats to be their standard bearer. Both candidates stumped the county but Billingshurst was defeated, his vote being 1086 and that of his opponent 1598, Larabee also carrying the district by a heavy majority.

And then came the thrilling and momentous campaign of 1860. When the news of Douglas' nomination by the northern wing of the Democracy reached Manitowoc on June 24th great rejoicing occurred among the Manitowoc Democrats, among whom were many who considered "the Little Giant" the greatest statesman of the age. A flagraising, bonfire, parade and ball were a few of the varied modes of welcome which the information received, prominent among the participants being E. K. Rand, C. C. Barnes, T. Robinson, W. D. Hitchcock, H. Berners, A. Wittman, Temple Clark and others. The fact that at the time Lincoln was not as widely known somewhat dampened the enthusiasm of the Republicans until later in the campaign, when the candidate began to prove his worth. The Democrats were, however, not united since several of the prominent leaders supported the Breckenridge ticket, put up by the southern wing of the party. Chief among them were H. S. Pierpont and C. Kuehn of Two Rivers, C. W. Fitch, editor of the Herald and C. A. Reuter of Manitowoc. In choosing delegates to the congressional convention a compromise was effected whereby Mr. Pierpont, a Breckenridge and Joseph Vilas, a Douglas Democrat were chosen. The split was injected into county politics as well and as the year advanced the chances of Democratic victory decreased proportionately. However organization was perfected on both sides and the struggle went on unabated. As early as July the German Republicans organized a club with H. Baetz as president, followed by the Scandinavian Republicans, who chose Jacob Halverson as their leader, the Two Rivers Republican club and finally the Wide Awakes, a Republican organization formed in Manitowoc, whose distinctive insignia, oilcloth caps and helmets, made them conspicuous in all public demonstrations. A. Scott Sloan and Judge Larrabee, the candidates of the Republican and Democratic tickets for congress canvassed the county thoroughly. At Two Rivers a parade was formed by the supporters of the former, attended by thirty farmers from Cooperstown carrying "a rail symbolizing allegiance to Lincoln" and in which many "hard fisted factory operatives" as they were flatteringly called participated. Democratic clubs were also active and thus the campaign progressed with parades, speeches and illuminations. Finally the eventful November day arrived and Manitowoc registered its vote against slavery in no uncertain manner, breaking over accustomed party lines so to do. Lincoln received 2041 votes, Douglas 1947 and Breckenridge a meager 9, while for congress Sloan received 2078 and Larrabee 1948. The vote clearly showed that what Breckenridge sentiment there had been in the county earlier in the year had been dissipated by the threats of secession. The Republicans celebrated the victory by an enthusiastic demonstration on November 17, in which a parade headed by Marshal Robert Blake was a feature. The war then broke out and men's minds necessarily turned from mere politics, all supporting the government in its struggle for existence. The Republicans, however, did not retain their control of the county, a fact shown by the election of 1862, in which Wheeler, the Democratic candidate for congress, received 795 majority over Browne, his Republican opponent The county was now in the Fifth district together with Calumet, Winnebago, Green Lake, Marquette, Waupaca, Outagamie, Brown, Kewaunee, Door, Oconto and Shawano counties. Both H. S. Pierpont and George Reed were mentioned as possibilities for congressional honors in the Democratic district convention of that year, which was presided over by the former.

Opposition to Lincoln grew steadily owing to the length of the war and the campaign of 1864 was in reality started a year earlier. In February 1863 a Democratic club was organized at the Courthouse, with the protection of the constitution as its aim and "Conciliation and Peace" as its motto. Among the promoters were F. Becker, W. Bach, J. Crowley, A. Bleser, W. M. Nichols, J. C. Eggers, G. S. Glover, P. J. Blesch, M. Kuhl, R. O'Connor, A. Wittmann and George Reed, the last named being elected president. Similar clubs were organized throughout the county also. The movement was met by the Republicans in March in the formation of the Union club, which met at Klingholz Hall weekly, among the members being S. A. Wood, J. F. Guyles, Oscar Koch, P. P. Smith, S. W. Smith, Rev. Mead Holmes and O. H. Carpenter. Many Manitowoc Democrats attended the National convention of their party held in Chicago in August 1864, which nominated General McClellan for the presidency. The campaign which followed was a hotly contested one, although party lines were changed considerably as a result of the war and the issues arising therefrom. Joseph Vilas was put forward by the local Democrats for the congressional nomination but received only fourteen votes in the convention against twenty-nine for Gabriel Bouck of Oshkosh. The result of the election was a landslide for the Democrats, the home vote being 2248 for McClellan and 1179 for Lincoln, the vote of the soldiers in the field somewhat reducing the former's majority. Colonel Bouck secured a similar lead over Philetus Sawyer in the county, although the latter carried the district. By 1866 due partially to the latter's interest in Manitowoc harbor improvements the Republican vote increased to 1737, Martin, the Democratic candidate receiving 1891 votes.

The campaign of 1868 was a closely contested one in Manitowoc. Seymour and Blair clubs divided honors as to enthusiasm with Grant and Wilson organizations and several prominent speakers, including Gov. Fairchild and George B. Smith visited the county. At the congressional convention Joseph Vilas was nominated on the first ballot and he carried on the fight with great vigor against Philetus Sawyer, whom the Republicans had renominated. The vote for president was very close, Seymour receiving 2640 votes and Grant 2605. For congress, however, Mr. Vilas ran greatly ahead of his ticket, receiving 3204 votes as against 2043 for Sawyer and also carrying Calumet, Kewaunee, Marquette and Outagamie counties. He was, however, defeated in the district as a whole, his total vote being 12431 against Sawyer's 16816. In 1870 another change took place and Sawyer, popular in the county on account of his championship of the harbor, received 3000 votes, a majority of 1473 over Stringham, his Democratic opponent. By 1872, however, the Democrats had resumed their control of the situation and were able to put up a strong and winning fight for Greeley. Another Manitowoc man was in the congressional fight this time in the person of Henry Baetz, who was the Republican nominee. Manitowoc by the new apportionment was still in the Fifth district, which now included the counties of Dodge, Fond du Lac, Manitowoc and Sheboygan. The result of the election was as follows:—Grant 2289, Greeley 2677; for congress, Eldridge 2526, Baetz, 2443. Mr. Baetz was also defeated by a heavy majority in the rest of the district. In 1874 Burchard, the Democratic nominee for congress, received 3157 votes, Barber, his opponent, polling only 1923. The next campaign was a memorable one. A Hayes club, of which A. D. Jones was president was early organized and among the speakers secured by the Republicans were ex-Governor Salomon and Matt Carpenter. The result was an overwhelming victory for the Democrats, Tilden receiving 3908 votes to Hayes' 2700 while Bragg for congress received 3913 against 2692 for G. W. Carter, his Republican opponent. During the long electoral struggle that followed the election excitement was intense, the Democrats holding mass meetings in protest against the final decision of the electoral commission. In 1878 Gen. Bragg secured another large majority of 1085 for congress over Smith, his opponent, which was reduced in 1880 to 630 over Colman, Republican.

The presidential campaign of 1880 was somewhat featureless in the county, Gen. Hancock, the Democratic nominee carrying it by a somewhat reduced majority, his vote being 3676 while that for Garfield was 2988. Two years later a Manitowoc man again ran for congress and this time secured the prize. He was Joseph Rankin, a Democrat and one of the most popular and straightforward men that Wisconsin has ever sent to national council halls. In the eighties the Fifth district included Manitowoc, Kewaunee, Sheboygan, Ozaukee, Calumet and Brown counties. Rankin received 3228 votes in the county and 12,933 in the district, while his opponent, Howland, received 1483 votes in the county and 6108 in the district. The Prohibition district convention was held in Manitowoc that year and at the time about one hundred votes, the maximum of the party's strength, were polled in the county. In 1884 Congressman Rankin ran again, this time against Charles Luling, also of Manitowoc and defeated him by a majority of 1353 in the county and 6241 in the district. As elsewhere in the country the Blaine-Cleveland fight of 1884 was a bitter one but the latter's majority was very large, the vote being Cleveland 4203, Blaine 2525. Congressman Rankin died early in 1886, greatly lamented at Washington as well as at his home and it became necessary to hold a special election to fill the remainder of his term. Charles Luling was nominated by the Republicans and Joseph Vilas put forward by Manitowoc Democrats before their party convention but their claims were rejected, largely through the action of the Sheboygan delegates. Thomas R. Hudd of Green Bay received the nomination, the vote being Hudd 16, Vilas 8, Horn 3, Timlin 3. Local Democrats resented this action of their convention and the result was that Mr. Luling carried the county, his vote being 2338 as against Hudd's 1586, although the latter's majority in the district was 3781. Hudd carried the county in the fall at the regular election, his majority over Kuesterman, his Democratic opponent, being 1534. The Cleveland administration recognized Manitowoc Democracy by appointing William A. Walker United States district attorney, that gentleman thereupon removing to Milwaukee.

The presidential campaign of 1888 in the county was one of great enthusiasm, parades being frequent. The result was another majority for Cleveland, reduced somewhat but still substantial, his vote being 4218 against 2713 for Harrison, 127 for Streeter, Prohibitionist, and 19 for Fish, Labor, George Brickner, the Democratic candidate for congress defeating Kuesterman by about the same majority. Brickner again carried the county in 1890 by a majority of 1285 over T. Blackstock, a Republican. In 1892 a long deadlock occured at the Democratic congressional convention held at Fond du Lac. The delegates from Manitowoc supported A. J. Schmitz as did many others but after scores of ballots Owen A. Wells of Fond du Lac received the nomination. Manitowoc was now in the Sixth district, including the counties of Marquette, Fond du Lac, Winnebago, Calumet, Waushara and Green Lake. The Republicans in this campaign placed Emil Baensch in the field for congress. The result of the campaign was easily discernible by men of political experience even before the vote had been taken. The feeling against the McKinley tariff bill was strong and pariicularly so in the west. The Cleveland landslide was tremendous, his vote in the county being 4349 as against Harrison's 2276, a majority of 2073. Owing to the popularity of candidate Baensch he ran about six hundred votes ahead of his ticket, but failed of election in the district. The county soon underwent a general political change, due perhaps to the stringency of the times and in 1894 the contest for congress was again close, Wells receiving 3368 votes while S. A. Cook, the Republican nominee received 2923, he carrying the district. The Populist party about this time became a factor and secured many adherents in the two cities of the county, detracting largely from the Democratic strength. The silver issue then came to the front and many prominent Democrats, including John Nagle, editor of the Pilot, bolted the Bryan ticket. This defection spread throughout all portions of the county, causing a great change, which was doubtless augmented by the able speakers, such as General Bragg, Senator Quarles and others who were sent to the county to address the citizens. The result was a Republican victory, the first on national issues since 1860, the vote being as follows:—McKinley 4431, Bryan 3917, Palmer 163, the last being the Gold Democratic vote. J. H. Davidson, the Republican nominee for congress, also carried the county by a majority somewhat smaller over W. F. Gruenewald. In 1898 Mr. Davidson and J. Stewart were opponents, Davidson losing the county by 206 votes. In 1900 silver plus expansion was again before the people and Manitowoc county remained in the Republican column. The local campaign was a hard fought one and McKinley's majority was somewhat reduced, the vote being as follows:—McKinley 4317, Bryan 4167, Debs 169, Wooley 65, Mallory 4. Congressman Davidson also carried the county by a majority of 241 over his Democratic opponent, Mr. Watson of Fond du Lac, and in 1902 he was again re-elected, carrying Manitowoc county by 418 votes over Thomas Patterson. Summarizing it will be seen that the Republicans have carried the county in but three out of fourteen presidential campaigns, and in only seven out of twenty-seven congressional struggles.

PETER JOHNSTON

## STATE POLITICS.

Manitowoc county has voted for governors of the state largely as it voted for presidents of the nation. It is of interest, however, to note how and by whom the county has been represented in the legislature and on the state tickets of the various political organizations. In territorial days Manitowoc was represented in the council and assembly largely by strangers, mainly from Brown county. The vote of the county in 1837 was called into question in a contest for a seat in the council. At this election the county gave J. Dickinson 32 votes and A. J. Irwin 2. In 1840 J. W. Conroe was elected to the lower house from Brown county and held the position for several years, being the sole representative from Manitowoc until statehood was reached. C. V. Arndt of Green Bay, who was a representative of the Manitowoc interests was shot by another legislator in 1842 and the news of the tragedy created considerable stir when it reached his constituents. W. H. Bruce, then a resident of the Rapids and a friend of the murdered man, made a trip to the state capitol in the dead of winter in order, if possible, to assist in avenging the dastardly act. In 1843 a vote concerning the adoption of a state government was taken, the vote in the county being 5 for and 6 against the proposition, showing that little interest was taken in the matter at the time. On August 7 1846 the question again came up and Manitowoc registered its vote as 23 for and 4 against the proposition. A constitutional convention was called in 1847 and Evander M. Soper was sent to represent Manitowoc county. He served on the committee on banks and banking but otherwise took no prominent part in the proceedings. The labors of this convention were rejected in the state when the constitution was put to a popular vote, although it carried the county by a vote of 96 to 45, Manitowoc also registering her vote against the equal suffrage of the negro at the time. A second constitutional convention was called as soon as the work of the first had been rejected and this time the people accepted the document, Manitowoc county giving 122 votes for and 5 against the proposition. It was represented in this convention together with Sheboygan by Silas Steadman, an old settler of the town of Sheboygan Falls.

Then followed the first election. Manitowoc was placed in the First Senatorial district together with Brown and Sheboygan counties and H. C. Hobart of Sheboygan was chosen the first senator, becoming a leading member of the upper house. The vote for assemblyman resulted in a tie between D. Smith of Mishicot and Ezra Durgin. K. K. Jones in a letter to the Manitowoc Pilot published in 1860 describes the first state election in the county as follows:—"Within about three weeks after my arrival (May 1848) we had an election for a representative to the first state legislature. Col. Ezra Durgin and the lamented and noble Daniel Smith of Mishicot were opposing candidates. The result was a tie; a new election was called by John Plumb, a deputy undersheriff of Brown county. We, the Smith men, denied the legality of the call and generally staid at home and the Durgin men had it all to themselves. Next week under a call from the coroner, the late Hubbard, Uncle Dan's friends went in on their muscle and had an election all alone in their glory. I believe we claimed more votes cast at our election than theirs. However Col. Durgin took his seat and a very influential and energetic member he made. If Manitowoc never had a worse one to represent her she may well be proud of them all. The good old Whig party of those days in the county consisted of James L. Kyle, James Bennett, Harvey Case, Pliny Pierce, Daniel Smith, Alfred Smith, H. H. Smith, Fred Borcherdt and perhaps a half dozen others, whom I do not now remember, excepting our old friend McNulty who was then one of us. I was also counted in that squad. Col. Sherwood used to say he admired our courage but had a poor opinion of our discretion. Yet we used to make a heap of trouble in your wigwams at every election." At this same election Dewey, the Democratic nominee for governor, carried the county by twenty votes over Tweedy his Whig opponent.

Until 1857 Manitowoc was represented in the state senate by men from other counties, including Samuel Goodel of

Stockbridge, Theodore Conkey of Appleton, H. N. Smith of Plymouth and David Taylor of Sheboygan. In the assembly, however, during the same period the county remained as one of the units of representation. Charles Kuehn was unanimously elected in the fall of 1848 and the succeeding fall defeated James L. Kyle, the Whig candidate, by a vote of 182 to 132. In the election of 1850 G. C. O. Malmros received 229 votes for the position as against 214 cast for J. M. Sprague and 68 for A. W. Preston while in 1851 and 1852 E. Ricker defeated S. B. Sherwood and B. F. White respectively. In the fall of 1853 the Whigs were victorious, James L. Kyle receiving 543 and J. M. Sherwood 416 votes, although Barstow the Democratic candidate for governor carried the county by over 600 majority. In that year also the county gave 618 votes against and only 319 for the prohibitory liquor law then before the people. In 1854 a three cornered struggle occurred in the county for a seat in the lower house. James Bennett was placed in nomination by the newly organized Republicans, Lyman Emerson by the Democrats and J. M. Sherwood by the Independent Democrats. Bennett was elected, receiving 616 votes, while Emerson received but 313 and Sherwood 308. Manitowoc county played an important part in the formation of the Republican party in the state of Wisconsin during this year. It may be well said that the organization took definite form at a People's State convention held in Madison on July 31st. C. Roeser was a delegate to this convention from the county and was made the candidate of the new party for the position of state treasurer in 1855, he and Charles Kuehn his successful opponent in that year being the first men from Manitowoc to attain places on a state ticket of any political organization. The Democratic majority for governor was 376 and C. H. Walker, a Democrat, was sent to the assembly by an even larger vote. Charles Kuehn served two years as state treasurer and made a very efficient officer. By the new apportionment going into effect in 1856 Manitowoc and Calumet counties were placed in one senatorial district while the former was divided into two assembly districts, the first including the towns of Two Rivers,

Mishicot, Kossuth and Manitowoc while the second comprised the towns of Rapids, Maple Grove, Franklin, Eaton, Newton, Meeme, Schleswig and Centerville. Both candidates for senatorial honors in that year were from Manitowoc, Temple Clark the Democratic nominee defeating O. H. Platt by about 570 votes and in the assembly districts C. H. Walker and T. Cunningham, both Democrats, were successful. In the succeeding year these men were followed by H. C. Hamilton and J. B. Dunn, also followers of Jeffersonian doctrines, Hamilton giving away in 1858 to a Republican, William Aldrich, the defeat of the regular Democratic candidate being largely due to the independent candidacy of S. A. Wood, who received 111 votes, thus cutting down the vote of Temple Clark, the regular candidate of the party, to 741. For senator S. H. Thurber, a leading merchant, was successful in defeating Dr. Preston, his Republican opponent. Assemblyman Aldrich soon became very prominent in the legislature and was highly regarded over the state. The gubernatorial election of 1859 was a hard fought one between Alexander Randall and Harrison C. Hobart, the nominees of the Republican and Democratic parties respectively. Arrangements were made for a series of joint debates between them during the campaign and Manitowoc was chosen as the scene of one of the forensic struggles. Mr. Randall was unable to be present but sent as his representative Carl Schurz, who came to Manitowoc for the occasion. Each was given an hour and the debate was an event long to be remembered by all present, it being said that the result might well have been declared a draw. Hobart was not elected although he carried the county by 1430 majority and both districts sent Democrats to the assembly, Joseph Rankin from the First and Peter Mulholland from the Second. In 1860 owing to disaffection in the Democratic camps both returned Republicans, J. L. Fobes representing the First and Joseph Stephenson the Second, while B. J. Sweet, a Republican from Calumet county carried the county by over 400 majority for senatorial honors.

Then came another apportionment, the senatorial district, now known as the Nineteenth, remaining unchanged but the county being divided into three assembly districts; the first including Centerville, Meeme, Schleswig, Eaton, Liberty, Newton and Rockland; the second Rapids, Cato, Maple Grove, Franklin, Kossuth and Cooperstown and the third Manitowoc, Two Rivers, Mishicot, Gibson and Two Creeks. In two of the three in the fall of 1861 Democrats were chosen by small majorities, the favored ones being J. Cahill of the second and E. K. Rand of the third district. In the first, however, S. Rounseville a Republican was elected by 8 majority. The vote for governor was also Democratic that year. Edward Salomon of Manitowoc was the candidate for the Republicans for the position of lieutenant governor and by the death of Gov. Harvey in 1862 the former became the chief magistrate of the state, a position which he held until January 1864, he being one of the first of his nationality in the western states to hold such high office. In 1862 both Messrs. Rand and Cahill were reelected by increased majorities and D. Shanahan, a Democrat, succeeding Mr. Rounseville in the first district while Joseph Vilas, also of that party, became state senator. In 1863 the Democrats lost ground again, P. P. Fuessenich a Republican being sent to Madison from the first district, although T. Thornton and D. Smoke, both Democrats, represented the remainder of the county. H. S. Pierpont was the Democratic candidate for state bank comptroller in this campaign but went down in defeat with the others of his party. It was in this year also that the town of Maple Grove went unanimously Democratic, a feat which called forth considerable comment and the presentation of a flag on the part of the Democratic ladies of the county. The campaign of 1864 brought about other changes, the first and second districts returning Democrats, H. Mulholland and M. Murphy while the third elected C. B. Daggett of Two Rivers, a Republican. George Reed secured a gratifying majority for the senatorship and immediately occupied a prominent place in state affairs. He held the place six years, being reelected by large majorities in 1866 and 1868 and was particularly valuable as a member of the committees on finance and banking. In the fall of 1865 the state decided the question of negro suffrage, the vote in the county being 840 for and 1858 against the proposition. In the first district that fall three candidates were in the field, H. Mulholland, P. J. Pierce and N. Dittmar, the first two being Democrats and the last named a Republican. The result was that Dittmar was elected although the second and third districts returned Democrats, William Eatough and David Smoke.

No changes were made by the apportionment of 1866 as far as the county was concerned. Mr. Dittmar was reelected in the first and M. Murphy and T. Robinson chosen in the second and third districts. In the next year John H. Bohne, Richard Donovan and David Smoke, all Democrats, represented the various districts and a strong majority was registered for Tallmadge, the Democratic nominee for governor as against Fairchild. In the fall of 1868 the representatives from the first and second districts were reelected but in the third J. L. Fobes, a Republican, defeated D. Smoke by sixty votes. A year later Henry Baetz was chosen by the Republicans as their candidate for state treasurer and was elected, although the county of his residence went Democratic. Three Democratic assemblymen, John Barth, Michael Fitzgerald and C. H. Schmidt were also chosen. The political struggle for legislative positions in 1870 was a bitter one. Three candidates for senatorial honors were placed in the field, J. Carey by the Republicans, although he had been and was later a Democrat, W. Bach by the People's party and C. H. Schmidt by the Democrats. Schmidt was elected, receiving 2141 votes to Carey's 1411 and Bach's 1011, and was reelected two years later by a somewhat smaller majority, the number of the district then being changed to the Fifteenth, which it has since remained. For the assembly S. Samuelson, a Republican was successful in the first district, M. Fitzgerald was reelected in the second and Joseph Rankin chosen in the third. Assemblyman Rankin was again honored in 1871 but Samuelson gave way to Peter Reuther, another Republican, and Fitzgerald to Martin McNamara, a Democrat. A year later there were elected C. R. Zorn, O. S.

Davis and J. Rankin and in 1873 W. R. Taylor the Democratic nominee for governor secured a large majority and in all three assembly districts Democrats were chosen to the assembly, C. R. Zorn, B. S. Lorrigan and Joseph Rankin, the majority of the last named being over 800. John Schuette was the next incumbent of the senatorial position, defeating Joseph Vilas in a hard fought contest in 1874. B. Lorrigan was reelected in the second assembly district but C. R. Zorn was superseded in the first by Fred Schmitz, a Newton Democrat, while in the third R. D. Smart, a Republican was selected. The next year Democrats were chosen to fill all the positions, the winning candidates being C. R. Zorn, T. Mohr and William Tisch. Senator Schuette was one of the Republicans who supported Don A. Cameron in the heated struggle for the United States senatorship and did much to make that statesman's election possible.

The apportionment of 1876 changed the outlines of the assembly districts of the county considerably, Cato, Maple Grove and Franklin being taken from the second and added to the first, Centerville and Newton from the first and added to the third, Rapids from the second and added to the third and Gibson, Two Rivers, Two Creeks and Mishicot changed from the third to the second. Thus constituted the first district returned Thomas Thornton, a Democrat, the second Thomas Mohr, another Democrat and the third Peter Johnston, a Republican. Senator Schuette ran again but was defeated by Joseph Rankin, who remained the representative of the Fifteenth for six years thereafter, defeating Charles Luling in 1878 and H. H. Smith in 1880. Senator Rankin gained an enviable reputation at Madison, one which later lifted him into a seat in the national council chamber He was chairman of the Democratic state central committee for two years during his incumbency as a state official. In 1877 Manitowoc gave 600 majority for the Democratic candidate for governor, J. A. Mallory and chose three men of the same faith to represent it in the assembly, Thomas Thornton, W. F. Nash and Henry Vits. John Carey, Democrat, became the representative of the first district a year later, another Democrat, William Zander in the second and a Republican, W. H. Hempschemeyer in the third. Carey and Hempschemeyer were reelected in 1879 but F. Pfunder, a Democrat, succeeded Zander in the second. In 1880 a new set of men were sent to Madison, Thomas Gleeson from the first, Ira P. Smith from the second and C. E. Estabrook from the third, all Democrats but the last named. He was reelected a year later, but Gleeson gave way to Peter Phillips, a Republican and Smith to Henry Goedgen, a Democrat. In 1882 since Senator Rankin was running for congress it became necessary to choose his successor. The Republicans placed D. Nottage of Two Rivers in nomination, the Democrats J. Carey and the Prohibitionists E. J. Smalley, Carey winning by over 500 votes. He remained in office until his death in 1887, being reelected in 1884 and 1886. The assemblymen elected with Carey in 1882 were J. Miller, H. Goedgen and W. T. Albers, all Democrats. The first district reelected their representative in 1884 but Messrs. Goedgen and Albers were succeeded by John Robinson, Democrat and C. E. Estabrook, Republican, the latter defeating his Democratic opponent, John Franz by a close margin of four votes. By this time the elections for governor was changed to the even years and the assemblymen were elected as the senators had been formerly, that is to say biennially, while the senators were chosen every four years. In 1886 Manitowoc was quite prominent in state politics, C. E. Estabrook being chosen attorney general as the candidate of the Republicans and W. A. Walker acting as chairman of the Democratic state central committee. To the assembly the three districts sent D. Tracy, Isaac Craite and Reinhardt Rahr, all Democrats.

According to the apportionment which went into effect in that year Manitowoc and Kewaunee counties were combined in one senatorial district and W. F. Nash of Two Riva strong Democrat, was elected in 1888 by a large majority over C. F. Smalley. In the assembly apportionment the three districts were retained but many changes made, Centreville being transferred from the third to the first and Maple Grove and Franklin from the first to the second, thus reducing the third district to Manitowoc, Rapids and Newton. The towns of Franklin and Carlton in Kewaunee county were also made a part of the second district. In the first district, thus constituted, E. P. Scheibe, a Democrat, was chosen, in the second Isaac Craite reelected and in the third J. S. Anderson, a Republican, selected. In 1890 the Bennett law, compelling public school education, was an issue in Wisconsin and feeling among the supporters of the parochial institutions ran high. The result in Manitowoc county was a phenomenal majority of 2182 for George W. Peck as against W. D. Hoard for governor, a most sweeping Democratic victory and for the assembly three Democrats were also chosen by large majorities, P. J. Conway, J. P. Nolan and William Croll. Then by the apportionment of 1892 Calumet was again attached to Manitowoc instead of Kewaunee and the number of assembly districts was reduced to two, the first including the towns of Centerville, Cato, Eaton, Liberty, Meeme, Rockland, Schleswig, Rapids, Kossuth, Franklin, Maple Grove and Newton and the second comprising Manitowoc, Two Rivers, Mishicot, Two Creeks, Gibson and Cooperstown. Senator Nash held office until 1894, being succeeded by J. McMullen of Calumet county. In 1892 P. J. Conway and W. Croll were returned as assemblymen and two years later the latter was reelected although Mr. Conway was succeeded by F. C. Maertz, another Democrat. In that year, (1894) Manitowoc was well represented on state tickets, both the candidates of the Republican and Democratic parties for the office of lieutenant governor, Emil Baensch and A. J. Schmitz, being residents of the city. The vote for lieutenant governor in the county was Baensch 3223, Schmitz 3165, the former running several hundred votes ahead of his ticket and being successful in the state as well, securing an office which he held with great credit to himself for four years. Henry Stolze received 356 votes in the county.

The Republicans gaining control another apportionment took place in 1896, Cato, Centerville, Liberty, Meeme, Rapids, Newton and Manitowoc composing the first and the rest of the county the second district. Charles W. Sweeting, a Republican, was chosen to represent the first and Mr. Maertz was reelected by his constituents in the second district that year. In 1898 Sweeting was succeeded by Joseph Willott, another Republican, who was again elected in 1900, while in the second district Jonas Gagnon of Two Rivers was chosen twice to serve its interests. For the senate the choice fell upon Norman A. Knudson, a young Republican who gained the district by 19 majority. The apportionment of 1901 left the assembly districts unchanged with the exception of the transfer of the town of Cato from the first to the second district. Among the candidates for state offices in 1900 were George Dicke of Two Rivers and Max Goeres of Kiel, the nominees of the Social Democracy for the positions of lieutenant governor and insurance commissioner respectively.

Joseph Willott succeeded himself as assemblyman in 1902 while Mr. Gagnon made way for another Democrat, N. Terens of Mishicot. Senator Knudson not being a candidate for reelection, W. A. Knauf of Chilton was placed in the field by the Republicans while Samuel Randolph, Jr. was nominated by the Democrats. The latter carried both counties by a close vote and was consequently the chosen representative of the district in the Senate. For governor however the county registered its preference for Robert M. LaFollette. The Social Democratic vote of this year was considerable, amounting to over four hundred, and the county was represented on the state ticket of the organization.

### COUNTY POLITICS.

As was stated before the county of Manitowoc was organized as a separate political unit for all except judicial purposes in December 1838. The first election was held accordingly on March 4 1839 at the residence of P. P. Pierce near the village of Rapids. O. C. Hubbard and Horace Conroe were judges of the election and Peter Johnston and J. F. Este clerks. Two parties were in evidence even in this primeval community, the one composed of the partisans of B. Jones, who resided at the mouth of the river and the other made up of Conroe's followers. There were only thirty-five votes cast and as the Conroe party numbered seventeen their ticket was chosen as follows:—County commissioners, Horace Conroe, J. G. Conroe, J. Rigby; assessor, O. C. Hubbard; register of deeds, J. W. Conroe; collector, Peter Johnston. Under the law then in existence the county commissioners corresponded to the present county board but were elected from the county as a whole,—a system which obtained in Wisconsin until 1849 and again from 1861 to 1870. The office of collector corresponded to the modern county treasurer. The other county officers such as sheriff, district attorney, clerk of the court and county judge did not become necessary until Manitowoc was organized judicially while the county clerk was chosen by the commissioners. These latter met first on March 15, choosing J. W. Conroe as clerk and J. G. Conroe chairman. The principal business was the appointment of three constables, Joseph Estes, W. Flinn and Chauncey Calhoun. At about the same time the legislature of the territory changed the name of the township from Conroe back to Manitowoc and provided that polls should be established at the steam sawmill at the Rapids and at "the public house" at the mouth of the Manitowoc River. In May two precincts were laid out, W. T. Sheppard, S. C. Chase and John Glap being chosen judges of election in the Two Rivers and J. W. Conroe, H. McAllister and B. Jones in the Manitowoc precinct. Thus was the county legally established and in 1840 J. W. Conroe constructed a one story county and town house at the northern limits of the village of Rapids, it being 24 by 38 feet in dimensions. This structure remained for twelve years the seat of government. For ten years the county board was composed of three members, one retiring annually. The principal business before that body was the laying out of roads and school districts and the appointment of constables and other minor officials. Among the latter were Constables D. S. Munger, S. Peake, E. L. Abbott, J. Holsted, H. B. Edson, J. Edwards, F. Laduke and L. D. Sackett; Tax Collectors D. S. Munger, E. D. Beardsley, P. P. Smith and Evander Soper. The county was sparsely populated and little government, even of a local nature, was needed for some time, the work done being largely ministerial. The men who composed the board were, however, leaders in the community and served their constituents well. In October 1839 Horace and J. L. Conroe were succeeded by Benjamin Jones and Joseph Edwards, showing that "the mouth" was in the ascendant, although a year later J. G. Conroe was returned instead of J. Edwards while Rigny, one of the first board after several year's service gave way to R. M. Eberts, the founder of Two Rivers. No change in the personnel of the board then occurred until 1842 when Conroe was succeeded by Oliver Clawson and in 1843 Eberts gave way to H. McAllister, who was soon succeeded, however, by Evander M. Soper, while Joel R. Smith succeeded Benjamin Jones. In 1844 A. Hoyt took the place formerly held by Evander Soper and the next year H. H. Champlin that of O. C. Hubbard, who had served one year instead of Mr. Clawson, the latter however again giving way in 1846 to Daniel Smith of Mishicot. In 1847 the board was made up of Oliver Clawson, Daniel Smith and Charles McAllister, the first named followed by E. M. Soper the next year. The last board under this county system of representation was elected in the fall of 1848 and consisted of J. M. Sprague, Albert Wheeler and Peter Poh.

The year 1848 witnessed several important changes in the county government. The county officials, who prior to this time had been appointed or elected annually were now to hold for two years. The township county board system, which had been optional in Wisconsin Territory since 1841, was now made compulsory and finally by legislative act of March 2 1848 Manitowoc county was judicially separated from Brown county, the act taking effect after the second Tuesday in April. The county was made a part of the Third Judicial Circuit under Judge A. W. Stow and it was ordered that proper rooms should be provided for the court at an expense of not exceeding $100 per year. The first term of court was held by Judge Stow on September 15 1848. O. C. Hubbard was chosen sheriff and E. Ricker clerk to act until the first of the following year; E. H. Ellis, J. W. Colby and

J. L. Kyle were admitted to the bar and an indictment was found for trespass on state lands. The records having to do with the county were removed to the Rapids from Green Bay also in this year, the work being under the direction of John P. Champlin. In the fall the first biennial election for county officers took place. Several candidates were frequently in the field for the same office in these early days and the personal more than the partisan element predominated for some time. In fact it may be said that it was not until 1854 that the various candidates for local office generally alligned themselves under the banner of some political party. The officers chosen in this first election were as follows:—Sheriff, George W. Durgin; county treasurer, Pliny Pierce; register of deeds, A. W. Preston; county clerk, E. H. Ellis; clerk of court, Ezekiel Ricker; surveyor, E. D. Beardsley; coroner, Joseph Edwards; county judge, J. H. W. Colby. Elections were held in the odd years for several of the offices at the beginning and thus it was that in 1849 Adam Bleser became treasurer, and P. P. Smith clerk of court. In the same year a jail was built at a cost of $235.

By the county organization formed in 1848 four townships, Manitowoc, Manitowoc Rapids, Two Rivers and Meeme were set off and the first session of the county board occurred June 28, 1849, the members being Andrew J. Vieau of Manitowoc, John Stewart of Two Rivers, Charles McAllister of Rapids and T. Cunningham of Meeme. The polls in the four towns were respectively as follows:— The American House, the home of Sebastian Boldus, the Courthouse and the home of H. B. Edson. Early in 1850 the towns of Newton and Centerville were formed, the first election being held in private houses and in the fall Maple Grove was added. The first representatives from these towns were: —Centerville, Charles Koehler; Newton, F. Hacker and Maple Grove, M. C. Brown. In 1850 a full set of county officers were elected with the exception of county clerk, that official being chosen in the odd years until 1883. It was in this year also that the legislature added the slice of territory, now composing the northern tier of townships, to the county. The towns of Kossuth and Eaton, or as it was first called, Valders, were formed in 1851 with William Eatough and George Monroe as their first representatives, Kossuth being set off from Rapids. The board at about this time adopted the county poor farm system which continued in use for over ten years when the more popular township system of maintenance supplanted it. Little interest was shown in the political campaign of 1852, most of the officers being elected unanimously or as independent candidates. In this year the county suffered a serious loss in the burning of the courthouse at the Rapids. The fire was set on April 30th by an insane man named Benjamin E. Lynde, who was confined in the jail and both the structures were a total loss, although the records were fortunately saved. The fire and the fact that Manitowoc had by far outstripped Rapids led to the agitation for the removal of the county seat to the former place. The matter came to a vote on April 14 1853 in accordance with legislative permission granted a month earlier. Ten townships registered their opinion in the matter, Mishicot, or as it was first called, Saxonburgh, having been organized with F. Borcherdt as chairman late in 1852. The vote resulted in an overwhelming majority in favor of the change, being as follows:--

| Town | For | Against |
| --- | --- | --- |
| Manitowoc | 278 | 2 |
| Eaton | 24 | 0 |
| Rapids | 8 | 52 |
| Newton | 74 | 1 |
| Kossuth | 71 | 4 |
| Meeme | 41 | 1 |
| Centreville | 2 | 0 |
| Two Rivers | | No returns |
| Mishicot | | " |
| Maple Grove | | " |
| Total | 498 | 60. |

Strange to say, however, the battle was only half over when the removal was decided upon for the question immediately arose on which side of the river the structure should be placed. The people residing on the north side suggested Union Park but the site finally chosen on South Eighth Street was a strong competitor from the first. The legislature of 1853 authorized a loan with which the building should be erected at a cost of not to exceed $5000, which sum was raised to $10,000 two years later after several public meetings had been held to consider the wisdom of the increase for the proposition had met with considerable opposition. Delays followed and for three years the question of a site was a mooted one in village politics. Finally, however, the south side triumphed and in 1857 the courthouse was constructed, John Meyer being the architect. An attempt had been made at construction a year or two before under the direction of a building committee but a defect had been found in the foundation and a new committee, consisting of G. Lee, E. D. Beardsley and S. Hill was appointed under whose direction the work was completed.

The campaign of 1854 was a most bitter one. By this time the Republican party was a factor and many who had formerly been Democrats flocked to the new organization. To make matters more complicated a well defined movement of defection occured in the Democratic ranks. The county convention of the party was a scene of discord and after it was over independent nominees were placed in the field for the offices of county treasurer, district attorney and sheriff. The Republicans thus succeeded in electing their entire ticket with the exception of the register of deeds. The vote is an interesting one as illustrating that men and not the party was the principle of division at the time. It was as follows:

| Office | Rep. | | Dem. | | Ind. | |
|---|---|---|---|---|---|---|
| Sheriff | F. W. Adams | 536 | A. McCullom | 369 | S. Carpenter | 338 |
| Treas. | G. Kremers | 682 | W. Bach | 520 | S. Kelley | 58 |
| Register of deeds | F. Salomon | 481 | A. N. Baker | 755 | | |

District attorney
W. Hamilton 836 N. Wollmer 394
Surveyor F. Armsby 1248
Coroner S. Bates 881 A. Preston 581
County clerk
C. Roeser 714 C. A. Reuter 506

The Democratic party in the county soon, however, recovered from its internal dissensions and in 1855 elected C. A. Reuter, their candidate for clerk of court by a large majority, while in 1856 they were victorious all along the line, notwithstanding the fact that there were independent candidates for both the offices of sheriff and county clerk. In 1855 the town of Schleswig, or as it was first known, Abel, was formed and H. F. Belitz chosen as its first representative in the county board. Cooperstown, Rockland and Franklin were also set off soon after, being represented respectively by J. R. Weber, Louis Faulhaber and Alanson Hickok. In 1857 the various wards of the villages of Two Rivers and Manitowoc were recognized as units of representation in the board, there being at that time three such divisions in Manitowoc, although the first and third together were given but one supervisor at first, and two in Two Rivers. Thereafter as the towns grew each ward was given representation as it came into existence, thus preserving the balance between the rural and urban interests. In early judicial affairs politics were largely tabooed. Judge Gorsline received the almost unanimous support of the county in the spring of 1856 for the circuit bench and at his resignation the year following Judge David Taylor of Sheboygan was appointed. At this time Kewaunee county was attached to Manitowoc for judicial purposes. As county judges the successors of Ezekiel Ricker whose death occurred in 1854 were George Reed who resigned, then George C. Lee who also relinquished the office after a short incumbency, Isaac Parrish, who served until 1858 and Charles H. Walker who defeated Parrish for reelection by a majority of 1013 votes.

The Democrats retained their power in 1857 when they elected their candidate for clerk of court and in 1858 when al-

C. P. MUNGER

most the whole county ticket was victorious. During the latter campaign there was again disaffection in the ranks, not sufficient to change the result at the polls however. Prominent among the bolters were Col. Sherwood, G. W. Barker, W. F. Eldredge, William Eatough, M. Playfair and Patrick Flynn and they placed D. H. Van Valkenburgh in the field as sheriff against Louis Kemper, the regular Democratic nominee and A. N. Baker as register of deeds against Jere Crowley. The votes for these two independent candidates, however, did not much exceed one hundred, although Baker's vote caused the election of Henry Baetz, the Republican nominee for register of deeds. On the other hand the Democrats secured almost exclusive control of the county board, all but five of the members being followers of the party. In 1858 Cato, Gibson and Liberty, the last first known as Buchanan, were created and given representation in the board, the first chairmen of the towns being Alanson Hickok, Jason Pellett and Ole Oleson. Finally in 1860 the town of Two Creeks, first called Rowley after an earlier settler, was set off it being the last of the eighteen townships to come into existence. H. Luebke was its first supervisor. In that year also the county board authorized the building of a brick structure for the county offices, as an annex to the courthouse. B. Jones secured the contract for $5000 and the building was erected on the southeast corner of the square. The year 1860 witnessed more factional strife and bitter contests in county politics, the campaign being perhaps the most virulent in Manitowoc's history. At the Democratic convention the trouble first began to show itself, largely from the fact that some, among them Editor Crowley of the Pilot, openly asserted that the gathering was in the hands of the Breckenridge followers and that they were trading with the Republicans. Judge Pierpont, as leader of the Breckenridge supporters, presided over the convention and Reuter, the regular nominee of the party for treasurer, was also of that faction. The result was that the bolters placed M. Kuhl in nomination for the position of county treasurer as opposed to Reuter and P. Hogan to oppose Alanson Hickok, the regular nominee for county clerk. Thus handicapped the Democrats went into the struggle against the Republicans and the result was a defeat in the case of every nominee by majorities ranging from two to seven hundred. Candidate Kuhl developed a remarkable strength, considering that he was an independent nominee, receiving 786 votes while Reuter received 1260 and his victorious Republican opponent, O. Koch 1907. S. A. Wood, the Democratic candidate for district attorney was about the only one on the ticket that secured anywhere near the regular party strength. The war then beginning led to many changes in local politics. The Breckenridge and Douglas Democrats drew together gradually and this fact, allied to that of the opposition of H. S. Pierpont to harbor taxes led to his election to the office of county judge in the spring of 1861, In the meanwhile the Union Democrats, including such men as Henry Sibree, Lyman Emerson and others joined the Republicans on all issues and gradually became an integral part of the party. In the fall of that year Conrad Bates was put forward as the Union candidate for clerk of court but was defeated by Jere Crowley, his Democratic opponent by 192 votes. The first election of a county school superintendent also occurred at this time, B. J. Van Valkenburgh, the Democratic nominee defeating Fred Borcherdt, whom the Unionists supported.

By this time another change had been made in the system of county government in the state. By act of March 28, 1861 the county boards were made to consist of three supervisors, one elected from each assembly district, while the chairmen of the towns retained only such functions as pertained to the equalization of taxes. Under this law the first board was elected in Manitowoc in November. In the first district John Carey, Democrat defeated F. R. Gutheil, Union. In the second district Lyman Emerson was chosen unanimously while in the third Nels Sorenson, Democrat defeated S. A. Wood, Union. The board met in the spring of 1862 and elected Mr. Emerson president but soon both he and Supervisor Sorenson resigned, necessitating the calling of a special election, which resulted in the choice of Alanson

Hickok in the second and Jason Pellett in the third district, both being Democrats. J. O'Hearn succeeded Hickok in November 1863 and as thus constituted the board continued to exist until 1866. The campaign of 1862 was somewhat of a complicated one. Men that had recently changed political allegiance were placed on tickets in strange companionship and the result was a remarkable divergence in the number of votes received by the candidates for different offices. There was no open bolting, however, and the Democrats elected all their officers except the county treasurer for which position Oscar Koch defeated H. S. Pierpont by a narrow majority. As the war proceeded the Democratic party continued to grow stronger in the county, only the towns of Manitowoc, Kossuth, Gibson, Liberty, Eaton and Rockland giving majorities for the Republican ticket in 1862, of which three, Kossuth, Gibson and Liberty, went over to the opponents a year later. During the war a number of resignations occurred among the county officers due to enlistments for military service, among the number being Sheriff Murphy, Superintendent of Schools Van Valkenburgh, County Judge Walker and Register of Deeds Baetz.

In 1863, 1864 and 1865 the Democratic county tickets were entirely successful by large majorities, due partially to the fact that many of the Republican candidates were former Democrats. In the fall of 1865 a new county board was chosen consisting of F. Schmitz, B. S. Lorrigan and G. Damler, who administered affairs ably. After the war had closed the Republicans regained considerable strength and in the fall of 1866 succeeded in electing Henry Baetz as county treasurer, besides making a very respectable showing in the contest for the other offices. The following fall according to an amendment of the county supervisor law a supervisor at large from the county as a whole was chosen to sit in the county board, the Democratic candidate, J. S. Eggers, carrying the election by seven hundred majority over C. W. White. Messrs. Gallogly, Mohr and Koehnke were also added to that body from the first, second and third districts respectively by virtue of another amendment to the law, which increased its total membership to seven, this action being taken for fear that dictatorship might be the result of too close a corporation. The board thus constituted remained in office until 1870 when a return to the system, whereby each township was represented by a supervisor, was made.

The county election of 1868 was another close contest. The Republicans developed considerable strength, reelecting Henry Baetz as treasurer and putting in office P. P. Fuessenich as county clerk and Fayette Armsby as surveyor while the Democrats elected the rest of the ticket. In the spring of that year Judge Taylor, the Democratic candidate for the circuit bench had also been defeated by Campbell McLain. On the other hand W. W. Waldo was chosen county judge by 2500 majority over H. Sibree, the Republican candidate, in the judicial election of 1869 while Democratic successes in the fall also presaged a change. The campaign of 1870 was nevertheless a very bitter one. This time both the Democratic and Republican camps suffered defections in the form of a third or People's party movement. This faction placed Ira P. Smith in nomination for sheriff, A. Chloupek for treasurer, J. Garry for register of deeds, G. A. Woodin for district attorney and J. Oswald for coroner, endorsing J. Thombs, the Democratic nominee for county clerk. The result of the election was unsatisfactory to all, the division of offices being about even. Quirin Ewen, P. P. Fussenich and F. Armsby, Republican nominees for treasurer, county clerk and surveyor were successful while from among the Democrats John Franz, A. Wittenberg, E. B. Treat and F. Simon secured the positions of register of deeds, sheriff, district attorney and coroner. Then came the Fuessenich scandal, the only deep blot on the history of Manitowoc politics, which had an injurious effect on Republican success for many years as well as casting a shadow on several leading Democratic politicians. Rumors that P. P. Fuessenich, the county clerk had not been using honest methods in the discharge of his duties led to an investigation early in 1871 and it was revealed by a committee of the county board, appointed to investigate the matter, that for six years a system of illegal appropriation of public funds had been going on. It was proved that over $20,000 of the county money had thus been squandered and it came to light that Fuessenich, the chief offender had made away with other sums besides. Before hearing the testimony the clerk handed in his resignation and fled the country, nothing further ever being heard from him. The matter created much excitement at the time and led to the institution of many reforms in the administration of public business.

Fuessenich's resignation made a special election necessary in the fall of 1871, Gilbert Burnet being chosen by 63 majority over H. S. Pierpont, the former being a Republican. Considerable trouble was experienced over the refusal of the county board of canvassers, through some irregularity, to count the returns from Cato and Pierpont was at first declared elected. On quo warranto proceedings, however, the vote of the town was admitted and Mr. Burnet seated. Despite the effects of the Fuessenich scandal the contest in the fall of 1872 was most intense and the result was another division of offices. The People's party of the county held a convention, H. S. Pierpont being the leading spirit but no nominations were made. P. J. Pierce was announced as an independent candidate for sheriff but later withdrew. R. D. Smart, the Republican candidate for that office ran several hundred ahead of his ticket and was elected over Edward Conway. A. M. Richter, another Republican, was chosen county clerk and the vote for treasurer resulted in a tie between Quirin Ewen, Republican and A. Wittenberg, Democrat, each receiving 2458 votes. The rest of the offices went to the Democrats. The tie in the case of treasurer made a special election necessary and one was accordingly held in December in which Mr. Ewen defeated his opponent by 101 votes. On the other hand the Democratic majority in 1873 increased to over 2000 on the vote for clerk of court and in 1874 their ticket was successful with the exception of county treasurer, to which position Quirin Ewen was again elected, this time by 256 majority over G. Damler. Ewen, however, died before his term expired and his opponent was chosen by the county board to fill the vacancy. From this time on until 1882 only three Republicans were succeessful in securing county office, the Democratic majorities being in the neighborhood of one thousand and in some cases, as in the election of county judge in 1877, there being no opposition. The first of these three exceptions was Prof. G. F. Viebahn, who in 1879 was chosen school superintendent over John Hussey by a majority of 561. The second was R. D. Smart. who owing to his personal popularity and disaffection in the Democratic ranks defeated J. P. Wickert for county judge in the spring of 1881 by 870 votes. The third was John Bibinger, who in 1882 was elected sheriff over W. Wieboldt. A year before Judge Norman Gilson had been chosen circuit judge over Campbell McLain, his Republican opponent, by a majority of 3102, one of the largest ever given in the county for any candidate. In 1882 the Prohibitionist put up a county ticket but did not develop essential strength. At this time the odd year elections for county superintendent and clerk of court ceased and thus political energies could be more centralized.

Early in the eighties many Manitowoc county men, notably William Rahr, urged the building of a county asylum for the care of the insane and at a meeting of the county board in May 1884 $25,000 was voted for that purpose. A three story brick structure was built on spacious grounds southwest of Manitowoc and the institution was opened in January 1885 with Gustav Mueller as superintendent. The asylum has since been managed by trustees and has proved most successful, many patients from other counties as well as the local insane being cared for. A county jail was erected in the early nineties and the old courthouse remodeled, the county office annex being removed. The latter part of the decade 1880-1890 saw as few Republicans in office in the county as had the earlier years of it. County Judge C. H. Schmidt, who had defeated Judge Smart in 1885 died in 1838 and Emil Baensch, a Republican was chosen to fill the vacancy. A year later, his term having expired, he defeated Hubert Falge by 1253 votes, the most decisive Republican victory for some time. Democratic landslides occured in 1890 and 1892 but by 1894 the beginning of another change in county politics came about and the years of exclusive Democratic rule were brought to an end. In that year the Populists put up a county ticket, which secured about three hundred votes, forming no inconsiderable element as the first third party movement in the county since the Prohibition ticket of 1882 with the exception of a few local candidates on the Labor ticket in 1888. The Democrats secured every office with the exception of sheriff, to which Henry Schmidt was elected over Daniel Tracy. Then came the campaign of 1896, resulting in a victory for all of the Republican nominees except the county clerk. In 1898 a reaction took place, the Republicans securing only the county treasurership, to which Peter Kaufman was elected, but in 1900 the party again gained ground, electing the sheriff, county clerk, district attorney, treasurer and surveyor while the Democrats secured the register of deeds, coroner and clerk of court, the county superintendent being chosen on a non-partisan basis. Owing to an error in the returns from the fourth ward of the city of Manitowoc E. S. Schmitz, the Democratic nominee for district attorney, was seated by the board of canvassers but after continuing in office for two months and after some litigation had been commenced a compromise was effected, whereby the Republican candidate, A. L. Hougen, took the position. A municipal court was established in the county in 1895 and both this and the probate court were for some time governed by non-partisan principles, owing to the balance existing between the two parties in the county but in 1901 the matter was again taken into politics, a Republican, A. P. Schenian being chosen municipal judge and a Democrat, John Chloupek becoming judge of the probate court. Michael Kirwan of Manitowoc succeeded Judge Gilson on the circuit bench in 1899, defeating Attorney Prescott of Sheboygan by a sweeping majority.

The election held in the fall of 1902 again witnessed an almost equal division of the spoils, the Democrats succeeding in electing the sheriff, register of deeds, clerk of court and coroner, while the Republicans chose the county clerk, treasurer, district attorney and surveyor, while for county school superintendent Fred Christiansen received support from both parties. The Social Democrats put a full county ticket in the field and made a very considerable showing.

Thus in summarizing it will be noted that the Democrats, with few exceptions, have been victorious in county politics. And yet the divisions that have occurred in the apportionment of the offices within the gift of the people show very clearly that the true test that has been applied was the man and not the party. Factional strife that was so bitter in earlier days, leading to scurrilous abuse and insult through the columns of the public press has largely ceased of late years. On the whole the study of the political complexion of the county in its varying changes is an interesting one and the record of the public officials has been with some few exceptions fairly good. Particularly might this be said of the members of the county boards, who, it may well be admitted, have been representatives in the best sense of the word. A list of the various officials of the county, the members of the county board and the chairmen of that body will be found in Appendix C.

## CHAPTER X.

### VILLAGE AND CITY GOVERNMENT.

Manitowoc county contains two cities, Manitowoc and Two Rivers and two villages, Reedsville and Kiel, that have been incorporated under the state laws, the former under special statutes and the villages in accordance with general laws. Both Manitowoc and Two Rivers had twenty years of village existence before entering upon a civic life. It is the purpose of this chapter to study the political and administrative history of each of them.

#### MANITOWOC.

The village of Manitowoc was an integral part of the township of the same name and indistinguishable from it until March 6, 1851 on which date a law was signed which authorized its incorporation. Even earlier this step had been proposed as the township, because of the fact that there was no other legal entity, was obliged to do much improvement outside of the scope of a rural community. Thus the travel across the Manitowoc river became so important that in 1848 it became necessary to supersede the primitive ferry by a bridge. In this first bridge, which was an inexpensive structure, there was no draw since at the time there was no necessity for one. At this time the business portion of Manitowoc was almost entirely on the north side and as many families resided on the opposite side a ready means of communication was very necessary. The charter provided that the village should be divided into two wards, that portion south of the river to be known as the first and that on the north side as the second. A president, marshal and treasurer for the whole village and three trustees and one assessor from each ward were to be chosen the first Tuesday of each April. The town supervisors were to appoint a polling place for the first election and all who were qualified voters of the town within the limits defined were given the suffrage. The president's duties were enumerated, including the keeping of the seal, signing licenses, justice of the peace powers and casting votes in case of a tie in the village board. General ordinance powers were conferred upon the board and it was annually to appoint a clerk, street commissioners in both wards, four fire wardens, a sealer of weights and measures, sexton, harbormaster and chief engineer of the fire department.

The first election was soon held, George Reed being chosen president, Gustavus Richter treasurer and A. Wittmann marshal. On May 12th the first meeting of the village trustees was held, the chairman of the county board administering the oath. The membership of this first board consisted of C. Hottelmann, J. F. Zinns and Evander M. Soper of the first and M. Fellows, J. Bennett and Jarvis E. Platt of the second ward. At the first session a map of the village was ordered to be made, by-laws were drafted and S. A. Wood was chosen clerk. The work of the board for the first few years was largely along pioneer lines. A cemetery had early been established at what is now the corner of North Eighth and Park streets, but this being too near the center of population a movement for a new one was early on foot, under the name of the Evergreen Cemetery Association. It was incorporated in 1856 and its rights the village bought out some years later. The ground purchased overlooked the Manitowoc river and has since been used for burial purposes. The grading of streets was another problem pressing for solution from the first and work was immediately begun, the hill on North Eighth street being removed in 1854 and other thoroughfares being opened later, although business for some time was centered on York and Commercial streets, which were laid out much wider than any of the others. George Reed was succeeded as village president by James Bennett in 1852 and the latter was reelected a year later. During his term authorization was received for the draining of extensive marshes east of South Ninth and north of Jay streets and much improvement took place. Fire companies made up of volunteer bands of male residents were organized and, although at first there was little apparatus, nevertheless the needs of the day were met. A public square was laid out between North Seventh, Park and North Sixth streets, later christened Union Park, the ladies of the city raising enough money in 1852 to fence it in. A few years later Washington Park was set off on the south side, surrounded by Eleventh, Washington, Marshal and Twelfth streets. Mr. Bennett was succeeded by William Bach, a Democrat of considerable popularity. He in turn, after a year of service, gave way to Charles Esslinger in 1855, who remained in office two years. As the treasurer of the Manitowoc & Mississippi at the time he received a hearty support from men of all parties although the elections were contested in the early days, as later, according to national party lines. A public meeting was held in December 1856 to ask for incorporation as a city but little came of the movement and the panic of the next year, coupled with the failure of the railroad plans to materialize, put a damper on municipal hopes. Up to March 1857 four amendments had been made to the village charter. The first and second, in 1852 and 1853, changed minor clauses in the original document, the third in 1856 altered the boundaries and the fourth in 1857 provided that each ward should elect a representative to the county board. In the last named year James Bennett was again elected president, this time on the Republican ticket. The year witnessed much dissatisfaction as to the proportion of taxes the village was obliged to pay under the equalization made by the county board and an injunction was secured against paying over the funds but it was dissolved later. It was during Bennett's term also that the village purchased two new hand fire engines at a cost of

$5000 and an engine house was constructed on the north side. The Badger Engine company was formed to man the apparatus, purely voluntary in character, and in February, 1855 a bucket company was also organized with E. K. Rand as foreman and C. Esslinger as first assistant. A complete plat of the village was made by Fred Salomon in 1857 being accepted by the village trustees as official.

President Bennett gave way in 1858 to Charles Esslinger. An amendment passed by the legislature in that year created the third ward, although it and the first were united for some years as far as representation in the county board was concerned. By another amendment passed the next spring the board of the village was given increased powers over the highways. It was seen by this time that a better bridge across the river was a necessity and on August 10 1859 a public meeting was called to consider the question. As a result a new structure with a draw was thrown across the river on Eighth street, being opened to the public the following February. Bridges were authorized the same year by the legislature at Ninth and Commercial streets but they were not constructed, nor was that at the west end of York street, authorized two years later. The next president of the village after Mr. Esslinger was S. A. Wood, who was elected twice on the Democratic ticket. During his incumbency the fire companies, now two in number, reached a more complete organization, gaining a recognized place socially as well as in their field of usefulness. Their annual reviews and balls were among the events of the year and it was not an infrequent occurrence for them to receive and pay visits to and from similar organizations in neighboring towns. The Badger company temporarily disbanded in 1861 but was succeeded in the second ward by the Clipper City Engine company, with Louis Kemper as foreman.

In the spring of 1861 two village tickets were placed in the field, G. B. Collins representing the Republicans as candidate for president and W. Rahr, Sr. the Democrats. Collins carried all three wards and was elected. He fulfilled his duties during the troublous times at the opening of the war with great ability and was succeeded in 1862 by James Bennett, now for the fourth term president. New streets were graded rapidly at this time and an amendment to the charter was secured facilitating such action. At the next election Oscar Koch, the Republican candidate, succeeded in defeating Joseph Vilas although the latter carried the second ward and in 1864 A. D. Jones was honored with the confidence of his townsmen, he also being a Republican. The activity of the village was consumed mainly at this time with the raising of bounties and interest was centered in the war. A new fire company was organized in the second ward during the year, known as the Union Engine Co. No. 1, Jonah Richards being chosen foreman and among the members being enrolled many of the most prominent villagers. In 1865 Joseph Vilas and O. Torrison were the opposing candidates for the village presidency, the former carrying all three wards, owing to his championship of the harbor projects then pending. During the last months of his term the charter of the village was recodified and passed by the state legislature. Few changes of importance were made, the principal features being the making of the marshal an appointive instead of an elective office and the addition of several powers to those already possessed by the trustees, including that over the improvement of parks and increased financial discretion. In the election of 1866 S. A. Wood, the Democratic candidate, was elected president, carrying all but the second ward, in which J. D. Markham, his opponent, was successful.

As the effects of the war disappeared village activity began to take on a more definite character. Great interest was manifested in the volunteer fire department which at this time had reached a high standard of efficiency. It consisted of Badger Engine company No. 2, stationed on the south side, of which F. Becker acted as foreman, Phoenix Hook & Ladder company, G. Phillips, foreman and Protection Bucket company, A. Pfeffer foreman. This mode of enlisting citizens in public service was a beneficent one and formed a remarkable feature of the times. An important change was made by an amendment to the village charter passed in

March 1867 by which it was provided that the office of village treasurer and marshal should be abolished, the town treasurer and constable filling their places and the assessors were made appointive instead of elective. The latter change was permanent but the former only temporary, the original provisions being restored a year later. After a year's service Mr. Wood was defeated and therefore succeeded by Henry Baetz, the latter remaining in office two years, carrying the village in 1868 over William Bach by a large majority. The legislature granted the village a new charter in the spring of that year, which was much more complete than any previous one. Among other things it provided for the creation of the fourth ward out of territory formerly comprising the western part of the second ward, for the annual election of a police justice, for the choice of a fire chief by the department itself and for the appointment by the trustees of a village attorney. The powers of the board were also considerably augmented, they being given control of the harbor, succeeding the commissioners, of whom mention is made elsewhere and being assigned the duty of acting as street commissioners in their respective wards. Among other provisions were the power to raise a tax for a bridge on Tenth street and to utilize one fourth of the time in the public schools in instruction in foreign languages and the creation of a board of equalization, consisting of the president, treasurer, clerk and assessor. Another amendment was passed a year later providing for the appointment of one street commissioner per ward and also authorizing a vote to be taken on the question of consolidating the village into one school district and of erecting a central high school. An interesting question came up in President Baetz's administration. An alley in block 262 was vacated by the trustees and it was sought to legalize the act by means of a special act from the legislature, which was accordingly granted. Governor Fairchild, however, vetoed the act after which the senate immediately passed the bill over his head by a vote of 22 to 3 and the assembly took similar action by a vote of 66 to 22. The next and last president of the village was Charles Luling, a Republican. Even before this the question of incorporation as a city had been agitated and as a result of efforts along this line the legislature on March 12, 1870 finally granted a charter. The document comprised forty-eight pages in the statute book of that year and was quite complete.

It provided for annual elections on the first Tuesday in April at which a mayor, treasurer, police justice and three aldermen, one justice of the peace and one constable for each ward were to be chosen by the voters. The board of aldermen was given the power to appoint a clerk, marshal, policemen, harbormaster, assessor, bridge tenders, sexton, sealer of weights and measures, fire chief, city attorney, surveyor, fire warden and one street commissioner per ward and at first the mayor had no veto power. The four wards remained as theretofore and four school districts were also authorized. Limits of taxation were fixed, that of the ward funds being two per cent and the board of equalization was made to consist of the mayor, clerk, treasurer and assessor. Petitions for the laying out and vacation of streets as well as for public park improvement were provided for and full powers over the harbor were defined. The first election under the charter occured as specified, the candidates for mayor being Peter Johnston, Republican and C. H. Schmidt, Democrat. Johnston carried all four of the wards and thus became the first magistrate of the newly created municipality, Otto Troemmel being chosen treasurer. Mayor Johnston was reelected in 1871 over John Franz, the latter carrying only the third ward. With the beginning of city life came much activity. An iron bridge was begun over the river at Tenth street, which reached completion in October 1872, the total cost being $25,000. This structure was 450 by 31 feet and was the first iron bridge in the county. Considerable improvement at the cemetery was also accomplished, efforts made at drainage on the south side, notably near Sherman's Creek and a new steam fire engine, the Manitowoc, purchased in 1872, after which public cisterns were placed at convenient places throughout the city. Loans were necessary to carry out these improvements and legislative authority to borrow was easily secured. By an amendment to the charter the city was divided into four districts for street purposes, each under the charge of a commissioner, appointed by the board and by another adopted in 1873 methods of fixing salaries were provided and the power of maintaining a dredge given to the municipality. River improvement and the fixing of dock lines played an important part in city affairs at the time as is elsewhere pointed out.

In 1872 Charles Luling defeated S. A. Wood for mayor by 508 majority and was succeeded a year later by another Republican, A. D. Jones, who was reelected in 1874 by 412 majority over George Pankratz, in 1875 by 267 majority over John Franz, in 1876 unanimously and in 1877 by 80 majority over E. K. Rand. During Mayor Jones' administration the work of public improvement continued. A new bridge was constructed at Eighth street at a cost of $27,000, another steam fire engine, the A. D. Jones, added to the department, being stationed on the north side and new engine houses were provided. The department was reorganized on a more modern basis with Fred Seeger as chief engineer, consisting of Steam Engine Company No. 1, Steam Engine Company No. 2, Badger Engine Company No. 3, Torrent Engine Company No. 2 and Protection Bucket company. Within a few years, however, the old volunteer organizations, the Torrent, Badger and Protection companies disbanded. Some changes in government were made by an amendment to the charter in 1875, the police justice being made appointive from among the justices of the peace and powers over street lighting and the regulation of railways being granted to the council. Two years later the legislature also changed the provision in regard to constituency of the board of equalization, one alderman from each ward being added. Complaint was again loud at about this time as before in the fifties as to the injustice with which the city was taxed by the county board.

The city election of 1878 was very close, John Schuette, a Republican defeating Adolph Piening, the Democratic nominee, by 36 majority. This marked the beginning of Mr. Schuette's six years at the helm of city affairs for he succes-

JUDGE H. S. PIERPONT

sively defeated Edward Conway, Henry Mulholland and George Pankratz, besides being unanimously chosen in 1881. His administration was marked by great advances, particularly in street improvement, drainage, fire department affairs and harbor improvement. The city charter was completely revised by C. E. Estabrook in 1879 and, as amended, was passed by the legislature. By this charter a city physician was added to the list of appointive officers, the office of police justice was abolished, the policemen took the place of the fire wardens, salary limits were fixed and the veto power given the mayor. In 1882 an amendment was passed in regard to the public grounds, streets and sidewalks, the council's powers in these regards being consideraoly augmented. Later in Mayor Schuette's term the question of instituting a system of waterworks was much agitated and a public meeting called to discuss the proposition but so much opposition was manifested that the project was dropped temporarily. In the spring of 1884 George Pankratz, the Democratic nominee for mayor defeated Mayor Schuette by 156 votes, carrying all but the first ward and a year later he defeated R. D. Smart by 127 majority. His successor was also a Democrat, Reinhardt Rahr, the youngest of Manitowoc's mayors, who defeated F. Sixta by 328 majority. The principal issue during his administration, which was an able one, was the waterworks question. In 1886 eastern capitalists appeared and at a public meeting held on October 18th it was decided to put the matter of granting a franchise to a popular vote, which was accordingly done on June 11th of the next year. By this time Thomas Torrison was mayor, having been elected by a majority of 141 votes over Reinhardt Rahr. The city divided on the waterworks question as follows:—

| Wards  | For | Against |
|--------|-----|---------|
| First  | 248 | 24      |
| Second | 56  | 31      |
| Third  | 283 | 52      |
| Fourth | 136 | 49      |
| Total  | 713 | 156     |

With this popular endorsement the franchise was granted and the Manitowoc Waterworks Company formed by the promoters, the system being installed during the succeeding two years. The pumphouse was constructed on the lake front near the south city limits, cribs and filters sunk out in Lake Michigan and a steel reservoir erected on North Water street. From time to time the system has been enlarged as patronage and public needs made extension necessary. Mayor Torrison was reelected in 1888 without opposition and continued his work in the advancement of the city's interests. Efforts were made to get a government building during his term and although unsuccessful, led to increased postal facilities. Saloon licenses were raised in amount to $200 at about this time but notwithstanding this fact for many years the city led all in the state as to the number of these institutions in proportion to population. It was decided that the city should be lighted by electricity and in February 1889 bids were received for that purpose. John Schuette was given the franchise and within a few months had a first class incandescent system in operation. The new waterworks system also led to a reorganization of the fire department and this was accomplished under the administration of Fred Schuette, who was elected in 1889 and again in 1890 and 1891 without opposition. The old steam fire engines were retired to reserve duty and a brick fire station was erected on Franklin street, a small sub-station containing a hose cart being placed on the north side. A system of electric fire alarms was also instituted and the entire department changed from a volunteer to a partly paid service. By legislative authorization a sewage system was put in, which was extended from year to year as necessity arose. A new charter was granted the city by the legislature in 1891 under which, with the exception of certain portions of the general law the council has adopted, it has since operated. Aldermen were reduced to two per ward by this act and the elections for city officers were made biennial. Considerable appointive power, including that over the chief of police, surveyor and attorney, was conferred upon the mayor and a board of public works was also instituted, consisting of the clerk, engineer and attorney. Paving, park improvement and bridge construction were provided for and other minor changes were designated. The limits of the city were extended also, the board soon creating the fifth and sixth wards, the former being the western portion of the third and the latter the western portion of the fourth ward. In the same year the legislature authorized the city to borrow $30,000 for the building of a new iron bridge across the river at Eighth street and accordingly the work was entered upon, the contract being let to the Wisconsin Bridge Company. The bridge at Tenth street was also rebuilt soon after. In 1892 the seventh ward was set off, consisting of that territory embraced in the extreme southwest portion of the city.

The election of 1893 witnessed a partisan contest for mayor Joseph Vilas representing the Democrats and Joseph Willott, Jr., the Republicans. The former was elected by 451 majority, carrying all but the second ward. City progress was largely retarded by the effect of the bank failures and the general panic during the years of his administration but towards the end the Wisconsin Central projects awakened a new interest in the future. Municipal ownership of lighting and waterworks was much discussed at the time, although no results followed in the way of a general public movement. Mayor Vilas was defeated by Thomas Torrison in 1895 by a majority of 424, the latter carrying every ward but the seventh. He was reelected two years later without opposition. During his term of office the city was particularly active in harbor improvements, the river being dredged at the expense of many thousands and extensive docking projects being carried out, of which ment.on is elsewhere made in these pages. Other improvements also went on apace. In 1899 the Democrats placed William Rahr in nomination for the mayoralty and he defeated George Burger, the Republican candidate, by 790 majority. Two years later Mr. Rahr was renominated, this time by the Republicans and defeated Henry Mulholland, his Democratic adversary, by 841 majority. His administration was one of remarkable vigor and was marked by great advancement. Among the improvements instituted were the reorganization of the police department, the installation of the police telegraph system, the placing of arc lights on the main streets, the renovation of the city parks, the paving of Eighth and Commercial streets with vitrified brick at a cost of nearly $40,000, the building of an engine house on North Eighth street at a cost of $10,000, the granting of street car and gas franchises and the opening of a public library. The question of building a new city hall was agitated but it was not thought advisable to go to that expense, although the rooms used for the city offices were thoroughly remodeled. Harbor improvements were also continued and additions made to Evergreen cemetery. On the whole the watchword of the city in recent years has been progress. In the spring election of 1903 Dr. W. G. Kemper, a Democrat was by a compromise agreement, unanimously chosen as mayor while the Republicans secured the city treasurership, the former incumbent, John Mahnke being reelected. Chief among the projects of moment engrossing the opening of his term were the building of the $25,000 Carnegie Library. A list of city officials of both Manitowoc and Two Rivers will be found in Appendix D.

### TWO RIVERS.

The village of Two Rivers was set off from the town of the same name and a charter granted to it on March 31 1858. It was divided into two wards, Washington street being the line of demarkation and the first Tuesday in May was fixed as the annual election day. The elective officers included a president, marshal, treasurer and three supervisors and one assessor per ward, while the clerk, harbormaster and minor officers were made appointive. According to the charter the first election was held in May 1858 and H. C. Hamilton, a Democrat was chosen president. He was succeeded by H. S. Pierpont in 1859, Edward Mueller in 1860, J. B. Burns in 1861, David Smoke in 1862 and then by John Oswald, who served as president three years. During this time the village was progressing rapidly. In 1862 the legislature authorized

MANITOWOC IN 1870

bridges on the East Twin at Main street and over the West Twin at Washington, Jefferson and Monroe streets. This act was repealed two years later and the village trustees given all authority over bridges, an authority which they soon acted upon, for the only bridge then in existence was that on Washington street erected by the county in 1849. Structures at a cost of $3600 were built at Washington and Walnut streets in 1865, J. Mann being the contractor. Street improvement was also pushed and adequate means of fire protection devised. Joseph Mann was elected president in 1866, after whom E. Mueller served another term, John Oswald two terms, Andrew Baetz one and J. M. Conine one. Then in 1872 B. F. Richter was honored, after whom Mr. Conine was again elected for two terms, serving until 1875.

In December 1868 the Two Rivers Excelsior Engine company was organized with H. Smith as foreman and also the Dexter Hook & Ladder Co. with George Burnell as foreman. A fireman's tournament was held in the village a year later and these organizations were very active factors for several years. In 1871, however, a steam fire engine was purchased and the department reorganized, a new fire station being erected in 1874 at a cost of $5000, the building also being used as a town hall. Several amendments to the charter were made during these years, one in 1868 in regard to the duties of the clerk and treasurer, one in 1870 containing minor provisions and one in 1871, changing the election day to the first Tuesday in April. Louis Zander became village president in 1875, then J. M. Conine served another term and he in turn was succeeded by B. F. Richter in 1877. A movement was then on foot looking towards the securing of a city charter and efforts in that direction were rewarded by the legislature in the grant of such a document on March 18 1878. By this charter three wards were created, Jefferson street being the dividing line between the first and the second and the third consisting of that portion of the city west and south of the West Twin. Annual elections were to be held on the first Tuesday in April at which a mayor, assessor, treasurer and two aldermen, one constable and one justice of the peace for each ward were to be elected. Each ward was given representation in the county board, this being a change from the system that had prevailed since 1870, by which the village as a whole was given but one representative in that body. The mayor was given no veto power but could cast a vote in case of a tie. The council was given the power of appointing a clerk, marshal, harbor master and other minor officers and also possessed the usual powers given to similar bodies. The city was constituted as one school district and one school commissioner was appointed by the council to represent each ward in matters pertaining to education. The first election held under the charter resulted in the choice of M. Maloy as mayor and E. Hammel as treasurer and the council was constituted as follows:—First Ward, U. Niquette and H. Lohman; Second Ward, R. E. Mueller and Joseph Schwab; Third Ward, Peter Stout and A. Wehausen. For many years the city officers in Two Rivers were kept out of partisan struggle, each spring a general caucus of citizens determining who should be the candidates and the election being merely a form of ratification. Mayor Maloy was reelected in 1879 and was succeeded a year later by W. F. Nash, Mr. Maloy being again chosen in 1881. Next Andrew Baetz held the office for two years, his administration witnessing the construction of a new bridge on Washington street and other improvements. Considerable money was also spent at and before this time in dredging the harbor. Mayor Baetz was succeeded by William Hurst for two years, who in turn gave way to B. H. Wilkens, who served four terms or until 1890, when B. F. Richter was chosen for a year. In 1891 two tickets were placed in the field, L. C. Traverse being the candidate of the Union Party and R. E. Mueller of the Democrats. The latter was elected, carrying all but the third ward. In this year the charter was wholly revised. Among the changes made were the creation of the offices of police justice, surveyor and school commissioners, five in number, the latter to be elected by the people and to hold office for three years, and the institution of a board of review, consisting of the mayor, assessor, clerk, and one alderman from each ward, whose duty it should be to equalize the city tax roll. Added powers were also given to the council in the way of maintaining parks and soon after improvements were made on the public square.

Mayor Mueller was reelected in 1892 and was succeeded by J. E. Hamilton, who held the office two terms and in turn gave way to William Luebke. During Mayor Hamilton's administration an election was held to decide upon the question of voting $17,000 for a new bridge at Walnut street and for harbor improvements. The project was carried by a vote of 241 to 132 and the bridge was built the next year at a cost of $14,000. The Populist party gained considerable strength in Two Rivers during the early nineties and in 1896 they placed a ticket in the field for the municipal offices. The campaign was an enthusiastic one and the new party succeeded in electing its candidate for mayor, Louis Zander, besides placing in office a majority of the councilmen. In 1897 Peter Gagnon was selected as mayor and has served several years, being succeeded by Peter Schroeder. Two wards were added in 1897, making five in all. In 1900 a vote was taken upon the question of granting a franchise for a waterworks and electric lighting plant and the proposition was carried, but owing to delays on the part of contractors the systems were not installed until 1902. A street car franchise was also granted at the opening of the new century. On the whole the city has been well governed and progressive.

### REEDSVILLE.

The village of Reedsville was incorporated under the general law on January 29 1892, having reached the required size to enable it to become a separate entity. The vote taken on the matter resulted in 86 for and 24 against the proposition. The village had been in existence since early days, having been named after George Reed but it did not grow until it was made a station on the M., L. S. & W. At the first election W. H. Noble was chosen president and August Schmelter treasurer and soon the village government was well started. The following gentlemen have officiated as village presidents:—

| | | |
|---|---|---|
| 1892–1894 | W. H. Noble |
| 1894–1896 | A. C. Maertz |
| 1896–1897 | J. E. Schultz |
| 1897-1899 | F. C. Stelling |
| 1899–1901 | F. C. Maertz |
| 1901–1903 | F. F. Stelling. |
| 1903 | Dr. Louis Falge. |

### KIEL.

On June 15, 1892 the village of Kiel in the town of Schleswig was incorporated and as such was given representation in the county board. Considerable public improvement has taken place and the locality has been served by its best men in public offices. The following is a list of the presidents of the village since its organization:—

| | |
|---|---|
| 1892–1893 | Charles Heins |
| 1893–1895 | Simon Hollensteiner |
| 1895–1897 | William J. Guetzloe |
| 1897–1900 | John Duecker |
| 1900–1901 | Michael Wagner |
| 1901 | H. J. Ammann. |
| 1902 | J. B. Laun. |
| 1903 | H. J. Ammann. |

## CHAPTER XI.

### CHURCHES.

Church life is an essential feature in the growth of every community. The stories of the struggles of a small but faithful congregation in the early years of existence is always interesting and there is often an element of the heroic in it. Manitowoc county has a past in this respect that will bear comparison with any similarly situated community and the growth of its spiritual interests has been from the beginning marked and rapid. An attempt is made in the following pages to describe the onward progress made by each denomination represented in the county.

EPISCOPAL.

As the oldest in point of continuous existence as an organized society the history of St. James Episcopal Church first demands attention. The Episcopals were early in the missionary field in Wisconsin and the efforts of Bishop Kemper will live in remembrance as long as that of the record of the state itself. One of his ablest coadjutors was Richard F. Cadle, who came to Wisconsin as missionary on the Oneida Reservation in 1834. In the latter thirties, probably in 1839, he visited the Rapids settlement and held what was the first Protestant service in the county. In his report submitted in February 1842 he speaks of a second visit as follows: "On the evening of Tuesday, December 7th (1841) I preached to a congregation of about sixty persons in a private house at Manitowoc Rapids, the county seat of Manitowoc county and situated on a river of the same name, three miles from its mouth. At the settlement where I officiated the population amounts to about sixty persons and at the mouth of the river the population is represented to be about three fourths of that number. Previous to this visit there had been no religious services at Manitowoc Rapids for the period of about a year and a half."

Eight years passed with an occasional visit by a missionary, among them two or three by Rev. Melancthon Hoyt in 1844. In February 1848 Bishop Kemper was making a tour of the Wisconsin parishes under his charge, being accompanied by a young Swede, Reverend Gustavus Unonius, then a recent graduate and the first of Nashotah Seminary. Upon reaching Sheboygan two members of the church, residing in Manitowoc arrived with the request that the bishop visit Manitowoc. This was impossible for him to do, so Reverend Unonius was despatched and held divine services. On the next day, February 28th, the resident members of the church met and organized a parish, naming it St. James Mission. The meeting took place at the home of Lemuel House, Colonel T. A. H. Edwards, the lighthouse keeper and Alden Clark, a merchant, being chosen wardens. It was decided to call Reverend Unonius to the parish and he accepted, assuming his duties on April 20th. At that time there were six families in the parish or twenty-seven communicants in all, including Lemuel House, E. H. Ellis, Richard Steele, Alden Clark, S. H. Sherwood and Colonel Edwards and the average congregation numbered about forty or fifty souls. The meetings were held in the upper rooms of a house, the lower part of which was occupied by the pastor and his family. Reverend Unonius remained in charge of the parish for a year, until April 1849, when he resigned and left for Chicago, where he organized a Swedish church. Born in Finland August 10, 1810 he came to America in 1845, going direct to Wisconsin and settling at Pine Lake. After several years of ser-

vice at Chicago he returned to his native land in 1858 and
was rewarded by a gift of 3000 kroner from the Swedish government in recognition of services rendered his countrymen
in America. He also held office in the customs service until
1888 when he retired on a pension and is now (1902) living
on a farm near Stockholm, beloved by all. In 1862 he published in the Swedish language a book entitled "Reminiscenses, Seventy Years in the Northwest of America," which
contains many interesting references to Manitowoc. It was
a noticeable fact that the Scandinavians who came to the
county and settled near the Rapids in 1848 and 1849 at first
united with the Episcopal church since the pastor was of
their race, eight of the original parish being Norwegians.
As soon, however, as there were sufficient of them they separated and established a church of their own, the Lutheran,
denomination. During Reverend Unonius' term four members
were gained by immigration and six lost by death. By his
resignation the church was left for some time without a rector as was also the Sheboygan mission, which he had attended. Said Bishop Kemper in his report in 1850: "Reverend Unonius was in this county about a year ago and is
remembered with much respect. When invited to a larger
sphere of action and particularly among his own countrymen
I readily consented to his departure from Wisconsin, notwithstanding that this diocese had peculiar claims upon his services. No one as yet succeeds him and yet Manitowoc and its
neighborhood present a scene of much usefulness to a selfsacrificing and laborious minister of the Gospel."

During the interim the Rapids communicants managed
to keep up occasional services and a regular Sunday school
but it was not until June 23 1851, the date of the appointment of Reverend G. P. Shetky that much interest was manifested. This clergyman was a very devout young man, fresh
from his theological studies, being ordained at Manitowoc.
He was however full of ambition and his first aim was the
building of a church. In the summer of 1851 he visited the
east to secure contributions and in a year $1074 had been
raised with pledges of $295 in addition. Plans were made by

Architect R. A. Gilpin of Philadelphia for an edifice that would seat two hundred and fifty persons to cost about $1,500 and a hundred foot lot at the corner of North Ninth and Chicago streets was donated by Benjamin Jones. The cornerstone was laid, all being in readiness, on November 24, 1851, Rt. Rev. Jackson Kemper, the missionary bishop officiating. Several presents were made to the church by eastern friends, the communion service being donated by acquaintances of Rev. Shetky residing in Germantown, Pa., the copies of liturgy coming from Philadelphia and the font from a gentleman in Albany, N. Y. In the meanwhile meetings were held by the congregation in the schoolhouse, the average attendance being about eighty and the communicants amounting to forty-three, while fifty children were in the Sunday school. Once in two weeks Reverend Shetky made trips to Two Rivers and held services at that village, the first taking place on October 19, 1851, attended by fifteen persons. The village of Rapids was visited at similar intervals, there being six communicants while Branch was the scene of monthly services. At a point fourteen miles west from Manitowoc there were seven Irish communicants who met occasionally to receive spiritual instruction from the minister, ten others usually attending, and there was a similar gathering occasionally in Meeme. In speaking of these visits later Reverend Shetky remarks in his report: "The impossible condition of the roads at this season obliged me to discontinue these monthly visits. I have no horse,—am too poor to keep one and am therefore obliged to perform all these journeys afoot." The strenuous life led by the young clergyman soon told upon his strength and, after a vacation, he returned only to resign April 1 1853. When he left a month or so later there were fifty-two communicants in his charge, twenty-eight of whom resided at Manitowoc. The church in the meantime had been completed, M. Fellows being the contractor, and it was consecrated July 25 1852 on the occasion of the festival of St. James. Rev. Shetky at first moved to Memphis, Tenn., and later attained prominence as a pastor in South Bend, Ind., Bay City, Mich. and in Philadelphia.

MANITOWOC RIVER BELOW CATO FALLS

Another short interim followed his resignation lasting until the arrival of Rev. George W. Thompson, in August 1853, he coming from Cincinnati to take up the work. At this time a mission was maintained at Robinson's settlement and the local church included thirty-three communicants. His ministry, however, was short for in 1854, while nursing cholera patients he fell ill of the dread disease and died on October 14th, his body being interred at Evergreen. After two months he was succeeded by Rev. Melancthon Hoyt, who had been in Wisconsin as a missionary since the early forties. A man of great energy he soon had the church in a very satisfactory condition and in the next year Bishop Kemper confirmed a class of eleven at Manitowoc and four at Two Rivers. At the latter place there had been organized St. Paul's Congregation and the cornerstone of a church was laid on September 3 1856. The first officers of the church were William Aldrich, senior warden; J. N. Fisher, junior warden; L. S. House, J. Teele and M. McDonald, vestrymen and services were held every Sunday afternoon. At Manitowoc the worshippers at St. James soon paid off the $500 debts still outstanding and additions were made to their structure at a considerable cost. During Rev. Hoyt's ministry the communicants increased to forty-three and the Sunday school remained prosperous. In the latter part of 1858 he resigned, continuing his labors in other fields for many years, finally removing to Dakota Territory. In April 1859 Rev. W. H. Cooper was sent to Manitowoc and remained until the following March, when he removed to Waukegan, Ill. He, also, officiated at Two Rivers, where the church had been completed, so as to seat three hundred persons, the last of the debt incurred in its construction being paid off some four years later.

The next clergyman to officiate was Reverend G. B. Engle, who came from Michigan in 1860. In his ministry services were held at Clark's Mills for some time. The great civil strife then broke out and Rev. Engle gave up his pastoral duties for a time to become chaplain in the Fourteenth Wisconsin, he being an ardent patriot. The war had a detrimental effect on the church life and St. Paul's congregation at Two Rivers became so depleted that the church was sold on May 14 1864 to the German Lutherans. In that year also Manitowoc was taken off the mission list, it thereafter being obliged to be totally self-supporting. In order to economize Rev. Engle, as he said in his report, sold his horse and discontinued his visits to Clark's Mills and soon after he resigned, moving to Indiana where he long resided. His successor, who took charge in January 1865, Rev. Lyman N. Freeman, came from Illinois and was most energetic. There were in that year nine baptisms and the Sunday school was comprised of twenty-two teachers and one hundred and thirty-seven scholars while there were three hundred persons in church connection. His ministry was injured, however, by certain charges made against his conduct, which were brought up before the standing committee at its meeting at Janesville in November. Investigations by Revs. Eastmann and Davis followed, as a result of which Rev. Freeman was cited to appear before the court of the diocese in June. This ecclesiastical trial, unique in character took place in the courthouse, Rev. Ashley of Milwaukee acting as president, there being besides four other judges. The accused was ably defended but was found guilty and withdrew from the ministry. He was followed by Rev. F. B. Dooley, formerly of the Michigan diocese, whose efforts were of a high order. During his incumbency a rectory was built, a parish school established with over fifty scholars, which was maintained for some years and the attendance at church largely increased. Rev. Dooley returned to Michigan in January 1870 and after a month or so, in which Rev. Ward supplied the pulpit, Rev. E. Peake assumed charge, he however removing to Missouri within a year. Several months passed without a pastor, when Rev. F. R. Haff of the Missouri diocese was appointed to Manitowoc. It was about this time that the church was called to mourn the loss of the venerable Bishop Kemper, whose relations with St. James had always been most amicable. Reverend Haff removed to Green Bay in the spring of 1873 and has since held a leading place among the Wisconsin clergy, officiating later at Trinity Church, Oshkosh. His successor was Rev. De Forest, who had that year been ordained and for three years he continued his ministry at Manitowoc.

In 1874 St. James, which had hitherto been in the Milwaukee diocese was transferred to the new Fond du Lac diocese. After Rev. De Forest's removal to Missouri the parish was placed under the guidance of Rev. M. E. Averill of Green Bay, who remained until 1881. The church and Sunday school membership had somewhat decreased during the latter seventies but the church was fairly prosperous and a mission was maintained at Branch. After Rev. Averill's service at St. James was completed, Rev. H. C. E. Costelle, who came from Albany, N. Y. took up the work. He revived the Two Rivers mission and did much for the advancement of the church at Manitowoc as well. During his ministry the Lydia E. Conroe bequest, comprising several acres of land in Manitowoc Rapids, was sold. Rev. Costelle left for Arkansas in March 1883 and died several years later in Quincy, Ill. Rev. H. T. Bray next assumed charge and remained until April 1886, being a man of fine scholarly attainments and an ardent worker. His successor was Rev. David Laseron, during whose pastorate of three years missions were sustained at Branch and Two Rivers. In December 1887 Rev. B. Talbot Rogers was appointed to St. James. By this time the parish numbered 250 souls and over 100 scholars were in the Sunday school. During the years of his ministry the number was vastly increased and the Two Rivers Mission was reorganized in 1901 with thirty members together with a Sunday school of about the same number. Recognized, however, as a man of great ability and attainments he was offered and accepted in 1894, the position of warden of Grafton Hall at Fond du Lac, where he has since maintained a high reputation as an educator. His successor was Rev. S. R. S. Gray, who came to St. James from the Milwaukee diocese on April 21 1895 and has since officiated. It was his aim to see the congregation have a new church edifice and funds sufficient for the starting of the enterprise were forthcoming in 1901. A site was chosen on the corner of North Eighth and State streets and the cornerstone of the new structure was laid on August 14th, the services being conducted by Rt. Rev. Weller, bishop-coadjutor of the Fond du Lac diocese amidst appropriate and elaborate ceremonies. The structure is of stone and cost in the neighborhood of $35,000. St. James church is today as at the beginning the only church of the denomination in the county and has an increasing membership. Several guilds made up of the ladies of the church are doing active work.

### METHODIST EPISCOPAL.

The early history of the Methodist Church in the west is one of struggle and in that struggle Manitowoc has played its part. Owing to a rule long prevailing in the denomination that a pastor should not remain in one situation more than two years there was not the opportunity for any one of the long list of resident ministers to identify himself with the community in any very large degree yet there are many of them whose memory will long be cherished. In 1837 Rev. Hiram W. Frink was appointed to a mission at Sheboygan which took in Sheboygan and Manitowoc counties and the villages of Brothertown and Stockbridge. There is, however, no record or probability that he ever formed any classes in the county and the mission was discontinued after the panic of 1837. In October 1843, however, Rev. David Lewis was assigned to the Manitowoc and Sheboygan mission and held services at the two places on alternate Sundays. He had two stations in Manitowoc, four in Sheboygan and two in Washington county. To reach these widely separated places Rev. Lewis was obliged to make long journeys on foot through the forest and often forded the Manitowoc river at Rapids when the feat was a dangerous one. A class of eleven members were formed at Manitowoc, among whom were P. P. Smith. The meetings were held in the upper story of B. Jones' warehouse in the summer while in the winter the congregation gathered at the home of Lighthouse Keeper Johnston, who was a Baptist. In July 1844 Rev. Lewis was succeeded by Rev. Garret N. Hanson, an earnest young man,

MANITOWOC RIVER NEAR RAPIDS

just entering upon the profession. After six years in Wisconsin he retired and died in 1856 at Fall River, Mass. In 1845 he was followed at Manitowoc by Rev. Samuel W. Martin at the end of whose term the village was dropped from the conference rolls.

In 1849 in company with Rev. Allen McIntosh Rev. Lewis was reappointed to Manitowoc and Sheboygan Counties, services being held at the Rapids in the Court House and at Manitowoc and Two Rivers in the schoolhouses. The next year Rev. Lewis alone was assigned Manitowoc County and he preached occasionally at Manitowoc Rapids, Two Rivers, Neshoto, Riley's and Mishicott, a small class being formed at Two Rivers. The pastor boarded with Henry Edwards and with his own hands during the fall and winter erected a parsonage, working upon it when not engaged in pastoral duties. Rev. Lewis was in later years the agent of the American Bible Society, then pastor at Fond du Lac and finally in 1874 retired, since residing in Sturgeon Bay. Born in New Jersey November 25 1815 he forms one of the striking examples of those hardy pioneer preachers whose heroism was only excelled by their practical piety. His successor was Rev. R. W. Barnes, who led a most successful ministry, the church membership increasing from 13 to 35, the Sunday school attendance from 24 to 50 and a library of 250 volumes being accumulated. Rev. Barnes was instrumental in securing funds for St. Paul's Church, a frame structure 35 by 40 feet which was erected on North Seventh Street during the succeeding years. He removed to Sheboygan Falls in 1853 and was succeeded by Rev. W. Sturgess. who remained a year and later officiated as pastor at various Wisconsin villages, being succeeded at Manitowoc by Rev. N. J. Alpin. In his ministry the church was dedicated, Prof. Cook of Lawrence University delivering the address on that occasion, May 3 1856. Rev. Alpin was born in Batavia, N. Y. in 1821 and was ordained while at Manitowoc. After forty years in the ministry he was superannuated. spending his last years in Waukesha. Rev. William Rowbotham took charge of St. Paul's in 1856, being followed by Rev. A. C. Squier a year later. Rev. Rowbotham removed to Mellette, South Dakota when he retired while Rev. Squier died at Sturgeon Bay.

In 1859 Rev. C. C. Symes was assigned to Manitowoc by the conference, which met that year at St. Paul's, he having charge of Two Rivers also. An Englishman by birth he was twenty two years old at the time and had been in America six years. After a year at Manitowoc he preached at Berlin, Lake Mills and Columbus and died at Manitowoc November 13 1870. For the following two years Rev. Rositer C. Parsons was the pastor, coming from Green Bay to assume his duties. He was born in Georgetown. N. Y. May 30 1817 and with his parents early moved to Ohio, where he attended Allegheny College and in 1854 came to Wisconsin, preaching at Port Washington, Milwauke and, after his Manitowoc pastorate, at Whitewater, Lake Geneva, Spring Prairie, Menomonee Falls and East Troy, finally passing away at Lyons, Wis., July 27, 1887. He had under his charge two churches, one built at Maple Grove some time during the later fifties and St. Paul's. His successor was Rev. L. N. Wheeler, who also remained two years and under his able management the church grew rapidly. Rev. S. S. Smith followed and the church, formerly in the Fond du Lac, was placed in the Appleton district. Rev. Smith was in 1899 the pastor of the Zion Church near Oshkosh. In 1867 Rev. Alexander C. Huntley assumed charge which he retained two years. He was another New York man, having been born December 27 1819 and moving to Ohio at the age of thirteen, entered the ministry in 1843. He preached in New York until 1857 when he removed to Wisconsin and for twenty eight years labored at various places, dying at Fond du Lac at the age of sixty six years. During the two years following the pulpit was filled by Rev. Loren L. Knox, a former Lawrence University professor, who had been in Wisconsin for ten years. Rev. Knox later retired and has lived many years in Evanston, Ill. His successor at Manitowoc for two years was Rev. James Lavelle, who in 1873 was transferred to Ripon and the next year withdrew from the conference. The wishes of the Manitowoc congregation were then gratified in the reappointment of Rev. L. N. Wheeler. He occupies a unique place in the history of Methodism in Wisconsin. Born in Waukesha June 28 1839 he entered the ministry at the age of nineteen, his first charge being Two Rivers. After his first Manitowoc ministry he was sent to China to take charge of the Foo Chow Mission, where he arrived after a long journey via Africa. He was instrumental in starting The Missionary Record and in a few years returned to America, Manitowoc again seeking and securing his valuable services. Later he preached at Lake Mills and Janesville, became the presiding elder of the Fond du Lac district in 1879, returned to China for three years and then preached at Beaver Dam, Bay View, Evansville and Fort Atkinson. In 1890 he went to China a third time in the interests of the American Bible Society and died at Shanghai April 9 1893. He served as chaplain of the Fifty First Wisconsin during the Civil War and was the author of several works, among them "A Foreigner in China."

Then came the ministry of Rev. Philo S. Bennett, also a leader in Methodism. Of New York birth he entered the ministry in 1837, coming to Milwaukee nine years later. After securing an advanced degree at Beloit he was made presiding elder of the Appleton district, acted as financial agent of Lawrence University and preached at Racine, Waukesha, Grand Rapids, New London and other places. He was a writer of power, having been a bitter opponent of slavery and in 1890 together with Rev. Lawson published the "History of Methodism in Wisconsin." He died in Appleton after several years of retirement on April 5 1895. The church membership of St. Paul's during his incumbency numbered sixty-six, but it was increased to seventy-two by his successor, Rev. J. W. Olmstead, who remained in Manitowoc two years. In recent years Rev. Olmstead has acted as agent of the Children's Home Society. In 1878 Rev. C. N. Stowers commenced a two years' pastorate, coming from Dakota Territory. He was born in Maine in 1835 and came to Wisconsin at the age of thirty-three years, acting for some years as professor of Lawrence University. He died some years since in Minneapolis. His successor, Rev. G. H. Moulton, who also remained but one year was a Canadian by birth and after his transfer from Manitowoc became the presiding elder of the Fond du Lac district, later removing to Nebraska. He was followed by Rev. J. F. Tubbs for a year and then came Rev. H. Stone Richardson, another commanding figure in Wisconsin Methodism. Born in New York on June 27 1827 he was early left upon his own resources and drifted to Albany, where he made his way through the State Normal School. For some years succeeding he traveled around the world, visiting Italy, Cuba, Texas and at one time being one of the Texas Rangers. In 1849 he visited California as a gold seeker and led a life of adventure for several years on the Pacific coast, serving for a time in the legislature. When the war broke out he enlisted as chaplain of a regiment and later became a major. After the conflict was over he entered the ministry and held charges in many Wisconsin cities, retiring after a successful ministry at Oshkosh. He passed away after a short illness February 9 1899.

The next Methodist pastor was Rev. J. D. Foote, a man of Connecticut birth and a graduate of Lawrence University. He entered the field in 1858 and in 1860 was made a regent of the state university, later becoming the chaplain of the Fifteenth Wisconsin. After some years spent in Kansas and Texas he returned to Wisconsin in 1883 and came to Manitowoc from Fort Howard. Later he visited California for his health and died at San Diego July 29 1899. His successor at Manitowoc was Rev. J. Wills, who is still in the active ministry and it was during his incumbency that the church was repaired and rededicated September 5 1886. The conference then sent Rev. William Clark for a year, who later removed to Sharon, and was succeeded by Rev. A. L. Whitcomb, who in 1888 was transferred to Oshkosh. During that year the church was served by Revs. E. B. Service, J. N. Funston and J. D. Cole. By this time the membership had reached eighty and there were over one hundred children in the Sunday school. For two years following Rev. J. H. Tippet officiated as pastor, then for two years Rev. T. D. Williams acted as such, followed for a year by Rev. H. J.

Duecker and then by Rev. O. P. Christian for two years, Rev. C. F. McGaha for one year and Rev. J. E. Garrett for a year. All of the last named six are still in the ministry in Wisconsin, except Rev. Duecker, transferred to the Southwest Kansas conference in 1896 and Rev. McGaha transferred to the East Ohio conference a year later. In 1898 the present pastor, Rev. William Hooton, assumed his duties at Manitowoc and has been very successful in his ministry. The church numbers about eighty members and a thriving Sunday school with one hundred and thirty pupils is an important adjunct as is also a ladies society. An Epworth League was started in connection with the church and the convention of the Appleton district of the society was held in Manitowoc in June 1898. The Woman's Missionary Society, in existence for seven years, is an active association and the district convention of the society was held in the city in May 1897.

As said before missions were early established at various points in the county. In 1858 Rev. L. N. Wheeler was sent to Two Rivers and Gibson, being succeeded by Rev. Walter McFarlane in 1860, who also remained two years. By this time an $800 church had been erected at Gibson and two Sunday schools were maintained by the minister. Reverend McFarlane was an ardent worker born in 1819 in Glasgow, Scotland and entering the Wisconsin ministry in 1856. After twenty years of pastoral service he retired and passed away at Evansville, Feb. 9 1896. During the war services at Two Rivers were discontinued and the Maple Grove charge, formerly dependent on Manitowoc, was combined with that at Gibson. A. C. Elliot acted as supply in 1864 but the congregation there grew smaller steadily and a few years later both were dropped from the conference list. An effort was made in 1870 to revive the Two Rivers class by W. Rose, a local preacher but after a year or so the attempt was given up. The Gibson church was again active in 1883 occasional services being held by Rev. H. Stone Richardson. The pulpit was later filled for several years by supplies, among them W. C. Morris, J. R. Joslyn, Alfred de Ford, F. Robertson and George A. Cooke. In 1886 under the last named the congregation numbered thirty members and a Sunday school of seventy-five scholars was maintained but soon after the church was finally discontinued. Thus today St. Paul's is the sole English speaking Methodist church in the county.

The Methodist church has always been expansive in character and thus it was not strange that an effort should early be made to establish its doctrines among the German immigrants who came to Wisconsin in such large numbers in the latter forties. Manitowoc and Sheboygan counties were made a working unit in this effort and as early as 1849 these two counties were on the Illinois Conference rolls although no regular pastor was sent to the region until 1851, when Rev. John Bischoff came to Manitowoc county and gathered together fourteen converts. After his departure a year later Rev. H. Senn assumed charge, succeeded in 1854 by Rev. Frederick Kluckholm, the German Methodists in the two counties then being eighty-two in number. It was Rev. Kluckholm who in reality was the founder of the church in the village of Manitowoc, the small building which for many years was used by the congregation being constructed in his pastorate. In 1856 he was succeeded by Rev. H. Withorn. By this time Sheboygan county had been taken from the circuit and efforts were made at the establishment of other churches in the county, notably in the town of Newton, a church being built there. In 1858 Rev. S. Schilfsgard assumed charge of the village work while Rev. C. Schneider looked after the interests of the country congregations. Later however the circuit was consolidated, Rev. John Salzer serving for two years, Rev. John W. Roecker for two and Rev. F. Feistkorn and Rev. Richard Fickenscher for one year apiece, followed by Rev. C. Leiprandt's two year pastorate, commencing in 1865. By this time the churches had been placed in the Chicago Conference and there were three congregations outside of the one in Manitowoc, having a large aggregate membership. This led to a division of the county in 1867 into two charges, Manitowoc and the Manitowoc circuit. In that year Rev. C. Stellner was assigned to the former and Rev. Henry Overbeck to the latter, Rev. Stellner remaining two years while the latter was succeeded by Rev. Conrad Eberhardt. In 1869 Revs. Theodore Strauble and C. Eberhardt shared the duties, the former remaining two years but the latter being transferred elsewhere, leaving the circuit vacant for some time.

In 1871 the work was assigned to Revs. J. J. Sandsmeier and Conrad Lampert, the former taking the city charge. Rev. Lampert soon left, being succeeded by Rev. Michael Enzminger while the city church was put under the ministry of Rev. Carl F. Allert in 1873, he remaining three years. Rev. Charles Rakow served two years (1874-1876) in the circuit after a year's interim being succeeded by Rev. E. Drescher, who also served two years. In the meantime Rev. B. Becker had become pastor of the city church and remained such until 1879 when Rev. J. J. Keller succeeded him for a year. By this time the circuit had diminished in size, only the Newton church being left with fifty members, while the Manitowoc church numbered seventy-five. Rev. Peter Schaeffer had charge of the Newton church in 1879 but in 1880 the two were combined, Rev. Charles Irwert assuming charge. It was he, whose efforts brought about the construction of a new brick church home at the corner of South Ninth and Hamilton streets, the cornerstone of which was laid in July 1882. His successors have been Revs. Anton Meixner (1883-1885), Ernst Fitzner (1885-1886), C. Roehl (1886-1891), A. F. Fuerstenau (1891-1895), J. F. Romoser (1895-1902) and Rev. J. F. Mueller the present pastor. The conference of the church met at Manitowoc in 1885 and again in 1900.

A Norwegian Methodist church was organized in Manitowoc in 1869, Rev. C. Jensen being chosen the first pastor. The charge included a church at Sheboygan also and both were placed under the Northwest Norwegian Conference. A small frame church was erected on North Sixth street and the membership was at first nineteen in number, gradually increasing as the years went by. Rev. Jensen was succeeded by Rev. B. Johansen in 1872, who retained the charge for two years, his successor being Rev. Charles Omann, who remained for a like period. In 1876 Rev. O. Wiersen was assigned to Manitowoc and Sheboygan, and was succeeded a year later by Rev. Gustafsen, who in turn gave way to Rev. O. L. Hansen after a year's ministry. Since 1880, however, there have been no regularly appointed ministers, occasional visits being made by itinerant evangelists. Reverend Peterson of another denomination of faith occupied the pulpit for some time in 1900.

### PRESBYTERIAN.

Among the churches in Manitowoc the First Presbyterian has always been prominent. The history of the organization dates back to June 26, 1851 on which day the church was founded at the home of Frederick Borcherdt in the village of Manitowoc Rapids. The instigating spirit in the movement was Rev. William Herritt, who was sent to the county as a home missionary in August 1850. Rev. Herritt was a graduate of Lane Seminary and had been licensed to preach a year before entering on his duties at Manitowoc. His first efforts were at Two Rivers, where he established a Congregational Church the following January but later he broadened his work so that the Rapids organization assumed life. The charter members were F. Borcherdt, Mrs. Wilhelmina Borcherdt, James and Isabella Patterson, Mrs. S. D. Herritt, M. E. Hall, Margaret Allen, Abigail Sherman, J. S. Reed, E. A. Sherman, D. M. Thomas, Moses Tufts and Misses Eliza and H. A. Tufts. For a little over two years Rev. Herritt had charge, making a circuit of over twenty miles each Sabbath on foot at first, although later he purchased a horse. Mrs. Herritt, who was an educated woman, later wrote a book containing the family's experience in Wisconsin entitled "A Keepsake," which contained many interesting facts concerning their life in the county. The Herritts removed in 1853, the husband dying at Quincy, Ill., January 19, 1867, being survived for many years by his wife, who made her home in Kansas City. In 1852 the church was removed to Manitotowoc and in the same year the Milwaukee Presbytery met in the latter village. The church was connected with that body from the beginning.

After meeting in the schoolhouse for some time it was decided that a church should be built. It was on the 30th of

March 1854, at a meeting presided over by Frederick Borcherdt, that the matter was definitely settled. Five trustees, since the organization perfected by Rev. Herritt had fallen into desuetude, were then chosen as follows:—Louis Sherman, James Patterson, Frederick Borcherdt, Hanson Rand and George Reed. On July 16, 1855 a contract was entered into by which arrangements were made for the construction of a building at the corner of North Ninth and Chicago streets, and it was not long before it was completed at a cost of $490, being known as "The Tabernacle." The efforts of the Enterprise Ladies Society of the church provided furnishings for the new house of worship at a cost of $100 and the structure was duly dedicated in November. In May Rev. Mead Holmes had been engaged at a salary of $600 a year and he entered upon his duties soon after. An energetic worker he soon had the little congregation in a flourishing condition. He paid particular attention to the Sunday school, later in life being a leader in this line and this important feature of church life was added in the same year. After four years of ministry at Manitowoc Rev. Holmes resigned and was succeeded by Rev. M. C. Stanley, who had been in Wisconsin since 1856 and who had been for some time pastor of the Congregational church at Two Rivers Rev. Holmes continued to reside at Manitowoc a number of years as a religious worker and writer, among his works being a volume entitled "A Soldier of the Cumberland," descriptive of his son's experiences in the war. Later the family moved to Rockford, Ill. where the venerable clergyman still resides. Rev. Stanley was a man of great integrity and strong principle,—a sturdy advocate of liberty before the war, attracting much attention in the village by his sermons against slavery.

Early in 1860 he removed to Milwaukee and was succeeded by Rev. John H. Dillingham, formerly of New York. Three years later he was, in turn, followed by Rev. A. G. Beebe, who served the congregation ably until 1865 when Rev. W. J. Stoutenberg assumed charge. In 1868 upon his removal to Michigan a new era was inaugarated by the calling of Rev. C. B. Stevens of Hancock, Mich. An energetic and yet practical leader he decided that the church should immediately seek better and more commodious quarters, giving largely of his own means to see that end consummated. In January a lot at the corner of North Eighth and State streets was purchased from Hiram McAllister for a consideration of $1500 and two years later the construction of the building began. In the meantime the church had increased in membership and the Sunday school under the charge of O. R. Bacon reached a high standard. The cornerstone of the First Church as it was called was laid on June 21, 1870 with solemn ceremonies. A parade, in which the Odd Fellows, Masons, Sons of Hermann and musical societies participated, was formed and when the site was reached President Louis Sherman opened the service. Songs, prayers and the reading of a text by Rev. Wilson of Two Rivers followed; then E. B. Treat of the building committee read the figures giving the cost and dimensions of the structure and a brief response was made by J. D. Markham, representing the trustees. The stone was then duly laid, taps of the trowel being administered by Mayor Peter Johnston, Rev. Stevens, Rev. Knox of the M. E. Church, Rev. Windemuth of the German Reformed and H. A. Raine of the Masons. In 1872 the structure, completed at the cost of $20,000 was ready for occupancy and for five years Rev. Stevens had the pleasure of preaching in the edifice, which his efforts had made possible. Then, in 1877 he resigned, being succeeded for three years by Rev. W. F. Cellars. In 1880 a call was extended to Rev. J. M. Craig, a very able and eloquent clergyman of Scotch descent, liberal in opinions and learned in the classics. During the next six years the church enjoyed great prosperity and it was with genuine regret that his flock received his resignation in July 1886, in order that he might accept a call to Holyoke, Mass.

After a few months interim the congregation called Rev. Guido Bossard, then a young man fresh from theological studies, whose scholarly attainments soon gained him general respect. He was ordained February 7, 1887 and remained until September 1890 when he left for Oconto, later establishing himself at La Crosse. In 1889 the Milwaukee Presbytery again met at Manitowoc. At this time the elders of the church were E. K. Rand, H. F. Hubbard and W. Thombs, L. M. Sherman succeeding the last named later and C. F. Smalley being added in 1892. Rev. O. H. Chapin of Delevan was called in 1890 and was a most popular pastor during his four years of service. In November 1895 he resigned to accept a call to a Milwaukee church, his successor being Rev. Emmet Rankin, who served from February 1896 to July 1899. Rev. Rankin was born in Paoli, Kansas in 1869 and graduated at the age of twenty from Parks College, Kansas City, later doing post graduate work at Princeton, besides pursuing theological studies at the McCormick Seminary in Chicago. Three vears after leaving Manitowoc he resigned from the ministry to assume the editorial chair of a leading agricultural paper. The next pastor was Rev. Walter Johnston, who came from Ironwood, Mich., a man of great eloquence and power. His ministry, however, was short as he accepted a call from Logansport, Indiana. His successor, the present pastor, Rev. D. C. Jones assumed his duties in April 1901. The church is largely attended and maintains a Sunday school. A society of Christian Endeavor was organized in 1887 and for many years it has led a successful existence, the convention of the Winnebago district being held in the city in March 1898. A Junior Endeavor is also an adjunct to the church as are also a ladies society and a young womans' guild. Extensive improvements to the church edifice were made during the winter of 1902, and the Presbytery met there in the spring of 1903,

On November 26, 1858 the First Presbyterian church of Eaton was organized. trustees being elected as follows:—J. M. Curtiss, J. Mott, G. Monroe, E. A. Brown and J. Tyler. This continued in existence for some time but during the war interest lagged and the services became infrequent. In 1869 a Presbyterian church was established at Cato, the elders being S. D. Robinson, later succeeded by R. McNutt, N. Darling, D. Robinson and O. Davis. No regular pastor served the church until 1893 when Rev. A. Rederus was called from Sioux City, Iowa. On May 19th two years later he revived the Eaton church at Niles, M. Johnson and W. Tyler being chosen elders. He continued to minister at both places until 1898 when he resigned, since which time the pulpits have been vacant. The Hope Bohemian Presbyterian Church was started at Melnik in 1892 by Rev. Joseph Balcar, who was ordained at Manitowoc, but he left after two years service for Ely, Iowa, being succeeded by the present pastor, Rev. F. T. Bastel. Occasional Presbyterian services in that language are held in Manitowoc also.

### ROMAN CATHOLIC.

The part played by the Roman Catholic Church in Manitowoc county has always been a large one and in membership the congregations professing that faith far outnumber all others. The parishes in the county are partly in the Milwaukee and partly in the Green Bay diocese, the latter having been founded in 1860 with the Manitowoc and Fox Rivers as the dividing lines. Green Bay was the center of early activity along missionary lines in Wisconsin and thus it was that Rev. Joseph Brenner was sent to Manitowoc county in 1850. An occasional visit from a Jesuit wanderer had been made before this time but it was not until Rev. Brenner's arrival that definite pastoral work began and perhaps no man better fitted could have been chosen for the work. Energetic and zealous at the end of his four years of service he had established congregations at Manitowoc Rapids, Two Rivers, Cooperstown, Meeme, Maple Grove and French Creek, holding services and building churches in each of these places. This was a wonderful accomplishment considering the circumstances,—the newness of the community and the poverty of the parishioners. The congregation at the Rapids included for some years the members of the faith at Manitowoc, the latter being obliged to go to the county seat to attend services, a church being erected at the Rapids in 1852. In the next year Father Brenner was called away from his duties and later left for the island of Java in the East Indies. A member of the Jesuit order the clergyman was forty-five years of age when he came to Manitowoc, having for some years previous resided at Green Bay where he gained a reputation as a linquist and writer. He died in the midst of his labors at Bombay, India in January 1885. His successor, Rev. H. J. Nuyts had also been previously stationed at Green Bay and upon assuming charge decided that a church should be built at Manitowoc. Accordingly the first St. Boniface, a frame structure 40 by 70 feet, was erected on a lot on Marshall street, it being capable of seating seven hundred people and soon after a small parsonage was built and a five acre burial site purchased at a point some distance south of the city. Rev. Nuyts continued in service at Manitowoc and Rapids for three years, when he left for Grant County, from where soon after he returned to his native Holland, dying at a ripe age.

His successor was Rev. Michael Beittner, who came in 1856 and officiated for a year. Father Beittner was of Bavarian birth and was ordained by Bishop Henni, officiating at New Coeln and Potosi before being sent to Manitowoc. After serving as pastor at Brighton, Jefferson and Racine for a time he returned to Bavaria, where he died May 28 1895. From April to August 1857 Rev. Joseph Maly was the priest of St. Boniface. He was born in Bohemia in 1828 and graduated from the Budweis Theological School at the age of twenty-eight, coming to America a year later. After a short residence at Syracuse, N. Y. he came to Wisconsin and for many years was engaged in work in Manitowoc County and later in Kewaunee county. In the fullness of age he then retired to a farm in Dane County. On August 23, 1857 he was succeeded in Manitowoc by Rev. Mathew Gernbauer, who remained until July 1859, being followed a year by Rev. Max de Becke, both serving the Rapids church as well. During the earlier sixties Rev. J. M. Pfeiffer acted as priest, resigning to take a trip to Germany and dying at sea on his return voyage September 30, 1863. During his absence Rev. E. A. Van Steenwyk of Two Rivers had officiated but the vacancy caused by the former's death was filled by the appointment of Rev. James Staehle, who remained in Manitowoc until 1868. During the next ten years Rev. Joseph Fessler was the resident priest. He was a German by birth and came to America in youth, studying at St. Francis Seminary. He was largely instrumental in the foundation of the convent at Alverno and after leaving Manitowoc went west, dying at Beaverton, Oregon June 20, 1896. On March 17, 1878 Rev. H. Jacobs assumed the duties of the parish and held the position until March three years later. He was born in Germany in 1841, came to America at the age of nineteen and soon graduated from St. Francis. After traveling in Europe he began his work in Fond du Lac County, where he returned to die after giving up his Manitowoc parish. For three months Rev. George Fessler of Alverno filled the vacancy and in May Rev. W. J. Peil the present incumbent assumed charge. Born in Racine October 3, 1849 he was ordained after a course at St. Francis, in 1872 and acted as assistant at St. Joseph's in Milwaukee for some months, later being stationed at Caledonia. A man of indomitable energy he soon made his influence felt. At his arrival there were one hundred families connected with the parish while at present there are about four times that number. His first aim was the building of a church as the older structure was becoming too small. The cornerstone of the new St. Boniface was laid May 5, 1885 with due ceremony, addresses being delivered by Fathers Willmes and Cleary, while the consecration occurred Nov. 25, 1886, Bishop Heiss officiating. The totol cost of the structure, which was 136 by 60 feet with a spire 136 feet high, was $30,000, the frescoing and other decorations being elaborate. The old church was used as a school for a time, Father Fessler having started such an institution in his ministry. An important adjunct to the church has been the St. Joseph Benevolent Society formed May 15, 1874. The first officers were: President, T. Mohr; Vice President, Adam Bleser; Secretary, N. Gentgen; Treasurer, C. M. Peters. It was incorporated two years later and celebrated its twenty-fifth anniversary in 1899, the event being attended by many thousands. During its existence it has expended over $12,000 in benevolence. Branches of the Catholic Knights, Catholic Order of Foresters and Knights of Columbus are also connected with the church. The present constituency of the congregation is mainly German and Irish and the work has become so extensive that for several years it has been necessary to have an assistant, Revs. Mueller and Salbreiter having filled the position. Another of the oldest Catholic organizations of the county is St. Luke's at Two Rivers. In 1851 R. M. Eberts and wife donated three lots in Block 51 to Bishop Henni for a church and accordingly Father Brenner established a mission on July 16, a frame structure being built to accommodate the worshippers. A majority of these were French Canadians although many Germans and a few Irish were in the number, necessitating representation of the various nationalities among the priests. After Father Brenner departed the following officiated:—Revs. W. De Yonge 1856-1857, Peter Menard 1857-1858, J. C. Perrodin 1858-1860, S. Senner 1860-1861, J. M. Pfeiffer 1861-1863, E. Van Steenwyk 1863-1864, Bonaventura de Goey 1864-1865, N. Hens 1866-1867, Jacob Gauche 1867-1870, J. F. Zawistowski 1870-1873, J. Gauche 1873-1877, A. Bogacki 1877-1879. The next pastor, Rev. George J. Veith, died suddenly October 1, 1881 while visiting in Green Bay and was succeeded by Rev. Mathias Welbes, who in 1891 was transferred to Kewaunee, being succeeded by Rev. J. A. Geissler. After two years Father Geissler departed and Rev. John G. Dries became pastor. On March 16, 1898, however, he died and Rev. Geissler was recalled, having since served the congregation. Father Dries was born in Luxemburg July 6, 1852 and came to America at the age of thirty, some years after entering the priesthood and at first ministering to congregations in Brown and Kewaunee counties. Father Geissler was born in Patterson, New Jersey April 4, 1854 and spent his early years at school in Belgium. His place in the hearts of his parishioners is high and he has done much for their advancement, the church now numbering 370 families. The cornerstone of a new church was laid July 12, 1891 and the structure, a fine stone one costing $25,000 was dedicated in October the year following. A benevolent society, taking the name of St. Joseph, was organized in 1872 and has done much good. A branch of the Catholic Knights also exists.

Another of the original churches of the county is that, known as St. Patrick's, in the town of Maple Grove. Fourteen Catholics met at the home B. S. Lorigan in 1850 and formed a church, which was visited at first by Rev. Brenner. A frame church was built and occasional services held by the priests in charge at Manitowoc until 1861 when Rev. Sebastian was made a resident pastor. He was a sincere patriot and did much towards filling Maple Grove's quota during the civil struggle. His successor in 1865 was Rev. Eugene McGinnity now of Janesville and largely through his efforts the building of a new church was undertaken, the cornerstone being laid November 1, 1868, the structure when completed being 100 by 46 feet. The succeeding pastors having been Revs. James Mahoney 1868-1870, Andrew Seubert 1870-1874, Louis Cornelius 1874-1875, C. Lemogie 1875-1879, Roman Schotter 1879-1881, W. J. Rice 1881-1887, Conrad Seule 1887-1893 and the present pastor Rev. T. J. Ryan. Father Ryan is of Irish birth and became a priest in 1884, ministering in Omro, Winneconne and Ripon for some time. A branch of the C. K. W. is in existence in connection with St. Luke's.

A fourth church to be established by Father Brenner was St. James' at Cooperstown. A building was erected in 1850, six years after the first permanent settlement in the township. Until 1865 it was visited by Father Brenner of Manitowoc and Father Maly of Francis Creek but in that year Rev. Augustin Lang took up his duties at the parish, succeeded in two years by Rev. William Mahoney. Rev. Eusebius Henzle, who came to the church in 1868, died February 20, 1870 and was succeeded by Rev. James Gauche now of De Pere for three years. A new church was erected in 1871, made possible by the energetic efforts of the building committee. From 1876 to 1884 Rev. August Rossochowitz, an exile from Germany officiated, being succeeded for a few months by Father Stirn of Francis Creek. The later priests have been Revs. J. A. Duermeyer 1884-1887, John H. Holzknecht 1887-1892, F. X. Steinbrecher and F. W. Geier 1892, John D. Schwartzmeyer 1892-1895. In 1895 Rev. G. J. Pellegrin assumed charge, a man of extraordinary attainments, of

MANITOWOC IN 1859

Belgian birth and a linguist of reputation. Born in 1846 he came to America at the age of nineteen and is a graduate of St. Francis Seminary. His successor was the present pastor, Rev. F. W. Geier. The congregation was incorporated in 1883 and now numbers one hundred and twenty-five families. Branch No. 101 C. K. W. is made up of members of St. James.

Father Brenner also organized St. Ann's at Francis Creek, the first church being built by his successor, Rev. Joseph Maly. Rev. F. X. Steinbrecher became the pastor in 1877 serving until 1885. Later Rev. William H. De Haan, a native of Amsterdam, Holland assumed charge, removing to Aniwa in 1896 and being succeeded by Rev. Lakoney, who in turn gave way to the present priest, Rev. J. Vorlichek. The congregation numbers seventy families.

St. Isidore's Church in the town of Meeme is another monument to the organizing ability of Father Brenner. In the fall of 1850 a few religionists gathered at the home of John Maltilor and formed a church. Henry Mulholland, Sr. donated a three acre plot upon which was constructed a chapel 50 by 30 feet, Bishop Henni naming it. It was visited by priests from surrounding churches until 1862 when Rev. Lawrence Kenney took charge. He induced his people to build a new structure, which was completed in 1864 and blessed by Bishop Henni on his memorable trip through the county that year when a total of 910 were confirmed at the various churches. Rev. Kenney died while at St. Isadore's and was buried under the new church. Rev. McGinnity of Maple Grove then looked after the parish for four years until the appointment of Rev. Thomas McDoneell who also died in the midst of his labors February 24 1869. After a vacancy of a year the following pastors officiated in the order named:—Revs. E. R. Goss 1870-1871, Dennis Tierney 1871-1874, J. R. Briller 1878-1879, Thomas Corry 1879-1880, R. J. Roche 1880-1882, A. J. Gerhard 1882, J. J. Smith 1883-1885, E. E. Graves 1885-1886, E. F. Pitt 1886-1890, M. B. Norton 1890-1894 and Rev. E. Henderson. The church numbers 500 families, largely of Irish descent. Branch No. 68 C. K. W. was established at Meeme April 14 1887.

The next church to be established in the county was St. Joseph's at Kellnersville. In 1852 fifteen Bohemian families settled at that village,—originally all Catholics. For six years they were attended by Rev. Joseph Maly of Francis Creek and a log church was built in the town of Cooperstown, dedicated to St. Wenceslaus, there being 150 families in the parish. After various vicissitudes a dispute arose over the property and the church, led by Rev. Gideon Manazek, became schismatic, the pastor being suspended from the priesthood. Reverend Manazek died in 1873 and was followed for four years by Reverend Sadimir Klacel, who continued the church in defiance of the diocesan authorities. Reverend A. Cipin of Carlton at last brought about a reconciliation and a new church was then built, one mile south of St. Wenceslaus and dedicated to St. Joseph. Among the later priests have been Revs. Ignatz Lager, J. Maly, F. Privoznek, W. Koerner, J. Jiranek, A. Cipin, R. Lakomey and F. Just. A division occurred during Rev. Koerner's ministry, several families withdrawing. Reverend Just is a Bohemian by birth and came to America at an early age. He also has a mission at Greenstreet under his charge.

In no community in the county has religious and secular life been more closely allied than at the village of St. Nazianz. Rev. Ambrose Oschwald, a native of Baden, a man of high intellectual order with tastes tending somewhat toward asceticism, was responsible for the founding of a colony at that village, communistic and religious in character. Gathering around him one hundred and fourteen of his followers, mainly from his parish in the old world, he set out for a new country in order that he might found a Utopia. He arrived in Milwaukee in August 1854 and was there induced to purchase 3840 acres of land in the town of Eaton, paying $3.50 per acre. Arriving at their new home on the 26th of the month the settlers set at work hewing down the wilderness and among the first structures built was a church, St. Gregory's. A convent for the women was soon constructed and in 1864 a monastery of the Franciscan order was added. The land was owned and worked in common and the whole domestic economy was under the guidance of Father Oschwald. The latter has been described as "intimate with the classics and history, learned in medicine and eloquent as a divine" and he was above all a consistent communist. A common treasury was established and certain rules and regulations adopted for the government of all. Father Oschwald was somewhat of an architect and his design of the settlement buildings were unique. The sisters' convent was a large three story building situated on Main street, plastered on the outside and painted a delicate pink. One wing was used as a chapel, containing two galleries and was capable of seating a large number of persons. The brothers' monastery was similar in construction and also contained a chapel. Around the grounds were various "stations," boxes on posts containing representations of sacred scenes and upon the summit of a little hill was erected a small chapel, resembling and named after the famous Mount Loretto, the interior decorations being quite elaborate. The first church soon became too small for the increasing number of the colonists and accordingly a larger one was built. The parishioners themselves engaged in different occupations, some tending in the fields while others made articles of straw, shoes, fancy work and a certain kind of cheese that became immensely popular in the market. All prospered until Father Oschwald's death, which occurred on February 27, 1873, whereupon dissensions arose and many of the communal features were abandoned. The sarcophagus containing the remains of the dead priest still lies in the basement of the monastery always guarded by a lighted lamp. Rev. P. A. Mutz was his successor, he having been ordained as one of the graduates of St. Francis some years before. The present pastor is Rev. Diebl. The village is still full of the old world atmosphere and religious influences are great. A branch of the C. K. W., exists in connection with St. Gregory's.

Among the older churches of the county is that of the Nativity at Tisch Mills. Founded by Rev. J. Maly it remained as a

---

The author desires to state that he owes the names and dates of the rural priests of the county to that admirable work, the Catholic Church in Wisconsin.

mission connected with Carlton, Kewaunee county until 1893. Among its pastors have been Revs. August Lang, A. Cipin, Joseph Kirpal, A. Vychodil and E. Kabat. Since its separation from Carlton Revs. F. Shimonek, F. Windisch, F. Kolen and L. Ulauschek have had charge of the parish in the order named. The church numbers 150 families.

In 1861 Father Schrauderbach of Sheboygan established St. Wendel's in the town of Centerville. Rev. Kleiber, a Bavarian, was the first resident priest, followed a year later by Rev. P. Stuecki of Sheboygan, who died Feb. 4 1863 and was buried near the church. A log structure was erected at first, then a frame building in 1864, which burned down thirty years later and was replaced by an elegant new church in 1895. A mission at Centerville was established also in 1861 by Father Schrauderbach and another, St. Fidelis', in the town of Meeme by Father Korfhage in 1872, both of which have since been under the care of the priests of St. Wendel. The pastors since Rev. Stuecki's death have been:—Revs. J. Welter 1863-1864, Bernhard 1864, M. Weiss 1864-1865, A. F. Zuber 1865-1871, H. F. Korfhage 1871-1875, Thomas Breiker 1875-1877, C. Schilling 1877-1880, J. P. Van Treek 1880-1882, H. Helfstern 1882-1893, Rudolph Ollig 1893, William Dejalle 1893-1899, and W. Wolf, the present pastor. About 100 families are under his charge.

St. Augustine's congregation in the town of Kossuth, made up of the settlers of Bohemian nationality who early came to the town, was started in 1862. The church is attended by priests from Francis Creek and Kellnersville. The congregation numbers about one hundred families.

In 1865 Ira Clark gave two acres for a church site at Clark's Mills and upon it was built the Church of the Immaculate Conception. Before 1865 occasional services had been held by priests from Maple Grove but it was not until that year that a priest was assigned the locality regularly, Father Fessler serving the congregation for some time. Then for some years it was a mission of St. Nazianz and Maple Grove until 1875 when Rev. John Wernert was assigned the parish. A brick structure, 75 by 13 feet costing $4000, was then erected and a parsonage completed. The succeeding pastors were Revs. Gerhard Hornish 1878, Clement Lau 1878-1879, Joseph Rhode 1879-1885, John Holzknecht 1885-1887, J. A. Duermeyer 1887-1890, George Brenner 1890-1895, E. Kabat 1895-1899. The present pastor is Rev. Ulrich. Branch No. 146 C. K. W. is located at Clark's Mills.

The Church of the Assumption was built by the Bohemian residents of Reedsville in 1866, there having been originally twenty-five families in the parish. It was first attended by priests from Francis Creek but in 1876 Rev. Julius Stroehlke assumed charge, being succeeded the next year by Rev. Maly for a few months, he in turn being followed by Rev. T. Spunor. During the latter's pastorate the cornerstone of a new church was laid, it being completed by Rev. John Videnka, who died in the midst of his labors on May 29, 1885. During the term of his successor, Rev. William Kraemer a branch of the Catholic Knights was established and a parochial school started and in 1896 Rev. Adelbert Cipin assumed charge. Rev. Cipin is a Bohemian by birth and entered the priesthood in 1873, serving at Ahnapee and Kellnersville before being transferred to Reedsville. Holy Trinity church at Kasson was established as a mission from the Assumption in 1875 and has since been so connected.

A Polish church, named St. Casimir's was established in 1868 at Northeim in the town of Newton. Fire destroyed the first structure in 1880 but it was rebuilt and is now a substantial edifice. The pastors of the congregation have been Revs. B. Buwzynski 1868-1870, F. X. Kralczywski 1870-1871, P. Koncz 1872-1873, Alexander Michnowski 1873-1874, Simon Wieczorik 1874-1877, C. Goerik 1877-1878, R. A. Bukowski 1878-1879, J. Musulwicz 1879-1880, Aenitas Goch 1880-1881, George Fessler 1881-1882, Felix Ozechowski 1882-1884, J. Deilkicaworz 1885-1887, J. Horbacz 1887-1888, John Maczyuski 1889-1891, Z. Luczycki 1891-1893, Henry Cichocki 1893 and the present pastor, Ignatz Paluch.

St. Mary's Polish Church was organized at Manitowoc February 24 1870. The frame building used formerly by the German Lutherans of the city was purchased three years later and removed to "the Hill," being dedicated September 6 1874. The congregation grew rapidly until now it embraces three hundred families. In 1888 an orphan asylum was founded and placed under the care of the Polish Felician Sisters and it has since become an important benevolent institution. In the same year it was decided to begin the construction of a new and costly church but after the foundation had been laid funds grew scarce and it was ten years before the structure could be completed, the dedication ceremonies occurring October 1 1899. The list of pastors of the church is as follows:—Rev. F. X. Kralczywski 1872, Peter Koncz 1872-1873, A. Michnowski 1873-1874, Simon Wieczorik 1875-1876, Erasmus Bartkiewicz 1878, Joseph Musylwicz 1879-1882, Felix Orzcechorisk 1882-1884, Joseph Deiticwicz 1884, Ladislaus Zuczcki 1886-1890, C. Monczysk 1893, Henry Cichocki 1893-1894. As the chronology shows there have been frequent vacancies but a new era of prosperity was inaugurated upon the arrival of Rev. Wenceslaus Krzwonos, the new priest, on October 1 1896. Born in Bouk, Galicia, September 28 1852 he was educated at Rycszow and at the age of twenty entered the Cracow Military Academy, later graduating and becoming a lieutenant in the Fortieth Austrian Infantry for four years, at the expiration of which time he came to America. After entering a Benedictine Monastery in Missouri he was ordained a priest and served at St. Joseph, Missouri and later at South Chicago. He left the church on account of factional troubles in April 1903. There are connected with the church St. Adalbert's Society and the Ho'y Rosary Society, both large in membership.

St. Michael's at Whitelaw or Pine Grove was established in 1872, a church being built a year later. It was a mission of the Clark's Mills congregation until 1876 when the first resident pastor, Rev. Godfrey Noever was transferred from the Rapids church, the latter at the time being discontinued and its congregation divided. Later Clark's Mills priests again had St. Michael's under their charge but Rev. Joseph Hemmer assumed the duties of priest at the place in 1896, being succeeded the next year by Rev. Joseph Mack. A branch of the C. K. W. was organized at Whitelaw in July 1894.

On November 9 1869 Rev. Joseph Fessler of Manitowoc induced four sisters to take the vows and steps were immediately taken towards the building of a convent at Alverno, the structure being completed in September of the following year. Sister Odelia was the first mother superior and the number of sisters gradually grew until it reached twenty five or thirty. To accommodate these and also the inhabitants of that part of the county St. Joseph's Church was constructed in 1874 and placed for a time under the care of Father Fessler of Manitowoc. On his removal from the state in 1880 Rev. George Fessler assumed charge, which he retained until 1885 when on May 28th he died at the age of thirty seven. During his pastorate, on September 1 1881, the convent burned, the loss being about $65,000 but by dint of great effort the structure was speedily rebuilt and continued its successful existence, many hundred young people receiving instruction. A chapel was built in 1890 to accommodate the sisters. The successors of Father Fessler have been Revs. A. J. Gerhard 1885, I. P. Van Treck 1885-1887, H. Neihaus 1887-1888, P. H. Welbes 1888-1890, M. Oberlinkels 1890-1892. Rev. Norbert W. Dieninger assumed charge in 1892.

Among the churches later established was St. Peter's and Paul's at Kiel. During several years it was a mission of St. Anna's in Sheboygan County but in 1892 Rev. G. Weisse was appointed, followed in 1896 by Rev. M. J. Schmitz, who had just graduated from St. Francis.

On May 10 1889 the Poles at Two Rivers, who were a part of the congregation of St. Luke's, separated and established Sacred Heart Church. Rev. F. Luczycki was the first priest, being succeeded by Revs. Chelkocki, Bozwiacki, Geruss, Podlicki, Mozejuski, Kubazeski and Pociecha. A new church was erected by the congregation in 1899. A church at Mishicot which, since its foundation in 1866, had been connected with St. Luke's also separated in 1898, Rev. A. Bastian and Rev. P. St. Louis being the first priests.

A Catholic hospital, named the Holy Family, was erected

in Manitowoc in the latter nineties at a great expense and forms one of the most important public institutions in the county, having been designated as a marine hospital by the United States Government. Sacred Heart Congregation composed of English speaking Catholics was organized in 1902 in Manitowoc under Father O'Leary's guidance. The building formerly known as St. James' Episcopal was purchased but efforts were immediately put forth to secure a site for a larger church, land being purchased at the corner of State and North Seventh streets.

### LUTHERAN.

Many of the first German settlers who came to Manitowoc County were members of the Lutheran denomination and it was only natural that efforts should early be made at the establishment of a church. Thus it was that in the summer of 1851 the residents of the town of Newton formed a congregation, led by Rev. C. F. Goldammer, a man of great spiritual gifts who saw many years of useful ministration in Wisconsin. A rough church was built and the worshippers, although few in number, took much interest in the enterprise. Rev. Goldammer was not a man to limit his usefulness and as early as 1851 he came to Manitowoc every second week to hold services with a few families. For years these gatherings took place in the old district school at the corner of South Seventh and Washington streets. Finally on April 9 1855 St. John's congregation was organized in the village with thirty families in church connection and it was decided to call Rev. Goldammer to the parish. He accepted and a church, parsonage and school were completed the following year the latter being enlarged in 1859 to meet the growing demands. The church was a frame structure 35 by 50 feet in dimensions, which was capable of seating about four hundred people. In 1858 Rev. Goldammer left for Burlington, Wis. and Rev. Philip Koehler accepted the work and responsibility for the next nine years. In 1861 the congregation had a membership of ninety-one families; in 1865 the report shows 184 families and 193 children in school attendance. By act of the legislature March 23 1866 the congregation was incorporated and in the same year a new school was erected, which continued to do duty for twenty-five years until it was taken away to make room for the present structure. Rev. Koehler left in 1867 and was succeeded by Rev. M. Quehl. It was during his pastorate that, the old church proving utterly inadequate, it was decided to build a new brick structure. The building was completed in 1873 at a cost of $16,000 and is one of the most commodious in the city. By this time Rev. K. Huebner had taken up pastoral work in the city but after two years' service he gave way, in 1874, to Rev. G. Thiele, later of Milwaukee. Rev. F. Pieper assumed charge in 1876, followed by Rev. R. Pieper in 1878. Two years later the Synod of Minnesota and Wisconsin met at St. John's and the church was again chosen as the gathering place in 1894. In February 1891 Rev. Karl Machmueller, the present pastor, assumed charge and has assisted materially in the development of church life. The congregation numbers 435 families and there are 250 children in attendance at the school. A thriving ladies' society is maintained in connection with the church.

As early as 1861 occasional Lutheran services were held in the village of Two Rivers but it was not until 1863 that St. John's Congregation was organized by Rev. H. Barthels, a missionary pastor of the church. In the same year "the little brown church" built and owned by the Episcopals was purchased from Bishop Kemper and was used as a place of worship by the new congregation. Rev. Barthels remained until the latter part of 1865 and was succeeded by Rev. Braun and under his pastorate a parsonage was built. In October 1869 Rev. Braun was succeeded by Rev. Zuberbier, who died in the midst of his activities in 1872, whereupon Rev. C. Jaeger assumed pastoral duties for six years, he now being a resident of Racine. His successor was Rev. P. Lucas, who passed away at Two Rivers July 28 1881, Rev. J. P. Koehler then taking up the work. He remained seven years, at the end of which time he resigned to accept a position as professor in the Northwestern Theological Seminary at Watertown. It was under his guidance that the congregation decided to build a new church edifice. The building operations, however, were carried on by his successor, Rev. A. F. Siegler, the dedication taking place in 1889. In September 1892 the present pastor, Rev. C. A. F. Doehler, assumed charge of the church and under his leadership it has prospered, numbering now about nine hundred communicants. The school, started at the same time as the church, was for ten years under the care of the pastors but from that time on teachers were hired and the institution now numbers 160 scholars. Two frame structures are utilized for school purposes, one of them being the old church.

The Newton church, the oldest in the county led a very successful career, celebrating its golden anniversary in September 1901. Among the pastors have been Revs. C. Wagner, E. Strube, A. Pieper and Christian Sieker. In the town of Centerville two churches of the Lutheran denomination exist. St. John's Congregation was organized in 1860 with forty members and a church was built the next year. Seven years later St. Peter's was organized and a church built. One pastor has continued to serve both, the list being as follows:— Revs. M. Quehl 1862–1867, C. Dowidat 1869 1875, F. Pieper 1875–1877, J. Haase 1877–1883, C. Jaeger 1883–1887, P. Sprengling 1887. St. John's numbers seventy-two members and St. Peter's forty-six. Among the other early churches was that established at Reedsville. Rev. Goldammer held occasional services in the neighborhood during his Manitowoc pastorate and in the early sixties Revs. C. Gauschwitz and C. Braun were sent to the parish, the latter leaving in 1865 to take up his duties in Two Rivers. There were about twenty-five communicants at the time and under Rev. A. Kluge, who came in 1865, the congregation was increased and in 1869 St. Johannes and Jacobus Church was organized. Rev. Kluge remained fifteen years and in 1879 a new church was erected, replacing the earlier one built twenty years before. Rev. A. Topel served as pastor for seven years, at the end of which time the present minister, Rev. Phillip Brenner, was called. A parochial school with seventy scholars is maintained. In 1878 a church was established in the town of Gibson with C. Jaeger as pastor, he being succeeeed by Rev. P. Kionka,

The Larrabee church dates from 1884, the pastors since that time having been Revs. H. Prohl 1884–1888, H. Bruss 1888–1890, and the present minister, H. Mueller. The same year also witnessed the beginning of a church at Rosecrans, served consecutively by Revs. A. W. Kubel and Christian Sieker. At Niles in the town of Eaton a church was started in 1893 by Rev. W. Schlei, who has since officiated as pastor and in the same year Rev. H. Zarwell began his ministrations at a church established at Rube, being transferred to the Liberty Church later, his successor being Rev. F. Weertz. Rev. Schlei officiates at present, also, in a church built at Collins.

A mission church has existed for some years at Mishicott being served by Two Rivers ministers. Of late, however, Rev. Vater, a resident pastor, has had charge.

Not only were there many German settlers of the Lutheran faith but a large number of the Scandinavian race as well. In the latter forties many Norwegians settled in the towns of Liberty and Eaton and a few joined the Episcopal Church under Rev. Unonius. However they soon became strong enough to form a society of their own at Gjerpen, which was one of the oldest Norwegian settlements in the state. The church was organized October 4, 1850 and Rev. H. A. Stueb was called as the first pastor. Rev. Stueb was born in Bergen, May 13 1822 and came to America at the age of twenty-six and for many years was a leading figure in Wisconsin Lutheranism. After two years he was succeeded by Rev. J. A. Otteson, who was twenty-seven years old at the time, having come directly from Norway to his charge. Within three years he had established congregations at Manitowoc, Liberty, Maple Grove and Valders, making the circuit of the churches at as close intervals as time would allow him. Both Revs. Stueb and Otteson are still living and the former was present at the semi-centennial exercises held at Gjerpen in October 1900. In 1864 a church, the largest then in existence in the county, was dedicated at Liberty. The structure was 90 by 40 feet in dimensions and cost $4000, it being the scene of the Lutheran Synod two years later. Rev. L. M. Biorn had by this time undertaken pastoral work in the county, having the five churches under his supervision. For years the Manitowoc society met in the district school but in 1865 the construction of a church at the corner of North Eighth and State streets was commenced. When completed and ready for occupancy on Christmas day 1867 the building had cost $5000 and was capable of seating five hundred people, being 50 by 70 feet in dimensions. It was rebuilt and greatly beautified in 1899. Rev. Biorn continued as pastor of the church until 1879, when he resigned and was succeeded by Rev. C. F. Magelson. In 1880 the Synod of the church met at Manitowoc. In February 1893 Rev. J. A. Haugen assumed charge of the city congregation, remaining five years. At the end of his pastorate the congregation was divided, those denoted as the Missourians retaining the old church and calling Rev. P. R. Thorsen as pastor while the Anti-Missourians formed a new organization under the name of St. Paul's. This division, however, merely emphasized the separate organizations which had existed since 1874. The original St. Paul's Congregation had been organized on February 24th of that year and had constructed a church at the corner of North Seventh and St. Clair streets although the same pastor preached in the two churches for many years. In the fall of 1898 a new brick church was constructed by the parish three blocks west of the old site at a cost of $10,000, being dedicated March 19 1899. Rev. E. T. Rogne of Austin, Minn. was called to the pastorate and the congregation has led a very harmonious existence.

St. Paul's maintains a very successful branch of the Luther League, the Wisconsin convention of that organization being held in the city in the summer of 1901. A branch of the Luther Alliance is an adjunct of the older church and active ladies' societies are connected with both. A new Lutheran Church was erected at Valders during the fall of 1899, while the church at Gjerpen, which had been constructed in 1856 was thoroughly reconstructed in the same year at a cost of $10,000. Rev. C. Alfson has for some years past had charge of the country congregations.

## CONGREGATIONAL.

When Rev. W.' Herritt came to Manitowoc County in 1850 he set about establishing at Two Rivers a Congregational Church. On January 17th of the next year the plans were consummated by the foundation of the First Church, which was attached to the Milwaukee district, later being transferred to the Winnebago district. At first the congregation numbered but fourteen members although the average Sunday school attendance was about seventy. After Rev. Herritt's removal D. Pinkerton acted as pastor until 1857, when he was succeeded by Rev. M. C. Stanley. Just before the latter's arrival a church had been erected, one of the oldest in the county now standing. The pastor was called to Manitowoc a year after beginning his ministry and was succeeded by Rev. H. Pierpont, the father of Judge Pierpont, who increased the membership to nearly fifty and maintained a thriving Sunday school. From 1860 on, however, the church declined and having no pastor, finally passed out of existence. Rev. Pierpont removed to New York and died at Rochester in 1871. In 1867 Rev. Charles W. Wilson, a missionary of the Reformed Protestant Dutch Church of America arrived in Two Rivers and reestablished the congregation. After ten years of faithful labor he passed away and Rev. Thomas G. Pearce was called, he again instituting Congregational forms. The church membership at the time was but eleven. In November 1877 he was succeeded by Rev. D. M. Wooley, who in turn gave way to Rev. Sidney B. Demarest in March two years later. Rev. Demarest was a native of New York and was fifty-five years of age at the time he assumed pastoral duties at Two Rivers. He was a graduate of Western Reserve College and the Chicago Theological Seminary and officiated at several points in Wisconsin before his death, which occurred on August 14 1887 at Waupaca. His successor was Rev. David B. Spencer, Two Rivers being his first charge. He was an energetic young man and in a few months had increased the membership to fifty but in June he left for Hartland and the church discontinued services for a number of years.

In 1890, however, another effort was made, described in the Congregational Report as follows:—"At Two Rivers there was once a church but the life has gone out of it and its name removed from the names of the living. There has been this year a new church organized on the spot out of Methodists, Presbyterians, Congregationalists and Episcopalians under most happy auspices. Complete harmony exists among the Christians. They have sustained services five months, have called Rev. Alexander Chambers and will raise among themselves the larger part of his salary. This is practically a new church and the only one in the English tongue in a population of 3500 souls." Rev. Chambers accepted the call and soon the church was a thriving one of thirty members. He was succeeded by Rev. John N. Davidson, a local historian of some note, in 1893 and two years later a branch was started among the English residents of Two Creeks. Rev. Davidson resigned in February 1901 to accept a call from Dousman, Wis. and was succeeded by Rev. T. W. Cole, of Ivanhoe, Ill. The church today numbers about fifty members and a Sunday school of over one hundred pupils is maintained. A Christian Endeavor Society was established in 1893 and later another in connection with the Two Creeks church.

A Congregational church was established in Maple Grove in 1853 with fourteen members. Rev. Israel C. Holmes, father of Rev. Mead Holmes, was the first regular pastor and soon had a thriving Sunday school established. After about seven years, however, the services were discontinued and the congregation dissolved.

BAPTIST.

Although the Baptist denomination has not played a very prominent part in Manitowoc county there have been several churches of the sect within its borders. The only one in which the English language was used was established at School Hill in 1856 by Rev. Joseph Jeffreys. Rev. Jeffreys was a Welshman by birth and was ordained in Wisconsin. In his first report he said:—"This is an entirely new field among our Welsh people, settled in the forests along the lake shore" and told how "the Macedonian cry for help" had been sent to the Baptist convention of 1855. The pastor preached in Welsh at the morning and in English at the evening services but during the first year the congregation gained but one member. The minister remained two years and then there was an interim of seventeen years, in which there were no regular services held with the exception of a short time in 1863 when Rev. P. Work officiated. A new church was constructed in 1873 and two year's later Rev. H. A. Sears was sent to the parishes of School Hill and Plymouth, Sheboygan County. He was born in Springfield, N. Y. in 1818 and had been in Wisconsin since 1843. He died at Beaver Dam soon after leaving his pastoral duties in Manitowoc. During his three years of ministry the congregation increased from thirty to fifty and a thriving Sunday school was established. Rev. W. H. Whitelaw was the pastor in 1879 and then there was a vacancy until 1881, when for three years Rev. A. T. Miller of Sheboygan Falls officiated on alternate Sabbaths, being succeeded by Rev. Edward Jones in 1884. Rev. Jones died while engaged in his duties a year later and after an interim of three years Rev. J. Phillips assumed charge for some time. In 1792 Rev. Miller of Sheboygan Falls resumed his visits to the church, being succeeded in 1894 by Rev. A. Goodwin, in 1895 by Rev. S. W. Wiltshire of Sun Prairie and in 1898 by Rev. Thomas Davis, services being held every fourth Sabbath. The church at present numbers over thirty members and is situated in the Milwaukee district.

A German Baptist church was established on South Seventh Street in the village of Manitowoc in 1866 by Rev. C. Kleppe, a missionary. He held meetings at various points in the county but died at his work in 1867. He was succeeded by Rev. Theodore Klinker, the church numbering then about fifty members and in 1872 Rev. R. Haab assumed charge, which he retained for two years, being followed by Rev. A. Freitag for a year. After a vacancy of five years Rev. J. Miller of Watertown became the pastor and soon a Sunday school was started. After four years he gave way to Rev. M.

Schwendener of Kewaskum but the latter's stay was brief and a long vacancy ensued. Rev. Freitag established another German Baptist church in the town of Kossuth in 1875, which soon grew to a membership of sixty. It was served jointly with Manitowoc until 1887, when Rev. M. Schwendener assumed charge. After a vacancy of five years Rev. G. Engelmann of Freedom, Wis. came to the church in 1892 but remained only a year. In 1896 Rev. P. Hoffmann of LeRoy became the pastor and has since acted as such.

GERMAN REFORMED.

The first attempt at the organization of a church of the German Reformed denomination in the county occurred in the town of Newton in 1851, at which time a church was built, served for three years by Rev. Goldammer. A church was also built at Centerville and the two were served by Revs. J. F. Kluge (1854-1858) and Chr. Schiller (1856-1862) but on March 10 1862 they separated. The organization in Newton is known as the Reformed Salem Ebenezer Congregation and has been served by the following pastors:—Revs. J. Blaetgen 1863-1866, T. Grosshuesch 1867-1873, G. Zindler 1874-1879, W. Walenta 1879-1883, T. Grosshuesch 1883-1887 and D. W. Vriesen 1887 on. A new church building was erected in 1876. The ministers of the Centerville church have been Revs. Jean Grab, F. Nullhorst, John Blaetgen, E. Scheidt, H. Schenk, W. Lienkaemper, E. W. C. Brueckner and R. A. Most. In 1867 a church was built at Kiel, Rev. Praikschatis being the first pastor. He was succeeded by Rev. Schoepfle, who in turn gave way in 1871 to L. W. Zenk. For twenty years the latter faithfully served the church and under his pastorate a new edifice was erected in 1889. His successor was the present pastor, Rev. John Roeck.

The church in the city of Manitowoc dates from March 25 1868, on which date the congregation was formed by twelve families. The first preacher was Rev. Jacob Lotka, who remained but a few months. During his pastorate a lot was purchased and a small frame church costing $800 was erected. Rev. Lotka's successors have been:—Revs. George Windemuth 1869-1870, Paul Schoetke 1871, Henry Ruster-

MRS. S. C. BLAKE
First White Girl Born in Manitowoc County

holz 1872-1874, E. W. Henschen 1875-1880, G. Zindler 1881-1886, D. R. Huecker 1886-1889, C. Bonekemper 1889-1891 and L. W. Zenk, the present pastor. In 1889 it was deemed necessary to build a new church and a brick edifice costing $7000 was accordingly erected. The present membership is about 350. A mission was established by Rev. E. W. Henschen at Branch in 1879 and a church built there, which is still in use. The membership is about sixty.

### EVANGELICAL ASSOCIATION.

In 1856 Rev. William Siekoreik, a missionary of the Evangelical Association visited Two Rivers and succeeded in forming a nucleus, which on July 16 1859 became a duly organized congregation. A church was built that year on Pine Street and Rev. Peter Held called to the pulpit, which he occupied for two years. His successors during the sixties and early seventies were Rev. William F. Schneider, J. Banzhaf, J. H. Hammetter, E. Bockermuehl, L. G. Stroebel, W. Wittenweyler, J. Koch, G. Schwantes, D. Herb and F. Dite. Rev. George Hun, the next pastor was succeeded by Rev. F. Huelster, under whose guidance a new church, 60 by 40 feet, was erected. His successor was Rev. J. C. Runkel, who left for Milwaukee in May 1885, being succeeded temporarily by Rev Nickel and then permanently by Rev. M. Finger. The latter left for Berlin in 1888 and then Rev. J. G. Kern took up the work for two years, when Rev. Richard Eilert assumed charge. After three years service he left and his place was taken by Rev. Droegkamp of Sister Bay and later by Rev. F. J. Siewert. The present pastor, C. W. Schlueter has brought the congregation up to a large number, it now embracing 180 members. Two churches of the denomination have been maintained for some years in the town of Cooperstown, they being attended by the resident pastors of Morrison, Brown County, Rev. A. Lutz being the present minister. Another church at Reedsville, is a part of the Calumet parish and is administered at present by Rev. H. W. Lutz of that county. Meetings are occasionally held in Rockland and Eaton as well.

### GERMAN EVANGELICAL CHURCH.

Late in the eighties a mission of the German Evangelical Church was organized in the town of Meeme, Rev. J. Holzapfel of Mosel, Sheboygan County officiating. This has been since maintained and is still a mission. On January 4 1891 Rev. J. K. O. Ritzmann, now retired, organized the St. John's German Evangelical Church at Manitowoc. The first pastor was Rev. Emil Albert, who left in the fall of 1893, accepting a call to a charge at Oshkosh where he still resides. His successor was Rev. John Heinrich who remained until the summer of 1896. For the succeeding two years the church was connected with other charges, being served successively by the pastors of Oshkosh and Brillion but this not proving practicable, the church again received a pastor in the summer of 1898, Rev. M. Rosenfeld. He remained until the fall of 1900, the present pastor, Rev. Carl Nagel, then in Ohio, taking up the work on November 1st of that year in answer to a call by the missionary board of the synod. In 1901 the church building was moved to the corner of South Fifteenth and Marshall Streets and completely reconstructed. The membership is rapidly growing. Another church of the synod is located at Reedsville, being under the charge of the Brillion pastor, Rev. E. J. Fleer.

### JEWISH.

During the later nineties the city of Manitowoc became the home of a goodly number of Jews, sufficient at last to warrant the holding of services. After a few informal gatherings, on March 14 1900, the Ansha Polia Sadik Society was incorporated by I. Green, M. Stein, J. Sklute, M. Green, M. Phillips, M. Davidson, A. Schwartz, J. Phillips, D. Balkansky, S. Salicavitz, P. Schorney and J. Golden and regular meetings have since been held. In 1902 a synagogue was built.

### CHRISTIAN.

During the winter of 1895-96 revival services were held by the Christian or Campbellite Church at Manitowoc. An immersion of a number of the converts of the sect occurred at the Little Manitowoc February 28 1896 and since that time the members have met regularly at private homes, F. J. Ives acting as leader for a time. During 1901 Elder Stark of the church made frequent visits to the congregation.

### CHRISTIAN SCIENCE.

Interest in the doctrines of Christian Science was awakened in Manitowoc to a considerable degree in the decade 1890-1900 and the result was the formation of a society in 1899. A hall was rented and regular meetings have since been held. Miss Jerauld has officiated as local reader and outside speakers have frequently been secured.

### MISCELLANEOUS.

There have been in the county several societies doing Christian work along interdenominational lines, whose record is of interest. Among the earliest of these was the Manitowoc Bible Society. This was organized at Manitowoc Rapids at a meeting held in the courthouse February 18 1849, its object being the distribution of copies of the Holy Book. O. C. Hubbard was chosen its first president and E. H. Ellis its secretary and treasurer. Its second meeting was held in the Manitowoc schoolhouse, among those present being Rev. D. Lewis and Rev. Herritt. It has continued a useful existence ever since, many copies of the Bible being distributed. In 1860, for instance, when B. B. Cary was the agent, 1197 were placed in the homes of the county. Annual meetings are still held and C. F. Liebenow acts as the agent. A similar society was organized in Two Rivers in 1873.

Another important society was the Manitowoc County Sunday School Association. A preliminary meeting for the formation of this society was held at the Presbyterian Tabernacle on Tuesday June 24 1861, which was opened by prayer by Rev. Mead Holmes. Rev. J. H. Dillingham was chosen permanent chairman and reports were received to the effect that there were forty Sunday schools, numbering 1500 scholars, a goodly proportion in a county which then had but 24,000 inhabitants all told. Messrs. Carey, Groffman and Canright were chosen a committee on permanent organization and the following were the officers first elected:—President, C. S. Canright; Vice President, George Groffmann; Secretary, Rev. Mead Holmes; Treasurer, H. A. Shove. A vigilance committee was appointed in each township and for some years annual meetings were held in June. The organization, however, was but short lived.

A branch of the Young Men's Christian Association was organized in Manitowoc in February 1888 and led an active existence for some years, using the Jones Library rooms. The first officers were:—President, Louis Sherman; Vice President, Gottfried Esch; Corresponding Secretary, Dr. J. T. Martin; Recording Secretary, Eugene C. Smalley; Treasurer, H. Esch, Jr. The organization disbanded in the early nineties. A Sabbath Observance League in Manitowoc led an equally short career a little later.

## CHAPTER XII.

## SOCIETIES AND ORGANIZATIONS.

In the history of every community the part played by the social, benevolent and fraternal orders is always of the utmost importance and in that regard Manitowoc County presents no exception. There is no doubt that organizations of this kind promote a feeling of interdependence and social cohesion that is very salutary in its effects. Many of the orders in Manitowoc have in the first years of their existence been compelled to undergo struggles to maintain their life but that fact has made their development in later years all the stronger.

### FRATERNAL.

#### MASONIC.

Most prominent among fraternal organizations are the Masonic orders. On February 16 1856 a dispensation was granted for the formation of Manitowoc Lodge No. 65 F. & A. M. The first officers elected were Rev. Melancthon Hoyt, Worshipful Master; Peleg Glover, Senior Warden; Thomas Windiate, Junior Warden; John L. Lee, Treasurer; D. F. Austin, Secretary and J. H. Roberts, Tyler. The original number of brothers were twenty:—W. H. Glover, Michael Fellows, C. W. Fitch, W. W. Waldo, F. W. Nolan, A. Wittmann. H. Rassel, G. S. Glover, D. H. Van Valkenburgh, W. J. Potter, Charles Palmer, E. D. Beardsley, S. W. Carpenter, W. Barber, T. C. Shove, P. P. Smith, E. K. Rand, R. B. Musson, M. Backus and P. Reiley. This lodge has continued in existence ever since, with a constantly increasing membership. In 1875 there were sixty-three members, in 1880 eighty-two, in 1885 the same, in 1890 eighty-four and in 1895 ninety-one. Rev. Hoyt was honored by being chosen grand chaplain of the state in 1856, a position held by another Manitowoc brother, Rev. Engle in 1863 and F. Borcherdt was Grand Pursuivant in 1860.

On June 17 1858 a dispensation was granted to Tracy Lodge No. 107 F. & A. M., composed of twelve German Masons, largely taken from the ranks of the older lodge. While the general committee did not recommend the establishment of a second lodge in so small a place as Manitowoc then was, the Grand Lodge permitted it and the lodge continued to exist for some years, the charter being taken back, however, in April 1868. The first officers were F. Borcherdt, W. M.; D. Gerpheide, S. W.; and August Wittmann J. W. Two Rivers secured a lodge, when a dispensation was granted July 15 1874 for Two Rivers Lodge No. 200 F. & A. M., the officers being Dr. A. J. Patchen, W. M.; A. Hudson, S. W.; E. W. Young, J. W.; J. M. Conine, Treasurer; H. G. Fischbein, Secretary; Evan Evans, Tyler. Among the other members were J E. Hamilton, C. H. Jennison, D. Nottage, D. Van Nostrand, Jr. and Alexander Wood. Grand Master Cottrill installed the lodge and it has increased in membership until it numbered in 1900 about forty.

Manitowoc Chapter No. 16 Royal Arch Masons was founded by a dispensation granted April 4 1857 by the Grand Chapter. About fifteen gentlemen were among the charter members and officers were elected as follows:—Rev. M. Hoyt, High Priest; Ury Blake, King and W. R. Marvin, Scribe. A. W. Bowman, a member of the chapter was chosen Grand Principal Sojourner of the state in 1859. Depletion in the ranks, however, caused the chapter to be dropped in 1863, but it was again revived with nine members eleven years later. Among the members who have occupied positions in the Grand Chapter are Dr. J. F. Pritchard, G. B. Burnett and Clarence Hill. At present its membership numbers about eighty. The Masonic Lodge in Manitowoc occupies an elegant suite of rooms in the National Bank building.

### ODD FELLOWS.

In his report to the Grand Lodge of Wisconsin Odd Fellows in 1849 Grand Master Baird said: "In the county of Manitowoc there is as yet no lodge of the order but probably application will before long be made for the formation of one, as I am informed there are several members of the order residing in the county." As proof of his prediction there came about the application and granting of a charter to Chickerming Lodge No. 55 in July 1850 and on April 16 1851 the lodge was instituted by Deputy Grand Master Adams and Godfrey Stramm of Sheboygan and Mark Brainerd and W. H. Cole of Sheboygan Falls. The membership numbered ten and upon the next day the following officers were chosen:—Noble Grand, W. W. Waldo; Vice Grand, E. D. Beardsley; Recording Secretary, J. L. Kyle; Treasurer, P. P. Smith. Said the report of that year, "The prospects of Chickerming Lodge, I think, are very good. Some of the best men of Manitowoc are members of the lodge." Among these "best men" were W. Bach, E. L. Abbott, G. W. Durgin, A. Baensch, K. K. Jones, Dr. Zeilley, W. Murphy, L. Sherman, O. Torrison, F. Salomon, C. W. Fitch and G. E. Lee. Among the earlier Noble Grands were E. D. Beardsley, J. L. Kyle and M. Fellows and soon the lodge became prominent in the grand lodge of the state, S. W. Smith being Grand Master in 1864, H. F. Hubbard in 1868 and Rev. J. M. Craig in 1885, the last two named also being representatives of Wisconsin in the Sovereign or National Grand Lodge. For two years in the later fifties there were few meetings held and during the war it was with difficulty that the lodge survived but since that time it has led a remarkably successful career. In

1875 its membership was 11, in 1880 114, in 1885 145, in 1890 127, in 1895 120 and in 1900 114. The lodge has owned its own hall for a number of years.

In 1853 Two Rivers Lodge No. 66 was instituted, meeting Saturdays. W. Aldrich was prominent in the order and in 1857 became the Grand Master of the state. The cornerstone of an Odd Fellow's Hall was laid on February 28 1874 and numerous festive occasions have been given by the Two Rivers lodge, to which Manitowoc brothers have been invited. The lodge numbered in 1875 59 members, 71 in 1885, 46 in 1895 and 36 in 1900.

Many of the Odd Fellows were Germans and thus in 1871 Manitowoc Lodge No. 194 was instituted by them, C. Zander being chosen Noble Grand and A. Greve Vice Grand. The lodge in 1900 numbered about sixty members. In 1872 Kiel Lodge No. 212 was organized, being consolidated with the Manitou Lodge of Rhine, Sheboygan County in 1900. There were in 1900 about thirty members. On February 16 1894 Reedsville Lodge No. 237 was instituted and the following officers chosen:—W. H. Noble, N. G.; W. G. Hagenow, V. G. J. F. Shay, Secretary; J. Dumas, P. S.; W. Mueller, Treasurer. A lodge of the Rebecca order was organized by the German ladies of Two Rivers in 1871 under the name of Lydia Lodge No. 22, but it was dropped after an existence of seventeen years. Fredonia Lodge, Daughters of Rebecca No. 58 at Manitowoc, organized in 1891 lasted but seven years. Its first cfficers were Lena Stolze, N. G.; M. E. Reardon, V. G.; Addie Boecher, R. S. and for a time it had about fifty members.

## I. O. G. T.

Manitowoc county was the scene of much activity on the part of the Independent Order of Good Templars in early days. The earliest lodge to be organized was that at Two Rivers, where on July 19 1855 Evening Star No. 3 began its existence, it being one of the first in the state. After a life of eight years it surrendered its charter. At Manitowoc Phoenix Lodge No. 119 was organized March 12 1859 by Local Deputy Ramsdell but its existence numbered but four years. On February 9 1861 Good Intent Lodge was organized at Branch by Local Deputy Whelan, among the members being Bryan Mason, Jane Eatough, David Greenman, Sarah Linscott, W. Eatough, G. Gibson, J. McIvor, J. Smith, Elnathan Phelps, Charles McAllister, Sarah Gibson, Caroline Smith and N. Pierce. The lodge discontinued meetings in 1864. Union Lodge No. 257 was organized at Manitowoc in 1862 but had scarcely begun its existence before it was dropped. In 1866 two more short lived lodges were instituted, Oasis No. 364 at Maple Grove and Olive Branch No. 365 at Cato. In the latter village another, Phoenix No. 163 was called into being in 1879, although it, too, soon ceased to have animation. Another attempt in the city of Manitowoc was made in June 1880, when Sprague Lodge No. 231 was instituted, C. F. Smalley being the local deputy but by 1884 it was dropped from the list. Briar Lodge No. 154 at Two Rivers was equally short lived as was Lodge No. 345 in the same city, organized by Professor Marsh in 1889. Two others, Larrabee No. 95 at Larrabee and Crystal Fountain No. 77 at Cato, also failed to remain active. Niles Lodge No. 358, organized in 1894, however, is still in existence. Various juvenile lodges have been in existence in the county also.

## SONS OF HERMANN.

It was on June 19 1856 that twelve German residents of the village of Manitowoc met together and organized Thusnelda Lodge No. 7 of the Order of the Sons of Hermann, one of the earliest to be organized in the state. It was not, however, the very earliest in the county, since Two Rivers Lodge No. 5 antedates it by some months. Within a few years lodges were also started at Mishicot and Kiel, while a second lodge, Koerner No. 24 was instituted in Manitowoc. This was combined with the older organization in the later nineties, the joint membership being about seventy. The annual state convention of the order was held at Manitowoc in 1899 and John Schreihart, a member of the local lodge, has been once a member of the grand lodge of the state.

## A. O. U. W.

Clipper City Lodge No. 148 of the American Order of United Workmen was organized at Manitowoc November 26 1878, followed by Mozart Lodge No. 23, made up of German residents, on August 21 1879. W. A. Walker was the first district deputy of the county and in 1884 became grand foreman of the state, a year later being promoted to the position of Grand Master Workman. By that time Clipper City Lodge had over seventy members. Interest in the work of the order has been kept up with the passage of the years and the Mozart Lodge is still active.

### MISCELLANEOUS.

Manitowoc Lodge No. 86 of the Knights of Pythias was organized on December 4 1890 and has since led a very successful existence. The original membership was less than thirty but it had reached about sixty by 1901.

Royal League No. 42 was organized March 7 1888 with twenty-nine members and its record has been one of rapid growth, the membership in 1901 having attained eighty-seven. F. Schultz, a member of the local lodge, has been a member of the state advisory council.

Manitowoc Lodge No. 69, Temple of Honor, organized in 1876 for many years was active but lapsed in the later nineties.

The only representative of the order of Royal Arcanum in the county is Lake Shore Council No. 505, instituted in 1881, whose membership has been quite large.

Lakeside Tent No. 65 K. O. T. M. was organized in 1895 with about twenty members. Its numbers greatly increased until by 1901 it had in the neighborhood of ninety members. Another lodge of the Maccabees was organized at Two Rivers in July 1901 while a ladies' hive was established at Manitowoc the same year. H. Hallock a member of Lakeside Tent has been honored with the position of State Finance Keeper.

A branch of the Catholic Order of Foresters was organized at Manitowoc in December 1894, Joseph Simon being chosen Chief Ranger. The order grew rapidly and it was not long before a branch was connected with almost every Roman Catholic congregation in the county, as shown in the chapter on church history, the same being also true of the Catholic Knights of Wisconsin, of which order Henry Mulholland of Manitowoc was one of the founders.

A more recent Catholic order, the Knights of Columbus, has also succeeded in having established in 1902 at Manitowoc a most energetic chapter.

In 1898 a local branch of the Equitable Fraternal Union was established at Manitowoc and the membership in a few years reached over one hundred.

The first lodge of Modern Woodmen to be instituted in the county was Minnehaha Camp No. 1285, which was started at Manitowoc in 1890 by Deputies Bull and Lincoln. A few months later a camp was started at Two Rivers and since 1898 camps have also been added at Kiel, Reedsville, Cooperstown, Gibson, Centerville, Mishicot, Cato, Eaton, School Hill and Two Creeks. The first county convention was held in January 1899, Halvor Halvorsen acting as chairman and the first county picnic occurred at Mishicot on August 26 1901.

Youngest, but not least, among the fraternal orders of Manitowoc rank the Elks, organized with great festivity on April 19 1901 with Ernst Wagner as Exalted Ruler of the local lodge. The membership soon reached a large number.

Among the various other fraternal organizations, which have in the past filled a place in local life, have been Clipper City Lodge No. 9 of the order of Druids, Hope Lodge No. 363 Knights of Honor, Manitowoc Council No. 1150 of the Legion of Honor and the National Fraternal League No. 28.

### LITERARY ORGANIZATIONS.

One of the first efforts made at self improvement along literary lines was due to a coterie of Manitowoc young men, who in the year 1856 organized the Young Men's Institute, it being incorporated by the legislature. The promoters were A. Ten Eyck, K. K. Jones, I. H. Parrish, G. L. Lee, W. Bach, B. Jones, E. D. Beardsley, C. H. Walker, W. H.

Glover, O. H. Platt, C. W. Fitch, S. A. Wood, A. Wittmann, E. K. Rand, S. W. Smith and G. W. Glover. The object was the holding of annual courses of lectures and in this aim the society was successful for a number of years. The first course offered included the following lectures:—K. K. Jones on "Manitowoc, Its Past History, Present Progress and Future History," Rev. M. Hoyt on "Master Moderate," I. H. Parrish on "Russian War," W. W. Bates on "Manitowoc History and Shipbuilding in All Ages" and A. Ten Eyck on "The Sandwich Islands." Later courses comprised such speakers as Rev. Camp, of Sheboygan, Col. C. Robinson of Green Bay, Professor Bent of Boston, besides B. R. Anderson, Dr. Easton and Rev. Engle of Manitowoc. In 1859 the Manitowoc Literary and Scientific Society was formed by Jacob Lueps, S. A. Wood, W. Bach, W. Vette, C. W. Fitch, C. Hottelmann, R. Klingholz, H. Baetz, C. Walker and F. Salomon, the work of the society being interrupted by the war, which so soon broke out.

A peculiar and yet most successful organization was the Burns Society, made up of many of the older Scotch residents of the county, which was formed in January 1860 to celebrate with story and song each recurrence of the birthday of the popular poet. Henry Sibree was chosen president, Peter Johnston vice president and G. W. Burnet secretary. For seven or eight years the association gathered at some congenial spot to do honor to their countryman. Among the members were Robert McGavin, John Robinson, E. K. Rand, J. W. Barnes, T. E. Sullivan, J. Vilas, G. S. Glover, R. McGuire, H. Mulholland, and M. Mahoney, some of whom, it will be observed, turned Scotch for the occasion. Similar to this was the gathering of old English settlers at the Windiate House in 1872, although the association formed was not kept up. The Norden, a Norwegian literary semi-fraternal association has also led many years of prosperous existence. Among the more recent literary societies have been the Friday Night Literary Club, the Newman Club and the Drummond Club. In 1890 the Clio Club, an association of ladies, began its work and has since been the leading organization of its kind in the city, having become affiliated with the State Federation of Women's Clubs. The Two Rivers Historical Association, whose purpose is evident from its name, was formed in February 1898 during the Wisconsin Semi-Centennial movement. Literary societies have also been organized in the two cities and in a large number of the country districts in connection with the public schools.

## MUSICAL ORGANIZATIONS.

It was only natural that among so many of the Teutonic race music should early be recognized as a bond that makes heart and soul akin. As an evidence of the realization there was formed in Manitowoc in the fall of 1847 a musical society, John Zins being chosen conductor. The first concert was given on Washington's Birthday of the following year. The singing society after seven years' existence was incorporated as the Freier Saengerbund in 1855, among the promoters being W. Rahr, A. M. Richter, A. Richter, J. Roemer, J. Lueps, A. Berner, O. Troemmel, G. Schulz, P. Leubner, Henry Baetz, H. Lohe, J. Scherflus, F. Seeger, M. Vollendorf and W. Bach. The governor vetoed the bill incorporating the society for some reason but it passed over his head in the Senate by a vote of 21 to 8 and in the Assembly by a vote of 62 to 9. In a few years two more societies, Concordia and Harmonia were formed and in Two Rivers still another, Liedertafel was instituted. The Bohemians at Manitowoc also formed a singing society and they secured the state festival of similar organizations in 1888. The Fourth Annual Saengerfest of Eastern Wisconsin was held in Manitowoc in June 1897, the event being largely attended, while Kiel, which also has a musical society, entertained the gathering in 1901.

Other musical organizations have also played an important part in the past. The earliest band organized was that of the Schmidt brothers, residents of Newton, succeeded by Prof. Bieling's Band, organized in the sixties, later led by Prof. Urban, the Lutheran Band, the Acme Band, Prof. Weinschenk's numerous orchestras, the North Side Brass Band, organized in 1868 and the Polish Band,—all of Manitowoc,—

the Two Rivers Cornet Band and various smaller organizations throughout the county. Among the miscellaneous musical societies of past and present may be mentioned the Monday Musical Club, organized in 1899, the Glee Club, the Lake Shore Mandolin and Guitar Club in existence during the latter nineties, and the various church choirs and choruses.

#### DRAMATIC ORGANIZATIONS.

To the German residents of the county, also, Manitowoc owes the development of what has been done in the amateur dramatic art. In an article, appearing in the Nordwesten, A. Wittmann once told in a graphic manner of the first attempt to hold a German play in the village of Manitowoc. It was on Christmas Eve in 1848 that the attempt was made, all the actors being young men recently arrived from the Fatherland. The play chosen was, "Eckenste, der Nante" and in the cast were A. Bodenstab, C. Malmros, Richard Klingholz, W. Bach and A. Wittmann. A vacant room in the store of Bach and Klingholz afforded an improvised theater, the dressing room being a side bedroom. The whole village turned out to see the production,—even the "Yankees"—and the affair, which was a grand success terminated with "schnaps." Thus passed the first effort at amateur dramatics in Manitowoc. It was not long before the German Theatrical Association was giving popular plays. In the sixties the Bohemians also began to give occasional amateur productions in their language, a practice which they have since continued. The Manitowoc Dramatic Association was organized in 1874 and for some years gave dramatic entertainments, while in the latter nineties the Young Peoples' Dramatic Club led a successful existence.

#### ATHLETIC ORGANIZATIONS.

Physical developments was an end early sought by the German residents of Manitowoc County and the result was the formation of the Gymnastic Association on May 17 1854 at Franklin Hall, the charter members being F. Salomon. Jacob Lueps, Col. W. Lozier, T. Clark and W. W. Waldo. Six years afterwards an association was incorporated as Der

Turnverein, the incorporators being Charles Frase, F. Ebbert, J. Hoyer, C. G. Heingart, W. Hempschemeyer, J. Deubler, H. Woerfel, G. Schweitzer, H. Schweitzer, H. Eckert and W. Leverenz. In 1865 a hall was built at the corner of South Seventh and Washington streets at a cost of $8000 and in this hall gymnastic classes were started in 1872, having been maintained under the guidance of competent instructors till 1900. State Turnfests have been held at Manitowoc in 1867, 1883 and 1895, the last being attended by three thousand visitors.

In June 1857 a Turnverein was organized at Two Rivers and a large hall was erected by it ten years later. Another similar organization was founded at Centerville by the German residents in 1857 and societies have also existed at Kiel and Mishicot. The Bohemians of the city of Manitowoc also took an early interest in gymnastics and in 1864 built a small hall for this and theatrical purposes. Two years later the society known as the Slovanska Lipa was incorporated by Albert Fischer, F. Kostomlatsky, W. Kostomlatsky, J. Janecek, F. Stupecky, V. Stupecky, J. Brandeis, J. Falda, C. Salak, J. Mazena, V. Clement, D. Sternard, S. Skarywarda, M. Wahrhaneck, J. Skarywarda and L. Shimoneck. A new brick hall was erected on North Eighth Street in 1884, being dedicated on November 1st with formal ceremonies, addresses being delivered by Carl Jonas of Racine and L. J. Nash.

Among the various athletic sports of the county shooting early took a prominent place. In February 1870 the legislature incorporated the Manitowoc Schuetzen Gesellschaft, composed of Fred Becker, A. Berner, G. Bloquelle, Fred Carus, P. P. Fuessenich, A. Grosstueck, W. H. Hempschemeyer, E. Hollander, R. Klingholz, P. Leubner, F. Stupecky, C. H. Schmidt, P. Wieboldt and W. Bach. The year preceding the Mishicot Schuetzen Verein had been formed, among the promoters being Louis Koehnke, H. Beyer, J. Lindstedt, S. C. Selk, P. Rau, W. Tisch and F. Halberg. The State Schuetzenfest was held at the village in 1876. In 1880 the Manitowoc Shooting Club was formed, succeeded nine years later by the Manitowoc Gun Club, which was active for some years.

The Two Rivers Gun Club was formed at about the same time, the club stocking extensive game preserves near that city.

Baseball was popular in Wisconsin, from an early time. In 1868 the papers recorded a game between the Manitowoc and Sheboygan Falls teams, in which the score was 104 to 59 in favor of the former, the victors being Clark, Sherman, Smith, Enert, Nelson, Powers, Guyles, Reed and Woodin. In 1874 the Clipper Boy's Club was organized and a year later the Lakeside Baseball Club. From that time on the national game gained in interest and teams were formed at Two Rivers and other points in the county, interest being particularly high in the early nineties. Football enthusiasm arose in 1895 among the high school students and has since increased, there having been three or four teams in the county each fall. In 1884 the Manitowoc Bicycle Club was organized, succeeded when the "safety" came into general use by a similar club with a large membership. In 1885 boating was much in vogue and the Manitowoc Boat Club was formed, of which G. Burnet was president and Albert Landreth vice president. A tennis club was formed in the nineties, a court on private grounds being utilized, and there have been also various other miscellaneous organizations, such as the Tenpin League, the Skat Club, the Riding and Driving Association, etc.

### AGRICULTURAL ASSOCIATIONS.

Perhaps no one kind of societies has done so much for the advancement of the county's interests as those, which have, in the past, had charge of the various county fairs. The first meeting of the Manitowoc County Agricultural Association was held on June 23 1857 and in October of that year the first fair was held, the site chosen being Washington Square. For nine successive years fairs were held at this spot and the association thrived, its presidents in order of service being Jacob Lueps, C. Esslinger, J. F. Guyles and H. McAllister. In 1869 an attempt was made to reorganize and D. J. Easton was elected president but it met with little success. Five years later the Central Agricultural Society was

MR. AND MRS. PETER STOKER

formed and for a number of years the fairs were held at Clark's Mills. These, however, failed of success and in November 1883 the Manitowoc Industrial Association was formed with the following officers:--President, F. Schuette; Secretary, W. A. Walker; Treasurer, O. Torrison. A plot of thirty-seven acres was purchased northwest of the city of Manitowoc for $3150 and buildings erected, the first fair being held in October of the next year, Governor Rusk honoring the occasion by his presence. Thereafter the fair became an annual institution and played an important part in the agricultural life.

During the Grange movement in 1874 a number of associations were formed by the farmers including one in Meeme. A County Dairy Association was formed in 1886 with W. Danforth as president and in 1898 the State Dairymen's Association met in the city, Governor Scofield being present. Since the organization of the Farmers Institutes many have been held in accessible places in the county, proving of much value. In this connection it is interesting to note that it was a Manitowoc man, C. E. Estabrook, who, when in the legislature, first introduced the system of institutes in Wisconsin.

### LABOR ORGANIZATIONS.

Perhaps the earliest labor movement in the county was the formation of the Mechanics' Association of Manitowoc in September 1859. C. S. Canright was chosen president, W. Rahr vice president, J. Crowley secretary and E. J. Smalley treasurer. A committee on resolutions was made up of T. F. Hodges, K. S. Auberg, F. Schneider, D. Wallace, J. N. Perry, H. Westphal and J. Hurst and the position of the society on such matters as store pay was stated. As Manitowoc, however, was not a manufacturing center, such movements did not thrive and many years passed without witnessing another. In Two Rivers, where there was much manufacturing from the beginning, labor was unorganized until 1894. In the spring of that year the Mann Mutual Aid Association was formed, consisting of three hundred members and in the fall a union of wood workers was organized. In

September of the following year the first strike was inaugarated among the employees of the Two Rivers Manufacturing Company, one hundred men going out. The grievances, however, were finally compromised. Another strike took place in April 1897 but the difficulties were soon amicably adjusted. These frictions naturally led to a considerable organization of labor in Two Rivers and a similar tendency was noticeable in Manitowoc a year or so later. Among the laborers organized in the latter city were the longshoremen, who instituted two unions, the cigarmakers, masons and their tenders, carpenters, brewers, moulders. barbers, machinists, painters, clerks, typesetters and engineers, both stationary and marine. A central trades council and a branch of the American Federation of Labor were also organized during the summer of 1901. The first observance of Labor Day occurred in the fall of the same year.

### BENEVOLENT SOCIETIES.

Aside from the various denominational aid societies there have been and still exist several benevolent societies, principally in the city of Manitowoc. In November 1865 the Charitable Association was formed with the following officers:— President, Mrs. M. Fellows; Vice President, Mrs. H. Rand; Treasurer, Mrs. J. D. Markham and Secretary, Mrs. W. J. Stoutenbergh. The organization continued its good work for many years. The South Side Ladies Aid Society was organized in 1883 and a similar society among the north side ladies soon after. The absence of poverty, however, has not made great efforts in this direction very necessary.

### BUSINESS ASSOCIATIONS.

In July 1885 a number of the business men of Manitowoc gathered together and formed the Business Men's Association, electing E. K. Rand president. After some years the association was revived in 1891 as the Manitowoc Improvement Association with 147 members. T. C. Shove was elected president, G. B. Burnet vice president, Emil Baensch secretary and W. D. Richards treasurer while the board of directors was composed of F. H. Haley, F. C. Buerstatte, F. Schuette, W. D. Richards and Ernst Wagner. After the panic and depression caused by the bank failures had been somewhat alleviated the business men of the city formed an Advancement Association, which was quite active in the dredging and other improvements. The Merchants' Association of Manitowoc is an organization of later birth. The Two Rivers Advancement Association was formed in December 1890 with J. E. Hamilton as president, P. Gagnon and Leopold Mann as vice presidents and E. Manseau as secretary and treasurer, the organization proving to be of much benefit to that city.

Several associations of a business nature, having for their object mutual benefits have played an important part in the later development of the county. In the seventies there were founded the Manitowoc Rapids Fire Insurance Company, of whom the chief promoter was Charles Klingholz and the Mishicot Feuer Versicherung Gesellschaft. In 1870 the legislature incorporated the Manitowoc Fire Insurance Company with a capital of $100,000 the incorporators being Joseph Vilas, C. H. Walker, J. Mann, F. Schultz, F. Kostomlatsky, C. H. Schmidt, Jacob Halvorsen and A. Piening. Similar institutions as protection against fire were formed in various townships of the county among the farmers, notably in Newton, where a society has been in existence since the fifties. In 1879 the Mutual Life Insurance Company of Manitowoc was formed, Carl Gelbke being chosen president and G. Dusold vice president. More recent and working along somewhat different lines has been the Manitowoc Building and Loan Association, organized in 1890 with a capital of $50,000 which has enabled many to construct homes of their own.

MISCELLANEOUS.

There have been several classes of organizations, deserving of mention that it would be difficult to classify. Among those devoted to conviviality might be mentioned the Heydey Club, organized in Manitowoc in February 1889, which, after an existence of eleven years disbanded, the Calumet Club, an organization similar in nature, formed the same year, whose life was still shorter and the various minor dancing and card clubs. An organization, which should have survived, but unfortunately did not was the Manitowoc County Old Settlers

Club, formed on January 16 1879. The meeting was called by H. H. Smith, the father of Two Rivers, J. D. Markham, W. W. Waldo, W. Bach, and C. Esslinger and P. P. Smith was chosen president and William Bach secretary. A grand banquet was held on February 21st, which was largely attended and it was then decided that there should be a permanent organization, with vice presidents for each township, the list being made up as follows:—Schleswig, J. Barth, F. Krieger; Centerville, P. Werner. E. Rossberg; Newton, F. Schmitz, C. Wernecke; Meeme, H. Mulholland, J. H. Bohne; Eaton, Patrick O'Shea, Fred Swenson, Maple Grove, W. Zahn, M. Finlan; Franklin, Bryan Lorrigan. G. Betzer; Rapids, R. Donovan, H. Wills, N. Fitz; Kossuth, Casper Ewen, William Robinson; Liberty, J. Stephenson, M. Taugher; Rockland, D. B. Knapp, S. Hagenow; Cato, Ira C'ark, Jacob Grimm; Two Creeks, Fred Pfunder; Cooperstown, Henry Nachtwey; Mishicot, Julius Lindstedt, John Terens; Gibson, Jason Pellett, Manitowoc, J. Fliegler, E. J. Smalley, R. Klingholz, P. P. Smith, W. Burmeister, M. Fellows, G. Pankratz, C. W. White, S. A. Wood; Two Rivers, J. M. Conine, A. D. Farnum, Leopold Mann, Joseph Schwab. With all this complete organization, however, the association did not live beyond its birth, no further meetings being held.

In 1866 during the anti-English movement among the Irish residents of the United States, Manitowoc was the home of a Fenian Circle. The officers were:—Center, Michael Mahoney; Secretary, John Langtry; Treasurer, R. O'Connor; Committee of Safety, E. Sullivan, G. G. Dwyer, Jere Crowley and Emmett Crill and weekly meetings were held in Glover's Hall. The circle was revived in 1869 but soon passed out of existence.

In March 1892 the Manitowoc Humane Society was formed, Emil Baensch being chosen president and P. J. Pierce officer, later Richard McGuire occupying the latter position. The society, however, soon ceased to be active. Several organizations among the Bohemians of the county, with fraternal features, have been important features of their social life, notably the C. S. P. S.

## CHAPTER XIII.

### EDUCATION.

The interest shown in education in a community is, perhaps, the best test of the character of that community. There is no place where the future can be so shaped as in the schoolroom. Manitowoc county has good reason to feel proud of her past in respect to her educational history, for it is a matter of common knowledge that she has stood among the foremost counties of the state and that her efforts have gained wide recognition. As regards her public, private and parochial institutions of learning there has always been a spirit of enterprise prevailing. The self-sacrifice of the pioneer in giving his child an education in the face of almost insurmountable difficulties, is worthy of emulation and forms a peculiarly American characteristic.

The first school established in the county succeeded the first settlement by a year. It was in the winter of 1837-1838 that a few pioneers at the mouth of the Manitowoc decided to light the torch of knowledge. This was done by the raising of a private subscription and the hiring of one S. M. Peake to instruct the children of the community, twelve in number, P. P. Smith being the oldest. The primitive school held its sessions in the Jones warehouse at the corner of Sixth and Commercial Streets and instruction continued only through the winter months. In the spring Mrs. L. M. Potter, who had formerly been a teacher in the government school at Green Bay, opened a school at the Rapids, which continued in existence for some time, among the pupils being P. P. Smith and others from Manitowoc. Two years later a public school was established at the Rapids, the town hall being utilized for the purpose. A gentleman by the name of Beardsley was the first teacher and among his pupils were Dr. La Counte, P. P. Smith, D. Sackett, Giles and Erwin Hubbard and Joseph La Counte. In 1844 the county board chose E. L. Abbott, O. C. Hubbard and Oliver Clawson school commissioners and divided the county into three districts:—Two Rivers, Rapids and Manitowoc, schools being established at each and elections for district officers were held on October 10th. During the next five years the population remained almost stationary and as late as 1849 there were only seven school districts in the county. The Manitowoc school district, known later as No. 1, by that time had grown to such proportions that a commodious building was necessary and in 1848 the legislature authorized it to levy a tax of $350 for a new school. The money was accordingly raised and the next year a two story frame structure erected on North Seventh Street. This building for many years was the usual public gathering place for the villagers as well. In the same year a private German school was established in the town of Kossuth and George Peterson started a similar institution in the village of Mishicot, both being supplanted by public schools a few months later. At that time the average school year in the county was seven months and only a little over one half of the children attended regularly, owing to long distances and poor roads. The first gathering of the county teachers and those interested in education occurred at the courthouse at the village of Rapids in May 1849. Albert Wheeler acted as chairman and K. K. Jones as secretary. State Superintendent Root was present and addressed the pedagogues, recommending new plans and particularly the system of teachers' institutes. The meeting adopted resolutions favoring the formation of a county organization and the following were chosen officers:—President, James Bennett; Vice Presidents, P. Pierce, of Rapids and B. F. Sias of Two Rivers; Treasurer, William Ham, of Manitowoc; Secretary, E. H. Ellis of Rapids; Directors, H. H. Smith, of Two Rivers, W. F. Adams, of Meeme, Alden Clark and K. K. Jones, of Manitowoc. Some attempts were also made at the introduction of the graded system of schools soon after.

The extensive Irish and German immigration of the early fifties had an important influence on the county in an educational way since the favor, with which both nationalities view the school, is too well known to need remark. These sturdy pioneers rapidly settled both the rural and village communities and the log schoolhouse was a necessary attendant upon their advent. By the end of the year 1850 the first schools in the present limits of the townships of Centerville, Cato, Newton, Rockland, Meeme, Mishicot and Liberty had been established and within a few years the starting of schools in the other townships followed. The reports of the state superintendent of public instruction show a remarkable growth in one year alone. In 1850 90 out of 169 children in the county attended school, in 1851 633 out of 769; in 1850 there was received from the state funds $118; in 1851 the amount was $560. Much of the state school lands were situated in the county, there being 22,321 acres as late as 1852. The wages paid teachers in the county at this time averaged $23.50, which was higher than that maintained anywhere in the state. Among the pioneer country school teachers were Mrs. G. W. Burnett, Misses Theresa Mott, Harriet Higgins and Jane Jackson and Asa Holbrook, James Evers, John Stuart and J. Cohen. An atmosphere was created favorable to education in the Irish settlements in Meeme, particularly under the tutelage of Henry Mulholland, Sr., and Patrick O'Shea, resulting in the production of a coterie of bright minds, whose names became well known in educational circles of a later period. In the village of Manitowoc progress was also rapid. The growing needs resulted in the formation of several private schools, among them one taught by A. Wittmann in 1854, another in connection with the German Lutheran Church started in the same year and a third taught by Rev. Melancthon Hoyt of St. James Church, established two years later. School District No. 1 was ably served in the early fifties by Jos. Vilas, who had just arrived in Wisconsin and in 1856 O. R. Bacon, one of the chief figures in the educational history of the county assumed charge. He was thirty-five years of age at the time and was a man of considerable ability. After six years at the head of the school he resigned, serving as a paymaster during the war and later went into business at Manitowoc, dying June 18 1882. By 1856 the village had become so large that a new district became necessary and Dr. A. C. Gibson was hired by the residents on the south side of the river to open a school, which was done in the Esslinger building on Franklin Street in May. Later a frame building was erected for its occupancy at the corner of South Seventh and Washington Streets. Dr. Gibson remained in charge until the fall of 1858, when he accepted a position in the Two Rivers school and was succeeded by Jared Thompson, who was a man of high scholarly attainments. The interest shown in education is evidenced by the large attendance at a teachers' gathering held at Sheboygan in 1859, the following from Manitowoc County participating, Misses A. Birchard, S. E. Butler, C. M. Cooper, E. Tucker and Messrs. O. R. Bacon, C. S. Canright and Jared Thompson, all of Manitowoc; Henry Mulholland of Meeme, Joseph Stevenson, of Buchanan and Misses C. Honey and C. Williams and Messrs. J. B. Lord and J. W. Peck of Two Rivers. In the fall of the next year the teachers of the county held a convention in the Presbyterian Tabernacle at Manitowoc.

By 1860 according to the state report there were 86 districts in the county, the average school year was six months, 3971 out of 7887 children of school age attended and $4972 was received from the state. The value of school buildings was at that time $15,769, while the average teacher's wages were $22.24 for males and $15.42 for females. By way of comparison the report of 1870 is taken, showing the result of ten years growth. At the latter date 7810 out of the 14254 children of school age were in attendance, the state aid had increased to $5647, the value of school property to $35,760 and the average teachers' wages to $40. 36 for males and $26.- 85 for females, there being 183 teachers in the county. In the First Ward School Professor Thompson was succeeded in 1860 by W. F. Eldredge, C. S. Canright acting as assistant. The former served until October 1861, when he entered the army. He was a young man of great popularity and after years of honorable service for his country he moved to Yankton, Dakota where he died in 1895. During the war the first district school was taught for some time by O. F. De Land but later was under the joint charge of four ladies, Misses Warbuss, Burritt, Squires and Bennett. The office of county superintendent of schools was created by legislative act in 1861 and in that year Manitowoc county elected the first incumbent of that position, B. J. Van Valkenburgh being the Democratic and Fred Borcherdt the Republican candidate. The former won by a majority of 280 votes but resigned to go to the war in October of the next year, C. S. Canright being chosen to fill the vacancy temporarily until the fall election, at which J. W. Thombs, the Democratic candidate defeated Henry Sibree. Superintendent Thombs was succeeded by Jere Crowley, who was elected in 1863 over W. F. Eldredge by 608 majority. Crowley served in this office until his death five years later, being elected over Joseph Smith in 1865 and over A. M. Richter in 1867. Under his supervision education was systematized and regular examinations introduced, the county being divided into five districts for that purpose. Seventy-four teachers' certificates were granted in the county in the first year of his incumbency, which number had increased to 93 in 1870, to 152 in 1880 and decreased to 114 in 1890.

The close of the war marked a great increase in educational facilities. In Manitowoc a Lutheran school was erected in 1866 and a year later a Roman Catholic school started. Private schools were maintained by Mesdames S. Hill and Barnes and by Miss Maria Martin. In February 1865 J. F. Silsbee became the teacher in the south side district. It was during his incumbency that an order from the state superintendent closing the German department in all schools that maintained such instruction created so much adverse comment. After some months he was succeeded by Prof. McMullin, who in turn gave way to Prof. Scudder, a graduate of the University of Wisconsin. At Two Rivers $5000 was voted for a new school in 1866 and a year later the new building was dedicated, J. F. Silsbee having charge. On October 29 1866 the Third Ward School in Manitowoc was started in a brick building 35 by 50 feet on South Tenth street with Miss Minnie McGinley as principal. The condition of the other schools also became so crowded that the small buildings were totally incapable of holding the pupils, so that on the north side the primary department was divided and taught by C. M. Barnes and Miss Mary Shove in two private houses on North Sixth street and on the south side the intermediate and primary departments were removed to the corner of South Seventh and Jay streets. A sub-primary or kindergarten was also established under Miss Anna Metz at about this time.

Michael Kirwan was elected county superintendent in 1869 over C. S. Canright by over seven hundred majority an two years later defeated O. R. Bacon, being elected a third time to the office in 1873 by a unanimous vote. During his six years of office the condition of the schools was much improved and the esprit du corps among the teachers maintained at a high level. Large teachers' institutes were held annually, that in 1870 being the first, in which great interest was manifested, over one hundred pedagogues being in attendance. During this time O. H. Martin, D. F. Brainerd, J. F. A. Greene, L. J. Nash and later J. N. Stewart had charge of the North Side High School, while on the south side B. R. Anderson and C. A. Viebahn were successful teachers in the First Ward and W. A. Walker and J. Luce in the Third Ward. At Two Rivers among the teachers during this period, that is down to 1875, were J. S. Anderson, G. A. Williams, W. N. Ames, Charles Knapp and John Nagle, the latter acting as principal until 1877, in which year also Two

Rivers voted in favor of the establishment of a free high school. In Manitowoc an effort was made to consolidate the schools and to establish a central high school in 1869 but it signally failed when put to a vote. The early seventies were also an era of schoolhouse building. In 1871 the First Ward School was constructed on South Eighth and Hamilton streets, the structure being dedicated on January 29th of the succeeding year. In 1868 the state legislature passed an act enabling the first or north side district to levy a tax not to exceed $25,000 in order to provide for the erection of a new school, which was then found a necessity. It was, however, four years before the residents of the district saw their way clear to build the structure, the cornerstone being laid with great ceremony on July 25 1872, orations being delivered upon the occasion by Judge Anderson, Hubert Falge and others. Principal Stewart, who was then at the head of the school later became the president of the State Teachers' Association, was the author of several educational works and taught for many years at Janesville. His successor was Hosea Barns, who had charge of the school from 1874 to 1877, later entering the Baptist ministry and finally retiring to his home in Kenosha County after a life of usefulness. By the last year of his incumbency at Manitowoc the new brick building below Union Park was ready for occupancy and the high school was duly instituted. Two Rivers also erected a school in the seventies, the value of the two structures then possessed by her being $12,000. Many parochial schools were started by the Catholics and Lutherans throughout the county, including the Roman Catholic School at Two Rivers in 1877, which has always been particularly well attended, St. Ambrosius Academy at St. Nazianz and the girl's school at Alverno. In 1875 W. A. Walker, who had been a teacher in the Third Ward, was elected county superintendent over A. M. Richter and served two terms, being reelected without opposition. By the end of his incumbency there were 108 schoolhouses in the county, valued at $104,366, besides nineteen private schools. The funds received from the state in 1880 were

$6528, the average teachers' wages being $44.13 for males and $30.15 for females, while out of 15,919 children of school age, 8428 attended the public schools.

Efforts were made in September 1872 to form a county teachers' association, but although officers were elected,—C. A. Viebahn being selected president, W. A. Walker vice president and Miss Emma C. Guyles secretary,—the organization did not prove successful. Reorganization took place in 1875, however, Hosea Barns being chosen president, John Nagle secretary and Miss Alice P. Canright treasurer, since which time annual meetings have been held and the association has played an important part in educational affairs. The instructional forces of the city schools underwent many and frequent changes during the later seventies and early eighties. In the Third Ward School Prof. Luce was succeeded by J. A. Hussey in 1876, who in turn gave way to O. S. Brown. In 1879 Principal Hussey ran for county superintendent on the Democratic ticket but was defeated by Prof. Viebahn of the First Ward School by 561 majority. Two years later Mr. Brown was the Republican candidate but met defeat at the hands of John Nagle, the Democratic nominee by a narrow majority, the latter having already filled out the term of Prof. Viebahn, since the latter had in 1881 accepted a position in the faculty of the Whitewater Normal School, which he has since held. Prof. Viebahn did much for education in Manitowoc County and was once honored with the presidency of the State Teachers' Association. Prof. C. E. Patzer soon became the principal of the Third Ward School and under his guidance it advanced rapidly. On the north side Prof Barns was succeeded for two years by J. P. Briggs, who in 1880 gave way to Prof. McMahon. The latter resigned to go abroad for study a year after he had accepted the position and J. M. Rait, who had been a teacher at Two Rivers, then assumed charge of the school for two years. In the first ward the vacancy caused by the resignation of C. A. Viebahn was filled by the selection of F. G. Young in 1880. After serving the district only three years he resigned, took a post graduate course at John Hopkins University and later became a professor in the University of Oregon. His successor was John Miller. who later resigned and the vacancy filled by the appointment of P. H. Hewitt. The latter for eight years conducted the school, placing it among the foremost by his incessant endeavors. Ill health compelled him to resign in 1894 and a year or so later he died of consumption. At Two Rivers J. M. Rait acted as principal of the high school from 1877 to 1881, being succeeded by A. Thomas for three years, he later giving way to Arthur Burch, who in turn was succeeded by C. O. Marsh in 1887. Mr. Burch was another county teacher who attained the presidency of the State Teachers' Association. A new high school was built in the village of Kiel in 1884 and among the principals, who have been in charge of the institution, are P. H. Hewitt, J. C. Kamp, A. W. Dassler, G. M. Morrisey and A. O. Heyer. About fifty pupils are in regular attendance. All during the eighties John Nagle was county superintendent of schools, being selected unanimously in 1884 and 1886 and defeating A. Guttmann in 1888 by 1354 majority. His administration was a strong one and he became known throughout the state as a leading educator, being chosen president of the state association at one time. By 1890, the end of his administration, the state aid had increased to $17,543, 7430 of the 14,891 children of school age were in attendance at school and the value of the buildings was $141,869, while the average of teachers' wages had reached the highest point attained before or since, being $49 for males and $32 for females, there being 155 teachers in the county at the time.

The history of education in the county during the last ten or fifteen years of the nineteenth century was one of rapid development. In the first district Prof. Rait resigned at the end of the school year in 1883 and moved to Minneapolis and as his successor E. R. Smith of Burlington was chosen. A man of wide experience and great intellectual power for seven years he continued to exercise a beneficial influence on the school and when he resigned to embark in business great regret was felt. His successor, C. Fredel, remained but two years and gave way to H. J. Evans, an energetic instructor, who introduced many reforms in the school and soon had it on the accredited list of the state university. The district had grown so large that at the annual school meeting held in 1891 it was decided to build another structure, which was accordingly done. The building committee consisted of L. J. Nash, G. G. Sedgwick and A. J. Schmitz and a site was chosen at the corner of North Main and Huron streets, the school being named after Chas. Luling. An addition to this school was built in 1899 at a cost of $12,000. In 1901 the average attendance in the high school was 180, in the Park School as a whole 569 and in the Luling School 360. In the fall of 1902 Prof. P. G. W. Kellar the present principal assumed charge. The First Ward School by the resignation of Principal Hewitt found it necessary to cast about for another man and Prof. C. E. Patzer was accordingly chosen, continuing at the head of the institution for three years. Mr. Patzer had served four years as county superintendent, defeating A. Guttmann the Republican candidate in 1890 and being chosen unanimously at the next election. He was a man of much administrative ability and secured a position for his school on the accredited list. Resigning in 1897 to accept a position as professor in the Milwaukee Normal School, he was succeeded by W. Luehr, who proved to be a very able instructor. In the third ward Albert Guttmann became principal in the fall of 1886 and during seventeen years of able service he has done much for the school. The old facilities proving inadequate in 1891 a new schoolhouse was begun on South Twelfth street, being completed in the course of a year at a cost of $25,000. In 1900 still another building was erected, this time in the Fifth ward on Twenty-First street at a cost of $20,000. In the fourth district, a small division in the southern part of the city set off in the seventies, a new school was also erected at about the same time. All the schools of the city are maintained under the old district and school meeting system, although much talk of consolidation, particularly in regard to the high school, has taken place.

Among the principals of the Two Rivers High School in the nineties were A. W. Dassler, E. R. Smith, E. B. Carr, O.

B. O'Neil and C. W. Van de Walker. For the county superintendency A. Dassler was successful in 1894 but after one term was defeated by E. R. Smith, who was a Republican. After an able administration he was in turn defeated in 1898 by F. C. Christianson who was reelected twice without a partisan contest. According to his report of that year the receipts from the state were $15,674, 8733 children attended school out of 15,783 of school age and there were 171 teachers in the county, the average wages being $44 for males and $31 for females. A county training school for teachers, the third in the state, was opened in September 1901 under charge of Prof. F. S. Hyer and Miss Rose Cheney in the Fifth Ward School and much interest has been taken in the innovation. Parochial schools have also kept in the van of progress. A new building for the Roman Catholic School in Manitowoc was constructed in the later eighties and the German Lutherans completed a similar structure in 1891. In nearly every village and hamlet there are church schools, the Lutherans maintaining ten in the county and the Roman Catholics an even larger number. A private school entitled the Lake Shore Business College was established by Prof. C. D. Fahrney in Manitowoc in 1891 but suspended after five years of existence. Some years later the Wisconsin Business College was established and led a successful career under the able instruction of Principal C. F. Moore. A school for the deaf and dumb was instituted by the city with state aid in 1893 but it ceased to exist after seven years.

Libraries always play an important part in education. On January 23 1868 in a letter to C. H. Walker, Col. K. K. Jones, of Quincy, Ill. offered to give Manitowoc a library, provided an association was formed and the maintenance of the institution assured. The offer was accepted with eagerness and a public meeting held on February 1st, of which Joseph Vilas acted as chairman and Henry Sibree as secretary. A committee was appointed, consisting of O. B. Smith, H. Sibree, D. J. Easton and A. D. Jones, to make final arrangements and an association was formed on February 29th with C. H. Walker president, J. F. Guyles vice president,

Peter Johnston treasurer and O. B. Smith secretary. The association was duly incorporated by the legislature, the charter providing for a board of nine directors, to be elected annually, any subscriber to the amount of four dollars being given the privilege to vote at the meetings. The library was installed in a building on York street and was well supported and patronized for many years, many social and literary functions being given for its benefit. It was maintained until 1888, when the several hundred books it then possessed passed into the temporary care of the Y. M. C. A., being later transferred to the rooms of the Calumet Club and then to the north side school until added to the new city library. Although attempts were made to revive the enterprise from time to time Manitowoc was without a library until 1899, when as the result of the work of Miss Stearns of the State Library Commission, assisted by many of the local ladies, interested in education a favorable sentiment was created and sufficient funds accumulated for the opening of the institution. The following were, in November, appointed the first city library board:—L. J. Nash, E. Schuette, N. Torrison, Dr. John Meany, John Nagle, Dr. A. C. Fraser, F. C. Canright, Mesdames J. S. Anderson and Max Rahr. Rooms were secured in the Postoffice Building and the library proved a most successful enterprise. Andrew Carnegie donated $25,000 for a city library in 1902 and the work of erection was soon decided upon.

In January 1891 Joseph Mann of Milwaukee donated $1000 to the city of Two Rivers for a public library and about $2100 was raised by others in support of the institution. It was opened soon after and has been well patronized, receiving at various times considerable municipal support. District school libraries have been quite generally established throughout the county also, forming a valuable adjunct to the regular facilities.

JOHN NAGLE

## CHAPTER XIV.

### THE PRESS.

Few realize the influence of the public press upon the history of a community. It does, not, however, require much consideration to perceive its importance as a factor, acting in its dual capacity as a director and mirror of public opinion. It is easily seen, also, how important, particularly in the study of local history, it is to peruse carefully the columns of the newspapers, for through them we have not only the principal but often the sole means of a true understanding of conditions and development. Manitowoc County has been fortunate in having in past and present men of influence, of intellectual capacity and high integrity connected with its various news publications. The names of such as Fitch, Olmstead, Smith and Nagle are not soon forgotten by those who for years have had the opportunity of reading their comment on current events. The newspapers of the county have always been remarkable for the prominence given their editorial departments, the true test of a paper's individuality.

The newspaper history of Manitowoc County begins properly with the year 1850. True it is that from such expressions as "our Manitowoc readers," appearing in 1849 in the Green Bay Advocate indications are given that it had a local constituency and Milwaukee and Chicago papers were taken by a few of the more opulent. The Madison Express too, did what little county printing was to be done in the forties. But on November 30 1850 appeared the first number of the Manitowoc County Weekly Herald, established by C. W. Fitch, a pioneer resident of Kenosha. This gentleman was of New Jersey birth, being thirty-one years of age at the time he came to Manitowoc and was well educated and possessed of considerable editorial talent. The type and outfit used was shipped to the city on the steamer Champion and had been purchased of Editor Cramer of the Milwaukee Evening Wisconsin, being sold later by Fitch to a Naperville, Ill. firm. The paper started out in modest form and the first issue contained the following salutatory:—

"When we agreed to hazard the undertaking we had never set our foot upon the soil of Manitowoc or seen an inhabitant of the county. We did so from reliable representations of its past history, present population, business advantages and prospective advancement. These, to our ken, were not overrated and are sufficient to warrant the commencement with the promise of a liberal recompense. If we are all right in these conclusions and we know we are unless we have greatly overestimated the enterprise and foresight of the people, we shall not have cause for regret." In politics it was announced that the Herald would be liberally Democratic, the principles enunciated being as follows: "Politically we advance the doctrine of the Democratic party and the time honored custom demands that we should make some exposition of our faith. One of the most prominent articles of the Democratic creed in the western states is the exclusion of slavery from free territory. To this we most cheerfully subscribe. As a matter of principle and policy we are in favor of preserving the free soil of our country from the reproach of human bondage. We are in favor of cheap postage, a low rate of duties and economy in the administration of the government. We are opposed to banks and in favor of an independent treasury. We are in favor of river and harbor improvements, of granting public lands to actual settlers with proper limitations, at the lowest possible rates and of reasonable exemption laws."

It is thus easily seen that the doctrines of the new publication were extremely healthy and likely to have a beneficent influence on village life. Of the venture the Milwaukee Daily Wisconsin said in its issue of December 2nd: "'The Manitowoc County Herald is the title of a newspaper just published at the thriving village of Manitowoc by Charles W. Fitch, editor and proprietor. It is Democratic in politics, of the Jeffersonian stamp and is one of the neatest papers issued in the west. It is bound to succeed so long as the editor makes as good a local paper as he does now. Our brief personal acquaintance with Mr. Fitch has been of the most agreeable cast and we welcome him to our state and the profession with our best wishes for his prosperity as a man, a citizen and an editor. We trust the people of Northern Wisconsin will give him a liberal support." In those days personal jibes and shots at fellow editors were much more common than now and the pages were enlivened by many a friendly tift with the Green Bay Advocate and the Sheboygan Lake Shore Journal. The Herald was immediately made the official county paper, remaining so until 1855. For four years the sheet held the field uncontested and in April 1854 it was enlarged and from that time on copies were sent to the State Historical Library at Madison and have since been preserved, the only file in existence.

On the 25th of April of the same year, however, competition appeared in the shape of the Manitowoc Weekly Tribune, of which S. W. Smith officiated as editor. Mr. Smith had for some years been a resident of the village and resigned as manager of the National Hotel to assume his editorial duties. Smith and Roeser was the name of the proprietors but the latter retired from the firm in October. The paper started out with the statement that the publication was "a step not taken without consideration," adopted as its motto "Ever Onward" and notified subscribers that subscriptions were payable in wood and other merchandise. It was at first independent in politics,—Smith having been a Democrat with strong Abolition tendencies,—then became Free Democrat in policy and by 1857 was definitely ranked as a Republican newspaper. Editor Smith was an interesting writer and the series of articles appearing in 1854 on "Sights and Shadows of a Soldier's Life," detailing incidents in his career as a veteran in the Mexican war, was ably written. Some years later when he took trips to Chicago, Cincinnati and Washington his descriptions of the journeys were indicative of great skill as a writer. In July 1854 Carl Roeser, Sr., who had been associated with Smith in the establishment of the Tribune started the first German paper published in the county, known as the Wiskonsin Demokrat, Smith and Roeser appearing as the first proprietors and later Roeser & Co. By this time that nationality was much in evidence in the newly opened regions and the paper filled a need that had long been felt. It was strongly Free Soil in its proclivities and Roeser being considerable of a politician and a candidate for the position of state treasurer of the new Republican party in 1855, the paper was given over largely to controversy on public questions. It preached the doctrine of violation of the laws of the land in regard to the escape of fugitive slaves while the Herald counselled moderation. This radical position of the Demokrat opened the way for the establishment of a paper in the German language, taking opposite views on these burning questions and accordingly the Weekly Nordwesten was started in September 1855 by Carl H. Schmidt. The principles advocated by it were stated by the Herald as Democratic principles, coupled with "denunciation of Know Nothingism and Abolition fanaticism." Another German paper was also started by Carl Pflaume in the same year as the Nordwesten, being entitled Der Buschhauer but after twenty-four months existence it was discontinued, the editor returning to Germany. With all these publications in the field a struggle for county printing was the natural result, the Herald being superseded by the Tribune in 1855, the latter enjoying the patronage until it again reverted to the Herald in 1860. The Tribune suffered by fire in December 1856 but the damage was soon repaired and J. N. Stone acquired an interest which he retained for two years, later removing to Neenah where he still edits the Neenah Times, being one of the veteran figures of the Wisconsin press.

The years 1857 and 1858 saw many changes in the newspaper field. Editor Roeser sold an interest in the Demokrat in April of the first named year to A. Wallich and himself removed from the city some years later, dying in Washington, D. C. in November 1897. Roeser was present at the initial meeting of the Wisconsin Press Association in 1857 and was chosen second vice president. In October Editor Schmidt of the Nordwesten tried an experiment in making his paper a tri-weekly, continuing it as such until April 1859, a Dr. Vette being associated in the editorship in 1858. Another innovation took place in 1858 in the establishment on May 31st of the Manitowoc Daily Tribune, published by Smith & Stone. In the words of the salutatory: "The issue of a daily paper is an event in the history of a village or city," and it might have been added as was done by the Madison Democrat in commenting on the venture: "A daily paper in a town the size of Manitowoc is a somewhat hazardous experiment." The sheet was a small one with little space devoted to local news and the price was fixed at twelve cents a week or five dollars a year. One of the first items it contained was that of the marriage at Two Rivers of Conrad Bates and Miss Dorothea A. Phillips, by Rev. M. L. Stanley, commenting upon "the liberal fee enclosed for the marriage notice." The Weekly Tribune in the meanwhile continued publication and another competitor was introduced the following year when, on July 11 1859, the first issue of the Manitowoc Weekly Pilot appeared. Jere Crowley, a veteran Irish newspaper man was the proprietor, coming from Neenah, where he had edited the Advocate. A vigorous writer, who had been reared, as it were, in a newspaper office, having occupied all positions from that of "devil" upwards, he formed a valuable addition to the journalistic coterie. The Pilot was from the beginning strongly Democratic and maintained its political stand through its entire existence.

The field was thus occupied when the campaign of 1860 came on, unparalleled as to its bitterness. The various newspapers represented the various shades of opinion in that campaign most characteristically. At one extreme was the Manitowoc Herald, flaunting the names of Breckenridge and Lane, the candidates of the Southern Democracy, upon its editorial pages throughout the campaign. The Pilot on the other hand supported Douglas, bolting certain nominees of the Democratic party in the county because of their Breckenridge sympathies. In a position mediate between the two was the third Democratic weekly, the Nordwesten. The Tribune and Demokrat, of course supported the Republican candidates. The conflict took on a personal aspect in many respects and General Smith was particularly attacked, being nicknamed "Tin Horn Smith" on account of certain experiences he had undergone in the northern wilds of Wisconsin. It seems that he was sent by the state to the fastnesses of Shawano County in January 1860 to protect certain timber lands from depredations. In preparing for the expedition he made elaborate plans, taking with him four men besides two teams, loaded with stores and impedimenta, furnished by the state. The bill for tin ware alone was $51.04, the schedule including three tin lanterns, one red signal lantern and a tin horn five feet long. Some one signing himself Enquirer sent a communication to the legislature asking for an investigation and remarking: "If this expedition is an invading army sent out to conquer Shawano County and annex it to Manitowoc I solemnly protest against any change in our county boundaries." The incident was the occasion of much discussion in that body, Smith being attacked by Gabriel Bouck and Col. Elmore and being as ably defended by Col. Cobb. Smith, himself, always denied the charges and in fact it later transpired that he had only misconstrued orders but the nickname clung to him despite all. Editor Crowley, too, considered himself aggrieved in the campaign. His race and record had been used against him and efforts had been made by a member of his own party to oust him from the position of Deputy United States Marshal, which he then held. The decision of the political struggle did much to quiet the controversies and the Civil War brought many changes.

In January 1861 Otto Troemel established another German weekly under the name The Union but as the war clouds

gathered he surrendered the pen for the sword, consolidating
his publication with that of Editor Roeser under the appelation
"Union Democrat." In the absence of the latter in
Washington on business during 1861 F. Kuemler occupied
the editorial chair but after three years of varied existence
the paper suspended in August 1864. The Herald had, early
in 1861, come out for Lincoln, turning in a direction exactly
opposite from its former course and even the Pilot seemed to
consider that the president should be supported in his efforts
to sustain the union during the early part of the war. It had
become the official county paper by this time, a position it
long occupied thereafter. This loss as well as the reduced
circulation due to the war was a hard blow to the Herald and
it grew less and less influential, although it supported the
Republican candidates in 1862, until finally it was obliged to
suspend on March 26 1863, the last issue, printed at Sheboygan,
containing the following valedictory: "The truth has
long been apparent that we have in Manitowoc a superabundance
of newspapers. We have only some thirty-five hundred
voters in the county and three fourths of the patronizers of
local papers require those printed in their own languages.
The support of the remainder is divided between three English
papers, the entire amount of which is only sufficient for
one. We confess that we have no ambition to pursue a business
that does not pay a reasonable profit upon labor and capital
and this will suffice for a full explanation of the course
we have taken. Our suspension will be brief. We expect to
resume it very soon in a less crowded field, where we shall
call upon our editorial brethren of the state for a renewal of
those liberal courtesies so characteristic of the Wisconsin
press. With our readers we part reluctantly and, in closing,
the memory of long years of pleasant intercourse, of kindnesses
innumerable, of cheering words and gracious deeds,--
makes the task harder than we would wish, harder than they
will ever know. May the shades of adversity's night never
fall upon their hearts or homes. From all we bespeak
forgetfulness of past grievances and here, at this resting
point, we bury the hatchet of old dissensions." The outfit

was sold to the Tribune and Editor Fitch at first moved to Racine, where he started the Journal in November. Later, in 1867, he took up his residence in Washington becoming a prominent correspondent, being employed by the Pittsburg Chronicle and Boston Post; still later he acted as confidential clerk of Senator Sawyer. He died in Washington October 2 1899. Mr. Fitch was one of the ablest writers that have ever been in the journalistic world in Wisconsin and was honored by being chosen vice president of the State Editorial Association in 1861 and president in 1863.

The war had a depressing effect on all of the papers in the county. Subscriptions fell off and the offices were constantly being depleted by enlistments in the army. The Daily Tribune, which had battled for success so nobly, succumbed in November 1861, becoming at first tri-weekly, then semi-weekly and at last in August 1863 being merged in the weekly edition. The daily edition was again started in 1865 but continued only a few months and another attempt made by the same publication during the Franco-Prussian War met a similar fate. During the sixties the Tribune underwent many changes of management. In 1864 Editor Smith accepted the position of quartermaster in the Thirty-Ninth Wisconsin and his chair was occupied by Rev. L. N. Wheeler, then pastor of the Methodist Church, and H. Sibree. The former retired in September as did the latter soon after when the editor turned the duties over to Julius Enert and Thomas Sullivan in April 1865. In October General Smith, after selling out to O. B. Smith & Co., the principal member of the firm being his brother, left for Warsaw, Missouri, where he resided until his death in October 1890. In partnership with John M. Read, formerly of Manitowoc also, he established the Warsaw Times which he continued to edit for many years. As an editor, politician and soldier he ranked high and Manitowoc sustained a loss in his departure. O. B. Smith and J. Enert continued to control the Tribune until June 1869 when they sold it to Fred Borcherdt, the next prominent figure in in county journalism. Both the old owners moved south establishing the Knoxville, Tenn. Tribune and in 1889 O. B.

Smith became a state senator in Florida, having removed to that state.

During the troublous times of the war the Nordwesten had been suspended, no paper being issued from 1861 until February 1865 when Editor Schmidt, who had been at the front, again took up the pen. In 1867 he commenced the publication of a Sunday story edition which has been continued as a feature up to the present day, proving remarkably successful. The Pilot, in the meanwhile, had perhaps held the leading position. An opponent of Republican principles and of Lincoln and his policies it had incurred the enmity of many radicals, who considered opposition as disloyalty. On the night of May 12 1863 the office was broken into and much of the type thrown into the lake, affording the boys royal sport diving for lead for some days. This warning, however, did not cause Editor Crowley to abate his opposition and in the next issue he offered fifty dollars reward for information regarding the perpetrators of the outrage and remarked editorially: "If the scoundrels who have committed the dastardly act have not already repented we hope that Hell will one day find them in one of its hottest provinces." Soon after the war closed Mr. Crowley began to grow feeble and he was assisted in 1866 and 1867 by W. R. Kelley and in 1868 by J. M. Read, later of Kewaunee. In 1869 he retired definitely, selling the publication of which he had been ten years the editor to E. B. Treat. G. C. Skeen, a former Milwaukee Sentinel editor, was employed by Mr. Treat as editor for some time but in August he assumed charge himself. In April 1870 Jere Crowley passed away, mourned by all as a sincere and honest man. It is due to him that the Pilot was given such a prominent position at the outset, so that its later success might be easy. Soon after the war A. Wallich and C. Troemmel had taken up the broken threads again and reestablished the Demokrat, this time under the name of the Zeitung, the first issue appearing in June 1868, Republican in politics, as before.

Thus it was that by 1870 the personnel of the editorial fraternity of Manitowoc had entirely changed, the old figures having disappeared with the exception of C. H. Schmidt. Nor did the changes stop there. In August 1870 Mr. Treat relinquished the Pilot to J. C. Bollmeyer, who then acted as editor until his office was destroyed by fire on March 2 1871. Soon after Ten Eyck G. Olmstead purchased the plant and continued to manage it alone until he associated with him John Nagle in the spring of 1876. Mr. Bollmeyer moved to Ohio where he edited the Wausion Expositer for some years and died in December 1898. The Tribune in the meantime was managed by F. Borcherdt but upon his appointment as consul to Leghorn, Italy in 1874 his son Edward assumed the editorship. For six months in that year it changed to a semi-weekly but resumed its old form in September, after which time John B. Miller was for some months associated in the management. The elder Borcherdt died abroad in 1877 and in April of the next year the Tribune discontinued publication, thus leaving the Republicans without an organ. Its valedictory was terse, stating in reference to reasons for the paper's suspension: "It is unnecessary to enumerate them, but the fact is that it does not pay to continue its publication." Edward Borcherdt became associated with John Nagle and together they purchased the Olmstead interests in the Pilot, the first issue under the new management appearing April 25 1878. Changes had also taken place among the German papers. Editor Troemmel of the Zeitung died in February 1873 and the sheet was accordingly sold to Henry Baetz and Col. Wedelstad, the latter acting as editor until July 1875, when he removed to Milwaukee, later taking a position in the state treasurer's office. Fred Heinemann purchased the paper, changing the name to Manitowoc Journal, but did not long continue its publication and in the latter seventies the German Republicans lost their organ. On March 8 1871 the legislature granted a charter to the Nordwesten Printing Company, John Franz, C. G. Schmidt, C. H. Schmidt, Henry Schweitzer, A. Piening, H. Menge and M. Kettenhoffen being the incorporators. Four years later Menge & Schweitzer took up the management of the paper, Mr. Schmidt still retaining the editorial chair and soon also resuming entire control. In 1878 the Nordwesten and Pilot were the only newspapers in the city. Two Rivers, however, had by this time secured a publication, the Manitowoc County Chronicle, established in 1872, in the championship of the so-called People's Party, then active in politics. Judge H. S. Pierpont was the first editor but did not remain long at the head, being succeeded temporarily in 1874 by George N. Woodin and selling his interest in April of the following year to William F. Nash, the present proprietor. Mr. Nash has made a reputation state wide as an editor and has served the people of the county ably in the state senate. The paper is Democratic in politics. The city maintained a second paper, the Weekly Tribune edited by Robert Boehm and Republican in politics, for some time in 1900, but it soon discontinued.

On April 24 1879 appeared the first number of the new Manitowoc Tribune, revived by Henry Sandford of Racine and published by W. Christie of that city. It was Republican in politics and immediately took up the struggle against the Pilot. The latter had, however, a tremendous advantage due to a long and continuous existence, careful management and a circulation of over two thousand. The Tribune, first published at Racine, was soon located in Manitowoc but Christie severed his connection with it, starting the Manitowoc Journal on June 15 1880, a three quarto Republican weekly appearing Saturdays, that existed a little over a year. Editor Christie was a former Chicago Tribune employee. In June 1881 a new German paper, the Post, was founded by A. Wittmann, independent in politics and in October of the same year the Lake Shore Times made its appearance, the outfit of the Journal having been purchased by Haukohl & Baensch. This, too, was Republican and continued under the same management until 1884, when J. S. Anderson purchased it. Under the latter's able editorship, and assisted no less ably by his wife, the paper took on a dignified and literary tone which made it very popular. In 1887 it was sold to H. G. Kress, who for two years was its editor, discontinuing its publication in order to engage in business in Spokane, Washington. Other changes also took place in the eighties; Edward Borcherdt retired in 1888 from the Pilot management and in January of the same year Editor Schmidt, the veteran of Manitowoc journalism, passed away. Under his management the publication had taken a prominent place among the German weeklies in the state and it was largely due to his efforts that the German Editorial Association held its convention in Manitowoc in 1883. The paper was continued by a stock company from 1888 until 1893, H. Falge and later C. G. Schmidt, a brother of the deceased, acting as editors. In the latter year it was sold under administration proceedings to Mrs. C. H. Schmidt and for some months H. E. Kummer was the editor, after which C. G. Schmidt again resumed his duties, later associating with him his son Adelbert Schmidt. In the Post management William F. Brandt was for some years associated, retiring in 1892 to engage in business independently. Editor Sandford in the meantime continued to conduct the Tribune until in 1895 he secured a position at Madison. For some time he edited it from that city but in March 1897 sold the plant to G. G. Sedgwick, Rev. Emmet W. Rankin and E. R. Barrett of Kansas City, Missouri. The paper was soon incorporated with the St. Nazianz Weekly, a six column folio that had been in existence since June 1895, the editor of the latter, H. C. Olson forming one of the new corporation then organized under the name of the Citizen Publishing Company. The name of the Tribune was also changed to the Citizen. C. W. Roberts of Racine later purchased Olson's interest and became the editor of the Citizen, Editor Barrett removing soon after to Missouri.

A new publication appeared on December 14 1893, issued from the office of the Brandt Printing & Binding Co., entitled the Manitowoc Times-Press, of which H. G. Kress was the editor, it being in reality a continuation of the old Lake Shore Times. It, too, was Republican and has since continued to be such and Mr. Kress has continued to direct its editorial policy. The paper was published for some time independently by Mr. Kress and a daily edition of short duration was put forth in the fall of 1898. The years 1894 and 1896 witnessed the addition of two German weeklies in the county, which have since maintained themselves with credit, viz., the Wahrheit, edited and owned by C. Otto Schmidt, appearing first in the last named year, being Democratic in politics and the Kiel National Zeitung, started in 1894, owned at first by Halhnek & Landen, being edited by the latter and later being transferred to H. A. Kuenne. It is independent in politics. Editor Wittmann of the Post was honored by being chosen president of the German Press Association in 1890. In May 1896 he sold his interests to Emil Baensch and William Gennrich and a year later he passed away after a life of usefulness. The paper after his death became Republican in politics. On March 21 1900 one of the saddest chapters in the history of Manitowoc journalism was recorded. John Nagle, editor of the Pilot, after a short illness, succumbed to an attack of typhoid fever and passed from mortal scenes. Beloved by all, staunch to friends and convictions he presented a notable figure. He had at one time been honored with the presidency of the State Editorial Association and his opinions, as they appeared week by week, were widely copied. His attitude in the Bennett Law controversy, where he took a stand opposite to that of his party, also marked him as a man of convictions and gave him a wide reputation. Soon after his death a company was formed, which purchased the Pilot and placed Sydney T. Pratt, formerly of the Milwaukee Sentinel, in the editorial chair. He remained in this position and was a part owner of the enterprise until May 1903, when the Nordwesten and Pilot were combined, E. W. Mackey becoming editor and Adelbert Schmidt business manager.

It was the occasion of much remark that for so many years a town of the size of Manitowoc should have no daily paper. The project was often considered in the early nineties but it was not until October 19 1898 that the Brandt Printing & Binding Co. issued the first number of the Manitowoc Daily Herald. M. C. Gettings of Monroe was the first editor and was succeeded after a few months by E. R. Barrett and then by E. W. Mackey, also of Monroe, who has ably conducted its columns. After a hard struggle it gained a distinctive place in the popular favor and has a circulation of over a thousand. In October 1899 the Herald-Press Publishing Co. was formed with H. G. Kress as president, Horal Nelson as vice president and W. F. Brandt as secretary and treasurer, the company publishing both the Daily Herald and Weekly Times-Press. The former is independent in politics. On May 12 1900 another daily, The News, appeared for the first time, Republican in politics with C. W. Roberts as editor, he having acquired the interests of the Citizen Publishing Company. For a time F. Ellis Reed was connected with the management and finally John McFarlane of Racine purchased the paper and has since conducted it and the Weekly Citizen in a most satisfactory manner.

There have been more or less of what might be called ephemereal publications in the county. A religious weekly, Concordia by name, was published in Manitowoc during 1875 and 1876 but was later removed to Green Bay. Rev. Roehl of the German M. E. Church edited a monthly designated Der Hausbesucher in 1888 devoted to pastoral affairs. Rev. Rogers and Rev. Gray of St. James during the nineties also edited The Diocese, another church periodical. A Polish weekly, Wezyotko Jezusa published by local priests was established in 1887 and attained a wide circulation but the hard times of 1894 caused it to suspend. Another Polish publication, the Biblioteczka Rodzinna, met the same fate after a five months' existence in 1903. During 1896 Walter Wittmann edited a Populistic weekly entitled the New Broom, published at the office of the Manitowoc Post. Amateur talent has also found means of expression in the publication of The Picket by the pupils of the North Side High School in 1883 and 1884, the New Era and So-To-Speak by the pupils of the same school and the various other small miscellany. On the whole the progress of the press in the county has been one of the brightest phases in its history.

## CHAPTER XV.

### THE PROFESSIONS.

Manitowoc County has had in its existence many men in professional life, who have gained distinction and an honorable place among their fellows. Some of them have been sought out for public service and broader fields of usefulness, while others have led a quieter but no less honorable existence in the sphere of their choice, many being laid to rest after lives of service to the community amidst general regret and deep sorrow.

#### BENCH AND BAR.

Such is the case particularly with the men who have represented the legal profession. And not only has the bar been a strong one in the past but the courts have maintained a standard of dignity and impartiality, that has been most creditable. In the earliest days there was little or no litigation and as a result the county was judicially a part of Brown County until 1848, when upon Wisconsin's arrival at statehood Manitowoc was given complete autonomy. On September 10th Circuit Judge Alexander Stow opened the first term of court at Manitowoc Rapids. Little legal proceedings engaged his attention except the admission to the bar of E. H. Ellis, J. L. Kyle and J. H. W. Colby, Manitowoc's first attorneys. Mr. Colby was immediately elected county judge, receiving 163 votes, while E. M. Soper received 113, and E.

H. Ellis was chosen district attorney of the county. This marked the first judicial organization, although of course even before this time there had been justice courts, some of the early justices, appointed by the governor, being B. Jones, P. Pierce, Peter Johnston, Frederick Borcherdt, D. S. Munger and S. W. Sherwood.

Mr. Ellis, the first district attorney was a son of A. G. Ellis, the editor of the Green Bay Advocate, the first paper published west of Lake Michigan. He remained in practice at Manitowoc for some years, being succeeded in his office by Mr. Colby, who was unanimously chosen in the fall of 1850, dying three years later. The fourth of the early lawyers was Ezekiel Ricker, who had been the first clerk of court and he succeeded Mr. Colby as county judge, defeating the latter by 177 majority in the fall of 1849. He died at the time of the second cholera scourge in 1854, as did also James L. Kyle, who had been chosen district attorney after Mr. Colby's death. Judge Ricker was of Maine birth and was only thirty-three years of age at the time of his death. He had studied law in Lebanon, Maine with Attorney General Clifford of that state and came to Manitowoc in 1846, serving in the assembly for two years after his term as county judge expired. Mr. Kyle was five years his junior, having been born in 1826 and had also served in the legislature. Said the Madison Argus of him: "He was a noble hearted man, incapable of dishonesty, of fine and portly proportions and nobility of intellect." Kyle was succeeded as district attorney by N. Wollmer, who had been in the county since 1847 and remained there until his enlistment in the service of his country, losing his life before Atlanta in August 1864. It was in the incumbency of his successor, C. H. Walker, who was admitted to the bar at about this time, that the first murder trial took place in the county. Judge Gorsline of Sheboygan presided over the circuit court at this period, he having succeeded Timothy Howe, who was the first regular judge of the district. The defendant in the case was an immigrant and he was charged with the murder of the barkeeper of the Franklin Hotel, it appearing that there had been an altercation be-

H. H. SMITH

tween them. The defense was in the hands of N. Wollmer, assisted by E. Fox Cooke, of Sheboygan, while the district attorney was aided by J. M. Shafter of the same city. After lasting some days the trial resulted in an acquittal.

By 1855 the number of lawyers had increased considerably and many of those, whose names were later prominent, were admitted to the bar. George Reed had located in the village at an early date and in 1853 became county judge, succeeded later by George C. Lee, who in November 1856 resigned, Isaac C. Parrish being chosen to fill the vacancy. All of these men were lawyers and led long and honorable careers. S. A. Wood and W. D. Hamilton were also admitted to the bar at about this time. Hamilton defeated Lee for the position of district attorney in 1856 and C. H. Walker succeeded Parrish as county judge two years later. J. D. Markham, who had been admitted to the bar shortly before, settled in Manitowoc in 1856 and began his long years of successful practice. Among the other lawyers of the time were W. H. Hammond, W. M. Nichols, Rice and Sweet, L. T. Warren, John A. Daniells, Parrish and Esslinger, of Manitowoc and Conrad Bates, D. W. Duncombe and William Aldrich of Two Rivers. Some remained in the county but a short time but a majority of them were permanent residents. As district attorney George Lee succeeded W. H. Hamilton, but after two years in office gave way to J. D. Markham, who served two terms or until 1863, when W. M. Nichols, the Democratic candidate defeated him. The fight for the position of county judge in 1861 was a three cornered one, B. R. Anderson and S. A. Wood of Manitowoc and H. S. Pierpont of Two Rivers being the candidates. Anderson and Pierpont were then newcomers to the county and for many years were prominent at the bar and in all political controversies. Judge Pierpont was successful and held the office until his resignation in December 1864. Up to the time of the draft cases of 1863, in which the entire legal talent of the county was engaged and of which mention is made elsewhere in these pages, no very important litigation arose in the county. There had been, however, several murder cases, including the Burkhart-John trial in 1856, the Peglow-Frantz and the Higgins-Gammel trials in 1857, the Erlinger-Zioler and Gage-Packard trials in 1860 and the Smoke-Shreve case in 1864, the last being a particularly prominent trial, J. D. Markham and G. Woodin acting as prosecutors and George Reed and Charles White defending the accused. Mr. White had opened an office in the village the year before. Many of the attorneys left the county during the war to fight for their country, among them N. Wollmer, C. H. Walker and Charles White and many, who later became attorneys, served in the great conflict. G. N. Woodin, who had been admitted to the bar but shortly before was elected district attorney by the Democrats in 1864 and served two terms, while George W. Barker succeeded H. S. Pierpont as county judge in the same year, holding the office six years. Among those admitted to the Manitowoc County bar in the sixties,—most of them immediately after the war— were W. E. Hoye, C. A. Boynton, H. Sibree, C. W. Morse, W. M. Ross, E. B. Treat, T. G. Olmstead, T. C. Shove, D. E. Markham, W. F. Eldridge, Arthur Wood, W. A. Place, R. P. Eaton, R. P. Cook and W. Bird. Hamilton, Treat and Nichols, Lee and Walker and later Lee and White associated themselves together in co-partnerships. In 1868 E. B. Treat was elected district attorney on the Democratic ticket, defeating C. W. White, and W. W. Waldo the following spring was elected county judge over H. Sibree, being succeeded by T. G. Olmstead, another Democrat, four years later.

Among the new men to enter the legal field in the seventies were Michael Kirwan, J. S. Anderson, L. J. Nash, O. F. A. Greene, W. A. Walker, C. E. Estabrook, W. J. and H. G. Turner, G. A. Forrest, W. H. Hempschemeyer, W. Glover, W. Bach, A. J. Schmitz, D. A. Shove, W. G. Lueps, G. Byron and H. F. Belitz, the last named being a resident of Kiel. Of these Messrs. Estabrook, Walker, Turner and Schmitz in later years transferred their residence to Milwaukee, Mr. Estabrook becoming attorney general of the state. On the other hand Messrs. Anderson, Nash and Forrest have remained for many years among the leaders of the local bar. After remaining in the city a brief space of time in company with L. J. Nash, O. F. A. Greene removed to Boulder, Col., where he died in 1899. Through death the county lost several able lawyers in the decade under consideration. C. H. Walker died on Dec. 14 1877 after a life full of usefulness, during which he had served as a soldier, a legislator and judge. In the same year George Woodin and D. E. Markham passed away and in that succeeding Col. T. G. Olmstead, who had served as county judge until 1877, when Michael Kirwan was unanimously elected to that position. Col. H. F. Belitz, of Kiel, who had also been admitted to the bar but seldom practiced, died at about the same time, while the death of E. B. Treat occurred some two years later. His record also as a teacher, soldier and attorney was of the highest order and his demise was greatly regretted. He had been succeeded as district attorney in 1873 by W. J. Turner, who had defeated his Republican opponent, J. S. Anderson, by a narrow majority. H. Sibree, who was the next incumbent of the office was also a Democrat, defeating C. E. Estabrook in 1874. Two years later another Democrat, A. J. Schmitz, then recently admitted to the bar, was successful over J. D. Markham and was reelected in 1878, defeating J. S. Anderson. Since 1868 Campbell McLean had been circuit judge of the district, comprising Manitowoc, having succeeded Judge David Taylor. His successor, Norman S. Gilson, of Fond du Lac, chosen in 1880, filled his position with great dignity and impartiality, securing the respect alike of the bar and the public.

In 1880 a valuable addition to the Manitowoc bar was made by the removal from Kewaunee of G. G. Sedgwick to the former city. E. G. Nash, another prominent local lawyer commenced practice with his brother a year later. Others, who during the eighties were admitted to practice, were H. L. Markham and R. H. Markham, sons of J. D. Markham, Byron Oakley, who died soon after, C. A. Blesch, Emil Baensch and R. D. Smart. Judge Reed, who had long been the Nestor of the county bar lost his life in the terrible Newhall House disaster in Milwaukee on January 10 1883. He had always been prominent in local and state affairs and his death was a heavy loss to the community. Henry Sibree, another legal luminary, passed from earthly scenes in April of the same year after thirty years spent in practice at Manitowoc. In the death of H. S. Pierpont, which occurred May 6 1890 Two Rivers lost her leading lawyer. Judge Pierpont was of New York birth and was admitted to the bar of that state, afterwards practicing in Illinois. Coming to Two Rivers at an early day he engaged first in mercantile pursuits but later turned his attention to politics, being a candidate for attorney general and bank examiner on the Democratic state ticket. As a county judge he was considered very able and later as the founder of the Two Rivers Chronicle gained a wide reputation as a writer. R. D. Smart, who had been elected county judge in 1881 over J. P. Wickert, also passed away in 1890. He was a man of very attractive personality, a fact attested by his repeated election to office, although a Republican, in a strongly Democratic district. His successor as county judge was C. H. Schmidt, who although he was not a lawyer, was a very able gentleman, having for years been editor of the Nordwesten. He died in 1888 and was succeeded by Emil Baensch, then a young lawyer of rising reputation. All during the eighties A. J. Schmitz and W. A. Walker held the district attorneyship, defeating successively G. G. Sedgwick, E. G. Nash, H. L. Markham and G. A. Forrest, their Republican opponents. Mr. Walker was chosen United States district attorney in 1887, removing to Milwaukee to enter upon his duties.

Judge Baensch's successor as county judge was F. E. Manseau, who with Isaac Craite had established himself as an attorney in Two Rivers in the early nineties. The former was obliged to resign, however, on account of ill health in August 1895 and J. S. Anderson was appointed his successor, serving continuously until 1902, when John Chloupek was elected to fill the position. The latter had been admitted to practice ten years earlier and had become district attorney upon the expiration of the term of A. J. Schmitz. The Republican landslide of 1896 put A. P. Schenian into the office, an able attorney, who had recently set up in practice in Manitowoc, although theretofore he had been an attorney in the west for several years. He in turn gave way to E. S. Schmitz, a brother of A. J. Schmitz, and in 1900 after some legal difficulty over the returns another young lawyer, Albert Hougen, was elected to the office by a small majority. A municipal court for the county was created in 1895, being first presided over by Isaac Craite, but he was succeeded in the spring of 1901 by A. P. Schenian, a Republican. Among the lawyers, who were admitted to the Manitowoc County bar in the nineties were E. S. Schmitz, A. L. Hougen, E. J. Onstad, C. H. Sedgwick, A. H. Schmidt, Adelbert Schmidt, E. L. Kelley, A. L. Nash, C. D. Fahrney, R. C. Burke, W. H. Joyce, Victor Pierrelee, Arnold Alexander and J. Healy, of Manitowoc; F. W. Dicke of Two Rivers and A. J. Chloupek of Melnik. In the same period Manitowoc attorneys, who passed away were W. Bach, W. H. Hempschemeyer, C. Esslinger, A. Manseau and H. G. Turner, the last named having for some time been a resident of Milwaukee. In 1898 Michael H. Kirwan was honored with an election to the circuit bench of the district, including Manitowoc, Sheboygan, Kewaunee and Fond du Lac Counties, being the first of the Manitowoc bar to gain that distinction.

In the last twenty years of the century there was a large number of important cases in the county, which gave an opportunity to bring out the legal talent of the bar. Among the litigations of importance have been the various criminal and civil trials growing out of bank failures, the Quay street railway damage cases and several lengthy murder trials. A Manitowoc County Bar Association has been formed, being a means of mutual helpfulness among the lawyers of the county. Several of the attorneys in the county have in the past written on legal subjects, notably L. J. Nash, who has on several occasions addressed the State Bar Association. He has also held the position of state bar examiner.

## PHYSICIANS.

The practice of medicine, one of the highest callings, which men have taken up, has had some able representatives in the county, many of whom have reached eminence in their profession. Dr. A. W. Preston was the first regular physician to take up his residence in Manitowoc, arriving in 1847. He was a man of considerable ability and his services in the cholera epidemic of 1854, when he was the only physician in the county, are worthy of much admiration. When the war broke out he enlisted as a surgeon in the Sixth Wisconsin and after serving three years secured a furlough to visit friends in New Hampshire, where he died in December 1864. His was a life worthy of emulation, full of sacrifice and service for others. Another of the earliest physicians was Dr. Ransche, who in the later forties, established himself for some time at the Rapids. Soon after 1850 Dr. H. E. Zeilley arrived at Manitowoc, while Dr. John Oswald settled at Two Rivers, where he led a long and honorable career. He was born in Germany, was educated at Goettingen and Berlin, settled first in Pennsylvania, then in Ohio, then in 1852 came to Two Rivers, where he died in 1878. He was many times chosen village president and was elected county coroner in 1868 and again in 1874. Dr. Zeilley was a surgeon in the Fourteenth Regiment in the war and later removed to Chilton. Other physicians, who commenced practice in ante-bellum days, were A. C. Gibson, R. H. Colbourn, C. Mueller, J. C. Saltzmann, D. J. Easton, C. Schenk and H. S. Balcom. The last three named served as surgeons during the war but of all only Drs. Balcom and Easton remained in the county for any length of time. Dr. Easton lived in the city until his death, which occurred in 1880 and was always prominent. A graduate of the Albany Medical and Philadelphia Homeopathic Colleges, at his settlement in Manitowoc he was the first physician of that school of medicine in the vicinity. Among his contemporaries in the county were Dr. H. W. Tucker of Clarks Mills, who although somewhat older came to the county the same year as did Dr. Easton, Dr. C. Creutzberg, of Rapids, Dr. Kellogg, of Branch and Drs. F. Simon, J. Steger, and B. F. White of Two Rivers, of whom only Dr. Simon was a permanent resident of the county. He removed to Manitowoc later and served six terms as a coroner. Dr. Tucker passed away in 1878 at a ripe old age, while

Dr. Kellogg removed to Wrightstown, where he spent the reclining years of his life.

At the conclusion of the war the medical fraternity received several accessions. In 1865 Dr. J. A. Brown settled in the village of Manitowoc. Born in Hartford, Connecticut, in June 1816 he graduated at an early age from the Scientific School at Lima, N. Y., matriculating later at the University of Michigan. After ten years practice in Illinois he removed to Manitowoc where he spent the remaining years of his life, dying November 25 1893. Another newcomer was Dr. Schallern. He was a Bavarian by birth but fled from the Fatherland after the revolution of 1848, becoming a surgeon at Ward's Island, N. Y. Later he served in the 51st Ohio during the war, after which he located at Manitowoc. Returning to Mount Vernon, N. Y. he died in 1878. Drs. Balcom, Simon and Easton continued in practice after the war, each finding an extended field of usefulness, while Dr. C. C. Crocker established himself at Two Rivers, where he continued to practice for many years. Dr. Coakley, a graduate of the Chicago Medical College, in 1872 also decided to locate in the county. He was killed nine years later by an unfortunate fall from his carriage, while enroute to visit a patient. Dr. Balcom had also passed away some years preceding. Dr. R. K. Paine opened an office at Manitowoc in 1874, being then a recent graduate of the Hahnemann Homeopathic School at Chicago. He was born in Fond du Lac, was educated at Wayland Academy and served in the Twenty-First Wisconsin. In a few years he had built up a very lucrative practice and has been honored by an election to the presidency of the Wisconsin Homeopathic Society. Dr. J. F. Pritchard also came to Manitowoc in the seventies and soon proved himself an able practitioner, being appointed later a division surgeon by the Chicago & Northwestern Railway Company and being honored in 1891 by the vice presidency of the State Medical Association. Another physician, who practiced at Manitowoc at the time, was J. C. Oviatt.

In the next few years several more were added to the list of the county practitioners. In 1878 Dr. Dawley started an office at Mishicot but his usefulness was cut short by death two years later. Dr. H. M. Hittner was his successor at that village and after twelve years of practice he too passed away. Dr. J. R. Currens came to Two Rivers in the later seventies and built up a large practice, which he has since maintained. As a member of the State Board of Medical Examiners he has gained considerable prominence. Dr. F. S. Luhmann, a successful Manitowoc physician, established himself in that city in 1880 and Dr. W. G. Kemper, another of the allopathic school began work soon after. Dr. Luhmann was elected coroner for seven successive terms, beginning in 1882, defeating among others Drs. O'Connell, A. C. Fraser and J. F. Pritchard and was again chosen to the position in 1898 by 268 majority over A. C. Fraser. Dr. Fraser, a graduate of McGill University, Montreal, came to Manitowoc in 1881 and soon gained an extensive clientage. He served as coroner in 1897 and 1898 and was chosen as attending physician of the marine hospital in 1900. Others, who established themselves in the county at about the same time were Drs. S. C. Blake, P. E. Nagle, A. V. Smith, A. J. Schweichler and H. Menson of Manitowoc, all of whom have removed to other fields, the first named being a physician of wide repute in Chicago, C. Bodenstab of Reedsville, R. S. O'Connell of Cato, C. W. Stoelting of Kiel and C. H. Oswald and Calvin Barnes of Two Rivers. Both Oswald and Barnes died early in their careers, the former in 1884 and the latter in 1887. In October 1882 a county medical society was formed, ten physicians being present at the first meeting. Dr. J. F. Pritchard was chosen president, Dr. J. A. Brown vice president and Dr. W. G. Kemper secretary. Meetings were held every three months and the organization has since proved very helpful. In the later eighties and early nineties an unusually large number of physicians located at various points in the county. Among them were Drs. W. E. Buschmann, J. Rehrauer, E. Tillson and J. D. Moraux of Two Rivers, the last three named not remaining permanently however, Oliver Hebert and R. Wittmann of St. Wendel, the latter removing to Kiel, J. P. Hayes and P. J. Taugher of St. Nazians, C. Bossard of Kiel, Louis

Falge and P. G. Kuensel of Reedsville, W. H. Vosburg of Cooperstown and H. C. Thiehle and Gilbert Karnofsky of Manitowoc. Dr. Thiele died in 1888 after eight years of successful practice. Still later Manitowoc was selected as a field by several other physicians, among them C. Jacobs, who became city physician, J. F. Mulholland, a throat, nose and ear specialist, J. A. Roberts, who moved to the city from Kewaunee, J. E. Meany, who was elected coroner in 1900, H. E. Bahr, an osteopath, Walton C. Hubbard, C. Gleason, H. Thurtell, G. W. Patchen, J. E. Barnstein, Max Staehle, C. F. Fuhrmann and A. N. Kittelson. The last two named, however, remained but a short space of time. In the county the following also established themselves:—J. B. Rick at Larrabee, J. Hoyer at Tisch Mills, A. F. Hahn and G. L. Karnopp at Mishicot, Jacob Marti and H. Schaper at Kiel, Charles Schaper, who died at Franklin in December 1901, James Burke at Hika, C. W. Schmitz and T. O'Brein at St. Nazians and E. C. Christianson, H. Farrell, F. A. Greiner and A. Jekelfalusy at Two Rivers.

DENTISTS.

The first member of the dental profession to establish himself at Manitowoc was Dr. E. M. Thorpe, who arrived in February 1857. He remained in practice until the war broke out. In 1862 Dr. A. J. Patchen moved to the city and commenced a practice, which he continued for many years. Born in Hadley, Vermont in 1830, Mr. Patchen came to Fond du Lac in 1849 and served during the war in the Fifth Wisconsin, later being captain of Company G of the Thirty-Ninth. As a dentist he remained in practice until 1887, when he was succeeded by Dr. H. L. Banzhaf. He died ten years later. Another dentist of the early days was Henry Van Winkle. Not till the eighties did others enter the field permanently, the first being Drs. Charles and Ernst Seeger, who soon gained a lucrative practice and later associated with themselves Dr. Joseph Miller, formerly of Kaukauna. E. H. Watrous also located in Manitowoc for some years at about this time. Dr. Banzhaf took into partnership Drs. Martin and

Hoover but neither remained permanently. Dr. Louis F. Seeger opened an office at Manitowoc in 1890 and was soon joined by Dr. G. E. Henry, but the former died in a few months, leaving the latter to conduct the business until 1897 when he removed to Port Washington, being succeeded by C. J. Reinfried. Another dentist, who in the nineties started in the practice of his profession in Manitowoc was Dr. C. E. White, but he too removed from the city in 1900. Others who have started offices in Manitowoc of recent years are Drs. E. M. Kapitan, E. J. Eisen, Frank Gehbe, E. M. Blumenthal, J. McMillan, H. A. Simon, M. L. Bast, J. Huwatschek, C. W. Seehaase, C. C. Wernecke, Albert Vits and N. T. Ziglinski. In 1900 Dr. Banzhaf was honored by being chosen as a member of the state board of dental examiners and in 1902 moved to Milwaukee to take charge of a dental school. In Two Rivers E. J. Soik and Eggers Bros. opened dental parlors at about the same time, while in Kiel L. E. Wiesler commenced the practice of his profession.

## CHAPTER XVI.

### BANKS AND BANKING.

The history of the various banking institutions that have formed a part of the business life of the county is not altogether without its deplorable and unfortunate chapters. It was several years after the settlement of the village that Manitowoc's commercial needs justified the establishment of such an institution but as business grew a bank became an obvious necessity. That it was early considered is witnessed by the fact that a correspondent of the Evening Wisconsin of Milwaukee in speaking of a rumored foundation of a bank in 1850 condemned "the idea as a wild cat absurdity." The absurdity of the idea, however, soon wore off and within a few years there were several small depositaries, among the first being that of N. Wollmer, which grew up gradually out of a notary public and land business. The building was located at the corner of Quay and Eighth streets and the business was continued until the spring of 1858, when it failed. Another institution that met a similar fate at about the same time was that of William Bach. But the loss of these small and primitive offices made the need of other and better banks obvious, a need which was met by the organization of three in the latter part of 1858. The first was the Lake Shore Bank, which opened its doors on December 18th in the building west of the present site of the Manitowoc National. H. C. Adams was president of the institution and G. W. Adams cashier. It started out in a successful manner, with resources estimated in 1859 at $61,618 and after two years it was removed to Two Rivers, but there after a year's existence it failed. At the time of its suspension the amount of its circulation was $22,680 and the value of its security about 66½ per cent. G. W. Adams, the cashier was arrested after the failure on a charge of obtaining money under false pretenses but the prosecution never came to a definite result. The second bank was that of T. C. Shove, who had been a clerk in the Wollmer Bank, and the third was the Bank of Manitowoc, which opened its doors December 22nd with C. C. Barnes as president and J. C. Barnes as cashier, with a capital of $100,000. In 1858 the Manitowoc County Bank was started at Two Rivers, which after some years of existence in that city was removed to Manitowoc in July 1861 where it continued in the place of business of the old Lake Shore Bank. C. Kuehn, formerly state treasurer, was the principal in this enterprise and at one time the bank had a circulation of over $90,000. After a few years, however, it too was obliged to suspend, being able to pay but 45 cents on the dollar. This business reverse led to the premature death of Mr. Kuehn, which occurred at his home, half way between Manitowoc and Two Rivers, on November 2 1865. These early failures were not felt so heavily in the county since depositors were few, most of the pioneers of the day being struggling farmers. Barter was the general substitute for money and the more so since the currency was uncertain.

The Bank of Manitowoc and the Shove Bank, however, weathered the stress of the war period, although the former was twice obliged to get legislative permission to reduce its capital. After the national banking act was passed, the Bank of Manitowoc was reorganized and in 1866 became the First National Bank of Manitowoc. For years these two banks sufficed to fill the financial needs of the whole county and it was not until January 1 1884 that the Manitowoc Savings Bank was opened at the corner of South Eighth and Jay

Streets with a capital stock of $50,000, owned by John Schuette, Henry Schuette, J. Staehle and C. Estabrook. In the same year the Shove Bank was reorganized into the T. C. Shove Banking Company, including several new stockholders and with a capital of $45,000. Seven years passed without an addition in the number of banks, at the end of which time, in 1891, the Bank of Two Rivers was opened to satisfy the growing commercial needs of that city. The original capital was $10,000 and the proprietor was Edward Decker, whose banking interests in Northern Wisconsin were quite extensive.

The next year witnessed the beginnings of a series of disasters which caused misery untold, the echo of which was years in dying away. At 10:45 p. m. of the 11th of April 1892 fire, caused by an explosion, broke out in the plant of the Manitowoc Manufacting Company and in a few hours the leading industry of the city, employing two hundred men, was no more. The loss was $175,000 and the insurance but $60,000. On the following morning the doors of the T. C. Shove Banking Company were closed. It then transpired that the latter concern had been carrying the factory for large amounts, the factory being in reality under the same management as the bank. It was thought at first that the misfortune was not so great as it proved to be and it was hoped that Assignee Piening would be able to pay the depositors, who represented $400,000, at least 80 per cent. But matters soon showed up in a darker hue. The Manitowoc Manufacturing Company made an assignment to W. D. Richards and on April 13th the Wisconsin Central Mills, another company backed by the bank, assigned to J. Staehle for the benefit of creditors. It was then realized that much of the assets of the bank, which were originally reckoned at $500,000, was worthless paper. In the bank was county money to the amount of $51,282.83, deposited by Treasurer Gielow and a part of the city funds, amounting to $10,000. The former sum included $11,573 of the courthouse fund, the balance being a part of the general county funds. The bondsmen of the county treasurer were H. Truman, G. Cooper, Max Rahr, W. Rahr, R. Rahr, T. C. Shove and Mr. Gielow himself.

Many of the other depositors were farmers, since the bank always paid a high rate of interest, and the stringency of money that followed was very noticeable. As the factory of the Manitowoc Manufacturing Company was almost an essential institution to the industrial life of the city, efforts were early made to rebuild it. On April 12th a committee was appointed by the Advancement Association to meet the assignee, consisting of J. W. Barnes, H. Esch, Jr., T. E. Torrison, G. B. Burnett, H. C. Richards, J. Nagle, J. Schuette and D. Boehmer. A meeting was held three days later but no action taken, although workmen were rapidly leaving the city, leading Editor Nagle to remark in that week's edition of the Pilot: "Died, on Friday evening April 15th 1892 of inanity and lack of enterprise the city of Manitowoc." In fact the magnitude of the disaster had seemed to paralyze all efforts. Soon, however, a committee was appointed to raise subscriptions for a new plant and by May $75,000 had been subscribed.

As April wore on, however, the true condition of the bank became evident. The liabilities were made public at $473,084 with assets amounting to $536,805.07, of which $374,207.84 was in paper, much being almost worthless, if not entirely so. Of the assets $224,206 was due from the Manitowoc Manufacturing Company and the condition of that concern was thus the determining factor in the size of the dividends. The inventory of the assignee revealed the fact that there were about $40,000 in liabilities besides the amount owing the bank, while the total assets amounted to only $193,000, including $60,000 insurance money, for which the assignees of both the bank and company receipted, there being much question as to its application. The liabilities of the Wisconsin Central Mills consisted of $75,000 in loans from the bank, $16,000 in mortgages and $3000 in accounts, the only assets being the mill property and some accounts. With these conditions revealed feeling grew high and on May 10th the creditors met at the Turner Hall, electing E. K. Rand president and H. L. Markham secretary. Upon legal advice a committee was appointed, consisting of Dr. R. S. O'Connell,

H. Stolze and H. Baeruth, who looked over the books and on May 20th a second meeting was called, two hundred depositors being present. Another committee was appointed, consisting of Emil Baensch, S. A. Wood, T. E. Torrison, H. Vits and C. Hanson, who hired an expert accountant to examine the books. In the meantime the assignee had made as advantageous settlements as he could with the other heavy debtors of the bank. The expert's report submitted in July revealed the fact that only $35,000 of the $50,000 capital had ever been paid in, that no stockholders' meeting had been held and that other irregularities were present. The arrests of the officers of the bank followed later in July and after many trials the president of the concern was found guilty, the supreme court refusing to reverse the decision. In the meantime dividends were paid in installments of 10, 15 and 4½ per cent, a total of 29½ per cent. Much collateral litigation grew out of the failure. The county sued the bondsmen of the county treasurer for the loss it sustained, being represented by Attorneys Schmitz and Kirwan of Manitowoc and Gen. Winckler of Milwaukee, while Nash and Nash of Manitowoc and Gabriel Bouck of Oshkosh appeared for the defendants. The suit had been begun only after much consideration at the spring meeting in 1892 and was conducted on the part of the county by a committee consisting of Supervisors Gleeson, Niquette, Danforth, Rand and Burt. The county was greatly pressed for funds during this year on account of the failure. It won the suit in both the circuit and supreme courts but finally the bondsmen asked for a compromise. This was granted, with only two negative votes, by the county board and the county received $12,000 or about one third of the net loss. By April 1896 Assignee Richards of the Manitowoc Manufacturing Company announced a final settlement of the affairs of that concern, the dividend being about 5½ per cent, the insurance having been transferred final'y to the bank. A final settlement of the Shove affairs was made in the summer of 1900 and Assignee Piening was discharged from duty.

On December 26 1891 the First National Bank of Manitowoc liquidated and the State Bank of Manitowoc was formed by the stockholders, a fine new brick structure being erected on the corner of North Eighth and York streets. Increased business followed and everything bore the outward semblance of prosperity until the spring of 1893. As early as May 18th a run began and on the morning of June 6th the following notice was posted on the bank doors: "Owing to a run on the bank, which has continued for three weeks, its officers have concluded to make an assignment for the benefit of all the creditors. This has accordingly been done and the president of the bank, C. C. Barnes, has turned over his private means and property, including his homestead to be used for the same purpose. J. W. Barnes, Assignee."

The day before the suspension $60,000 had been withdrawn from deposit and in the preceding week a total of $110,000. It developed that the bank had not the capital it had been supposed to have possessed and that it had lost heavily in lumber deals. The result of this failure was a run upon the other two banks in the county, which the Manitowoc Savings Bank easily averted by a display of its magnificent backing and to which the Bank of Two Rivers temporarily succumbed, making an assignment to J. E. Hamilton. Business was greatly hampered by this condition of affairs and as summer progressed industry became well nigh dead. The assignee of the State Bank made a report on June 29th, which showed the assets to be $237,254, of which about $100,000 was in worthless paper, while the liabilities were $157,755.25. Ten days earlier the bank of Two Rivers had re-opened for business and it was soon seen that its suspension had been more a measure of caution than of necessity. In July at the suit of certain depositors both the president and cashier of the defunct institution were arrested but the death of both, occurring soon after, put an end to the legal proceedings. Assignee Barnes settled up the affairs of the bank with great dispatch and by May 1894, a final settlement was made, the creditors accepting 62 per cent.

The banking necessities of the city, crippled by these two failures, opened the way to a new institution, which

SCENE NEAR RAPIDS

started business in the building formerly occupied by the State Bank on May 7 1894. It was known as the State Bank of Manitowoc and was incorporated with a capital of $50,000. On August 30th it was reorganized as the National Bank of Manitowoc with L. D. Moses as president and Clarence Hill as cashier and a capital increased to $100,000, the directors being all, with the exception of L. J. Nash, outside men. Cashier Hill was succeeded by G. J. Moses in 1899, who in turn gave way to F. T. Zentner a year later. Another bank was added March 6 1901 by the opening of the German-American on the corner of Jay and Ninth Streets, a new brick and stone building 30 by 80 feet being erected for its occupancy. It was incorporated with a capital of $100,000; L. D. Moses was chosen president, and F. T. Zentner cashier. The opening of the twentieth century also witnessed the establishment of a new banking institution in the village of Kiel under the name of the State Bank of Kiel with C. Heins as president and R. Kiel as cashier. Two Rivers was chosen as the location of a second bank when on January 1 1902 the Savings Bank with a capital of $25,000 opened its doors.

## CHAPTER XVII.

## BUSINESS AND INDUSTRY.

The growth of a community in commercial and manufacturing interests is always difficult to describe since it is well nigh impossible to balance properly the weight which different factors have had in the shaping of industrial forces. To the agricultural growth reference has been made and, of course, this was a most important element in making the county a center of export. Of the development of transportation facilities by both land and water sufficient has also been said. There remains, however, to be given a brief outline of the progress of the manufacturing and business industries of the county.

One of the earliest industries to be started was that of the brewing of beer, in which Wisconsin as a whole, even before the Civil War, had taken a leading place. In 1848 there were established the Rahr brewery at Manitowoc and the Mueller brewery at Two Rivers. The former burned to the ground some years later but was rebuilt and has since been enlarged year by year until it ranks among the largest in the state. In the next succeeding years the Pautz brewery, the predecessor of the present Schreihart Brewing Company was also established on a firm footing. Other breweries were started by Kunz & Bleser, C. Fricke and F. Willinger in

Manitowoc, J. Lindstedt at Mishicot, G. Kunz at Branch, Gutheil Bros. at Kiel, A. Chloupek in Kossuth, M. Schmidt in Rapids and C. Scheibe at Centerville. Of these only the Kunz & Bleser brewery and the Gutheil brewery at Kiel are still in existence. In 1900 a new industry along this line was started in the erection of a malting plant and elevator by the Manitowoc Malting Company, of which ex-Mayor William Rahr is the president.

Of the beginnings of the Two Rivers factory system mention has been made. It has achieved a world wide reputation as regards the sale of its woodenware and type. The Two Rivers Manufacturing Company was organized by H. H. Smith in 1860, although the manufacture of tubs and pails had been commenced by him previously, when in 1851 he and W. H. Honey had built a factory. Later Messrs. Smith and H. C. Hamilton worked up the industry to a most successful point and they were later joined by the Mann brothers, Joseph, Henry and Leopold, who in later years acquired the sole interest in the plant. Additions were frequently made and the factory now employs a small army of men. The business of wood type manufacture was started by J. E. and Henry Hamilton in 1881 and has since grown to extensive proportions. Although the lumber industry has largely disappeared from the eastern section of Wisconsin planing mills are still numerous in the county and in 1886 a beginning was made along these lines that meant much for the future. In that year the mill of Hubbard and Noble, devoted to the manufacture of staves, hubs and similar articles, was started in Manitowoc and in two years the concern was bought out by the Manitowoc Manufacturing Company, of which F. Haley became the manager, local capital being interested to a large extent, the object being the manufacture of school seats and furniture. This concern soon established an enormous business, considering its small means and employed several hundred skilled laborers under Managers Haley and Smith but the destructive fire before mentioned led to its insolvency and dissolution. Another extensive plant was erected a year later by private subscription, which after existing for a number of years as an independent corporation, was finally absorbed into the American School Furniture Company. Other plants of a similar nature in the county are the Eggers Veneer Company of Two Rivers, the Kiel Woodenware Company, the Manitowoc Building & Supply Co., the Western Toy Co., and the Noble Mfg. Co., of Reedsville.

Woolen mills were established in the sixties by P. Pierce at the Rapids and by J. Vilas & Company at Manitowoc but the water power was not sufficient or steady enough to make the venture a success. In 1881 a similar institution was opened by Denway & Pautz at Manitowoc but it was destroyed by fire after a short operation. The Two Rivers Knitting Company organized in 1901 is a more recent attempt at the manufacture of articles in clothing. Tanning has always been an important industry in the county as well. The Wisconsin Leather Company, organized by C. Whitcomb and R. W. Allen, Milwaukee capitalists, was the pioneer along this line and erected a plant near Two Rivers in 1851, maintaining it for many years and at Two Creeks G. Pfister & Co., also of Milwaukee, early established itself. In Manitowoc the Sherman Leather Co., started in business in 1854, the Schultz tannery seven and the Vits tannery ten years later, while the Dobbert plant was built in 1865. Other concerns have since been opened but a majority of them have discont nued. A new industry was started at Manitowoc in 1902, that of the manufacture of mattresses, the Manitowoc Mattress Co. being the name of the corporation. Glue is also an important product of the city, the Manitowoc Glue Co. being the founder of the industry. The Stolz Mfg. Co. and H. Drost Paper Box Co. help to make the city known by their products, tinsel and paper goods. Cigar manufacture, too, is an important industry.

The iron industry in its various forms has also engaged a considerable part of local capital. Among the earliest foundries to be established was that of E. J. Smalley, later known as the Smalley Manufacturing Company, started in 1857. It was burned out in 1875 but reorganized eight years later and commenced the manufacture of feed cutters and agricultural implements on a large scale. The Dumke foundry was opened in 1861 while the Richards Iron Works owes its origin to a small shop started by Jonah Richards soon after, and it in turn was closely followed by the establishment of a shop by Prochazka & Chloupek. The Manitowoc Boiler Works was started by William Hess and F. Vader in the latter eighties and has since been conducted and enlarged by the former, the labor employed being entirely of the skilled variety. The manufacture of axes was also commenced by Martin & Willott in 1872, since which time it has grown steadily, now being controlled by Joseph and William Willott. Along the line of metallic products must also be mentioned those made of aluminum. Two factories, the Two Rivers Aluminum Co. and the Manitowoc Aluminum Novelty Co. are devoted to this industry. In the early nineties the manufacture of pearl buttons was an important industry in Manitowoc, there being at that time several factories but changes in the tariff made it no longer profitable to engage in it. The manufacture of bricks was introduced into the county by F. Ostenfeldt, then of Calumet County, in 1876 and since that time some half dozen companies have started in the business, notable among them the plants owned by the Manitowoc Clay Co.

Manitowoc County has also taken an important place in the manufacture of food products. For many years its flour mills were famous. Among the first to commence an extensive business was the Oriental Mills, established by John Schuette and A. Wahle at Manitowoc in 1869. The Wisconsin Central Mills were built by A. Wahle and L. Haupt soon after and came into the possession of Jacob Fliegler, being discontinued after the panic in 1892. In the same year the Manitowoc Mills owned by Truman and Cooper and established in 1874 were discontinued. Other institutions of this kind were the Wehausen Mills at Two Rivers, built in 1878, the Klingholz Mills at Rapids and several smaller ones in various parts of the county. In 1875 residents of Manitowoc formed the Citizens' Wheat Buying Association and subscribed $12,000 for the building of an elevator at the foot of South Seventh street. The structure was later leased and then sold to private parties. In 1870 A. M. Richter commenced the manufacture of vinegar, which has since been a most important product of local export. But chief among food products originating in Manitowoc are canned vegetables and particularly peas. The establishment of this industry was due to Albert Landreth, an energetic seedsman, who in 1883 built a warehouse in Manitowoc. After many years spent in dealing in seed peas he conceived the idea of canning the sweet varieties of that vegetable for the market and built a factory for that purpose which commenced operation in 1890. His brands became famous and the industry soon grew to enormous proportions. Several companies have been formed to prosecute the business, among them the Manitowoc Pea Packing Co. in 1898, the East Wisconsin Canning Co. in Manitowoc two years later, the E. J. Vaudreuil Canning Co. of Two Rivers and the St. Nazianz and Centerville Canning Cos. Some of these have placed in the market other varieties of canned vegetables and the soil of the county has proved very adaptable to their growth. In 1900 the Manitowoc Pickling Company started operations and a year later the H. Johannes Co. of Two Rivers was organized for similar purposes. A large seed business has also been built up by the Madsen Seed Co., and the Manitowoc Seed Co.

In its mercantile life Manitowoc County has been well represented by men of integrity and business acumen and its retail and wholesale establishments are a credit to them. Two of the former, O. Torrison Co. and Schuette Bros., have had a phenomenal growth of over fifty years. As a jobbing point it is represented by Plumb & Nelson Co., wholesale grocers, the Rand & Roemer Hardware Co. and the T. Schmidtmann Sons Co.

## APPENDIX A.
## AGRICULTURAL STATISTICS OF MANITOWOC COUNTY.

| | 1840 | 1850 | 1860 | 1870 | 1880 | 1890 | 1900 |
|---|---|---|---|---|---|---|---|
| Improved Acreage | | 1,122 | 26,177 | 131,292 | 200,477 | 235,060 | 249,691 |
| Wheat | 225 bu | 3,214 | 42,232 | 517,146 | 803,258 | 582,780 | 484,460 |
| Rye | | 191 | 32,649 | 92,881 | 87,869 | 230,679 | 289,451 |
| Oats | 1,750 bu | 5,253 | 61,375 | 386,759 | 700,664 | 1,052,991 | 1,597,780 |
| Corn | 175 bu | 287 | 2,420 | 2,865 | 21,433 | 32,401 | 89,250 |
| Barley | | 96 | 4,796 | 30,176 | 119,536 | 276,331 | 619,490 |
| Buckwheat | | | 226 | 410 | 505 | 1,641 | 570 |
| Potatoes | 1,900 bu | 7,297 | 45,551 | 108,180 | 181,647 | 233,555 | 275,351 |
| Peas and Beans | | 85 | 5,608 | 80,410 | 124,012 | 213,239 | 218,605 |
| Hay | 67 tons | 460 | 3,416 | 26,937 | 23,058 | 70,059 | 64,841 |
| Wool | | | 1,308 lbs | 44,421 | 84,391 | 61,893 | 80,440 |
| Honey | | 2,853 | 489 | 1,421 | 10,073 | 50,022 | 36,740 |
| Butter (on farms) | | 8,000(x) | 136,457 | 575,319 | 772,647 | 818,216 | 706,907 |
| Maple Syrup | 2,900 | 80 | 67,394 | 9,864 | 2,030 | 148 | |
| Horses | 11 | 22 | 558 | 4,460 | 9,328 | 11,187 | 13,531 |
| Milch Cows | 81 | 1,877 | 1,198 | 9,351 | 14,505 | 25,816 | 27,656 |
| Sheep | | | 693 | 16,403 | 15,486 | 10,309 | 17,553 |
| Swine | 90 | 187 | 2,366 | 11,200 | 12,576 | 15,611 | 16,491 |

(x) Includes butter.

## APPENDIX B.

## MARINE STATISTICS.

### CLEARANCES AND TONNAGE.

| Year | Clearonces | | Tonnage | |
|---|---|---|---|---|
| | Manitowoc | Two Rivers | Manitowoc | Two Rivers |
| 1901 | 2112 | | 2,069,720 | |
| 1900 | 2089 | | 1,724,000 | |
| 1899 | 1990 | 1560 | 1,671,523 | 436,384 |
| 98 | 1943 | 1566 | 1,592,727 | 336,190 |
| 97 | 1643 | 1644 | 2,083,799 | 255,713 |
| 96 | 1101 | 814 | 609,811 | 239,400 |
| 95 | 740 | 959 | 466,260 | 202,405 |
| 94 | 965 | 2104 | 482,010 | 316,420 |
| 93 | 886 | 1937 | 415,594 | 80,155 |
| 92 | 1174 | 794 | 600,596 | 93,275 |
| 91 | 1040 | 316 | 546,136 | 43,928 |
| 90 | 998 | | 416,317 | 24,628 |
| 89 | 652 | 447 | 225,637 | 41,350 |
| 88 | 614 | 419 | 205,551 | 29,540 |
| 87 | 678 | | 211,853 | |
| 86 | 573 | 280 | 177,625 | 22,960 |
| 85 | 670 | 307 | 202,595 | 23,450 |
| 84 | 953 | 392 | 285,696 | 26,236 |
| 83 | 1030 | 421 | 305,984 | 27,600 |
| 82 | 1191 | 320 | 418,081 | 16,060 |
| 81 | 793 | 258 | 269,907 | 12,280 |
| 80 | 829 | 130 | 288,857 | 7,500 |
| 79 | 886 | 410 | 301,665 | 124,000 |

| | | | | |
|---|---|---|---|---|
| 78 | 872 | 375 | 323,997 | 137,000 |
| 77 | 587 | 400 | 157,876 | 150,000 |
| 76 | 863 | 390 | 300,047 | 159,000 |
| 74 | 994 | 490 | | |
| 73 | 1235 | 539 | | |
| 72 | 1289 | 326 | | |
| 71 | 1117 | 302 | | |
| 69 | 994 | | | |
| 66 | 689 | | 151,900 | |
| 59 | 1071 | | | |
| 55 | 815 | 115 | | |
| 51 | 399 | | | |
| 50 | 146 | | | |
| 49 | 145 | | | |

## CRAFT BUILT AT MANITOWOC.

| Year | Craft | Tonnage | Builder |
|---|---|---|---|
| 1847 | Schr Citizen | 60 | Joseph Edwards |
| 52 | Challenge | 68 | Bates & Son |
|  | Defiance | 110 | W. Ham |
|  | Convoy | 64 | Joseph Edwards |
| 53 | Mary Stockton | 275 | Bates & Son |
|  | Platt | 25 | Joseph Hughes |
|  | North Yuba | 140 | Bates & Son |
|  | Lomira | 120 | C. Sorenson |
|  | Willlam Jones | 154 | Joseph Harbridge |
|  | Blackhawk | 110 | Bates & Son |
|  | Gesine | 99 | H. Rand |
|  | Col. Glover | 123 | Bates & Son |
| 54 | Transit | 121 | H. Rand |
|  | Toledo | 100 | C. Sorenson |
|  | Clipper City | 126 | Bates & Son |
|  | North Star | 175 | C. Sorenson |
|  | E. M. Shoyer | 120 | C. Sorenson |
| 55 | Anna Thorine | 89 | C. Sorenson |
| 56 | Guido | 116 | C. Sorenson |
|  | Belle | 118 | Bates & Son |
|  | S. Bates | 139 | Bates & Son |
| 57 | Trial | 36 | H. Rand |
|  | El Tempo | 213 | S. Goodwin |
|  | A. Baensch | 75 | G. S. Rand |
|  | H Rand | 130 | G. S. Rand |
| 60 | Two Charlies | 110 | R. L. Bell |
| 63 | Chicago Board of Trade | 422 | R. L. Bell |
|  | Sea Gem | 103 | S. Bates |
| 64 | Nabob (Waukesha) | 310 | G. S. Rand |
| 66 | S. A. Wood | 314 | H. Burger |
| 67 | Fleetwing | 344 | H. Burger |
|  | A. Richards | 285 | J. Richards |
| 68 | J. Phillips | 147 | E. W. Packard |
| 69 | L. McDonald (Lily E) | 210 | J. Hanson |
|  | C. L. Johnston | 199 | E. W. Packard |
| 70 | J. A. Stornach | 143 | J. Hanson |
|  | J. B. Newland | 173 | C. Henderson |
|  | Industry | 55 | P. Larson |
|  | Eva | 15 | W. McCullom |
|  | H. E. McAllister | 237 | J. Hanson |

| | | | |
|---|---|---|---|
| 71 | K. L. Bruce | 34 | Hanson & Scove |
| | Espindola | 54 | P. Larson |
| | G. Knapp | 186 | P. Larson |
| | W. Keller | 263 | J. Hanson |
| | L. Meeker | 312 | Hanson & Scove |
| | C. Neilson | 315 | Hanson & Scove |
| 72 | Willis | 260 | P. Larson |
| | C. B. Windiate | 332 | J. Butler |
| | M. A. Muir | 347 | Hanson & Scove |
| | Minnehaha | 60 | M. Ornes |
| | T. H. Howland | 299 | Hanson & Scove |
| | M. L. Higgie | 310 | Hanson & Scove |
| | City of Manitowoc | 310 | J. Richards |
| 73 | C. C. Barnes | 582 | H. Burger |
| | Blazing Star | 279 | J. Richards |
| | L J. Conway | 90 | Larson & Son |
| | Felicitous | 199 | P. Larson |
| | Woodstock (R. Kanters) | 164 | P. Larson |
| | Falmouth | 234 | Hanson & Scove |
| | Hunting Boy. | 55 | Captain Christianson |
| | Lydia | 83 | Rand & Burger |
| | C Luling | 233 | P. Larson |
| | George Murray | 790 | G. S. Rand |
| | Mystic Star | 339 | J. Butler |
| | G. Pfister | 694 | J. Hanson |
| | H. C. Richards | 700 | H. Burger |
| | H. M. Scove | 305 | Hanson & Scove |
| | Thistle | 363 | Rand & Burger |
| | G C. Trumphoff | 347 | J. Butler |
| 74 | J. I. Case | 828 | Rand & Burger |
| | J. Duvall | 132 | Rand & Burger |
| | Julia Larson | 59 | P. Larson |
| | Merchant | 66 | P. Larson |
| | Mocking Bird | 159 | J. Richards |
| | Rap | 8 | J. Hanson |
| | Ramadary | 22 | Capt. Worden |
| | David Vance | 774 | J. Butler |
| 75 | H. B. Burger | 214 | Rand & Burger |
| | J. V. Jones | 236 | Rand & Burger |
| | L. A Simpson | 227 | Rand & Burger |
| | Success | 161 | Capt. Jorgenson |
| 76 | Lottie Cooper | 265 | Rand & Burger |
| | Rover | 23 | W. Dow |
| | Tennie and Laura | 57 | Captain Jorgenson |

| | | | |
|---|---|---|---|
| 77............ | H. Esch | 42 | J. Butler |
| ............ | B. Jones | 45 | Capt. Knudson |
| 80............ | Penobscot | 260 | Rand & Burger |
| ............ | May Richards | 511 | Rand & Burger |
| 81............ | Isolda Bock | 70 | Capt. Jorgenson |
| ............ | Melitta | 83 | Hanson & Rand |
| ............ | E. B. Maxwell | 360 | Rand & Burger |
| ............ | Olga | 308 | Rand & Burger |
| ............ | T. L. Parker | 628 | Rand & Burger |
| ............ | Tallahassee | 760 | P. Larson |
| ............ | Lalla Rookh | 60 | P. Larson |
| 82............ | Alice | 307 | Rand & Burger |
| ............ | Burt Barnes | 134 | Rand & Burger |
| ............ | W. A. Goodman | 324 | Rand & Burger |
| ............ | J. L. McClaren | 286 | Rand & Burger |
| ............ | Mishicott | 73 | Rand & Burger |
| 83............ | Emm L. Nielson | 90 | Rand & Burger |
| 84............ | G. J. Boyce | 319 | Rand & Burger |
| ............ | Linerla | 77 | Rand & Burger |
| 85............ | James H. Hall | 100 | Rand & Burger |
| 88 ........... | Lizzie Metzner | 77 | Rand & Burger |
| ............ | W. C. Kimball | 33 | Rand & Burger |
| 89............ | Cora | 381 | Burger & Burger |
| 90............ | S. O. Neff | 346 | Burger & Burger |
| ............ | Actor | 30 | Roeber Bros. |
| 92............ | Myrtle Camp | 49 | Burger & Burger |
| 1861............ | Strs. Sunbeam | 450 | W. Bates |
| ............ | Union | 434 | W. Bates & Son |
| 66 ........... | Northwest (Greyhound) | 621 | G. S. Rand |
| ............ | Orion | 600 | G. S. Rand |
| 68............ | Manitowoc | 569 | G. S. Rand |
| 69............ | Sheboygan | 624 | G. S Rand |
| ............ | Corona | 470 | G. S Rand |
| 70............ | Norman | 996 | G. S. Rand |
| 71............ | Muskegon | 618 | G. S. Rand |
| 72............ | Oconto | 505 | G. S. Rand |
| ............ | Menominee (Iowa) | 796 | G. S. Rand |
| 73............ | De Pere (Michigan) | 736 | Rand & Burger |
| 74............ | Chicago | 747 | Rand & Burger |
| 79............ | Imperial | 68 | Rand & Burger |
| 80... ....... | Ludington (Georgia) | 842 | Rand & Burger |
| 81............ | Rube Richards | 815 | Rand & Burger |
| ............ | Thomas H. Smith | 281 | Rand & Burger |
| 82............ | J. C. Perrett (Ames) | 537 | Rand & Burger |
| ............ | R. A. Seymour, Jr. | 131 | Rand & Burger |

| | | | |
|---|---|---|---|
| 86............... | Marinette | 61 | Burger & Burger |
| 87............... | E. M. Tice | 728 | Burger & Burger |
| ............... | A. D. Hayward | 304 | Burger & Burger |
| ............... | Rand | 191 | Burger & Burger |
| ............... | Francis Hinton | 417 | Burger & Burger |
| 88............... | Mark B. Covell | 261 | Burger & Burger |
| ............... | Petoskey | 735 | Burger & Burger |
| ............... | Fannie Hart | 476 | Burger & Burger |
| 89............... | City of Racine | 1041 | Burger & Burger |
| ............... | J. E. Hall | 343 | Burger & Burger |
| ............... | Isabella J. Boyce | 368 | Burger & Burger |
| 90............... | Indiana | 1177 | Burger & Burger |
| ............... | City of Marquette | 341 | Burger & Burger |
| ............... | Eugéne Hart | 407 | Burger & Burger |
| 91............... | Edwin Buckley | 414 | Burger & Burger |
| 94............... | Sydney O. Neff | 435 | Burger & Bur er |
| ............... | Lotus | 219 | Burger & Burger |
| 1903............... | Chequamegon | | |
| 1879............... | Barges I. Stephenson | 461 | Rand & Burger |
| 80............... | S. M. Stephenson | 511 | Rand & Burger |
| ............... | Henry Whitbeck | 498 | Rand & Burger |
| 81............... | A. A. Carpenter | 540 | Rand & Burger |

### TUGS.

| Year | Name | Tonnage | Year | Name | Tonnage |
|---|---|---|---|---|---|
| 1868 | ..Kittie Smoke............75 | | 1892 | ....Alice E. Shipman.......40 | |
| 73 | ..W. Richards............19 | | | ....Fearless ...............28 | |
| 75 | ..Frank Canfield..........48 | | | ...S. A. Dixon............29 | |
| 77 | ..Minnie...................40 | | 93 | ....Julia C. Hammel.......28 | |
| | ..I. L. Wheeler............51 | | | ....R. M Cooper..........27 | |
| 80 | ..M. A. Knapp............18 | | 95 | ....Sidney T. Smith........71 | |
| 81 | ..Arctic...................52 | | 97 | ....Sedonie ...............14 | |
| 82 | ..George Pankratz........63 | | 98 | ... C. W. Endress..........73 | |
| 83 | ..C. M. Charnley..........83 | | | ....Bradwell..............44 | |
| | ..Duncan City..............79 | | | ....Alphard................32 | |
| 84 | ..G. Williams..............46 | | 1899 | ....Two Myrtles. ........96 | |
| 87. | Wau Bun.................63 | | | ....R. E. Burke............73 | |
| 90 | ..H. Ludington........... 47 | | 1900 | ....Angler............... .14 | |
| 91 | ..George Cooper............53 | | | ....J. B. Bradwell..........62 | |
| | ..I. M. Leatham (Raber)....50 | | | ....J. F. May..............62 | |
| 92 | ..Anne Belle..............48 | | | | |

# APPENDIX C.

## COUNTY OFFICERS OF MANITOWOC.

### COUNTY JUDGES.

1848 1849, H W. Colby, Dem.
1850 1852, Ezekiel Ricker, Dem.
1853 1854, George Reed, Dem.
1855 1856, George C. Lee. Dem.
1856 1857, Isaac Parish, Rep.
1858 1861, Charles H. Walker, Dem.
1862 1864, H. S. Pierpont, Dem.
1864 1869, George Barker, Dem
1870 1873, W. W. Waldo, Dem.

1874 1877, Ten Eyck G. Olmstead, Dem.
1878 1881, Michael Kirwan. Dem.
1882 1885, R. D Smart, Rep
1886 1888, C. H. Schmidt, Dem.
1888 1893, Emil Baensch, Rep
1894 1895, Frank Manseau, Dem.
1895 1901, J. S Anderson, Rep.
1902      John Chloupek, Dem.

### SHERIFFS.

1848      Oliver C. Hubbard, Whig
1848 1850, George W. Durgin, Dem.
1851 1852, W F. Snyder, Ind.
1853 1854, D. H Van Valkenburgh, Dem.
1855 1856, F. W. Adams, Rep.
1857 1858, T. A. H. Edwards, Dem.
1859 1860, Louis Kemper, Dem.
1861 1862, Wyman Murphy, Rep.
1862      R. T. Blake, Rep.
1863 1864 Ira P. Smith, Dem.
1895 1866, George S. Glover, Dem.
1867 1868, Robert T. Blake, Rep.
1869 1870, Peter Mulholland, Dem.
1871 1872, Albert Wittenberg, Dem.
1873 1874, R. D. Smart, Rep.

1875 1876, Albert Wittenberg, Dem.
1877 1878, Peter Mulholland, Dem.
1879 1880, P. J. Pierce. Dem.
1881 1882, M. H. Murphy, Dem
1883 1884, John Bibinger, Rep.
1885 1886, M. H. Murphy, Dem.
1887 1888, John Bolen, Dem.
1889 1890, Frank Zeman, Dem.
1891 1892, John Bolen, Dem.
1893 1894, William Stephani, Dem.
1895 1896, Henry Schmidt, Rep.
1897 1898, Chris Muth, Rep.
1899 1900, Henry Lehrmann, Dem.
1901 1902, Pierre Burt, Rep.
1903 1904, Walter C. Pellett, Dem.

## TREASURERS.

| | |
|---|---|
| 1839 Peter Johnston | 1865 1866, P. J. Blesch, Dem. |
| 1840 1844, O. C. Hubbard | 1867 1869, Henry Baetz, Rep. |
| 1845 Evander M. Soper | 1869 1870, J. C. Eggers, Dem. |
| 1846 1849, Pliny Pierce, Whig | 1871 1876, Quirin Ewen, Rep. |
| 1850 1851, Adam Bleser, Dem. | 1876 1886, G. Damler, Dem. |
| 1852 S. W. Smith, Rep. | 1887 1894, C. A Gielow, Dem. |
| 1853 1854, William Bach, Dem. | 1895 1896, Henry Goedjen, |
| 1855 1856, Gerald Kremmers, Rep. | 1897 1900, Peter Kaufmann, Rep. |
| 1857 1860, C. A. Reuter, Dem. | 1901 Charles Hacker, Rep. |
| 1861 1864, Oscar Koch, Rep. | |

## REGISTERS OF DEEDS.

| | |
|---|---|
| 1839 Jacob W. Conroe | 1859 1862, Henry Baetz, Rep. |
| 1840 1841, Thomas W. Baker | 1863 1866, J. C. Eggers, Dem. |
| 1842 1843, Pliny Pierce | 1867 1876, John Franz, Dem. |
| 1844 Liberty Clough | 1877 1879, John Proell, Dem. |
| 1845 Paul M Champlin | 1879 1881, August Brasch, Dem. |
| 1846 Charles H. Champlin | 1881 . A. D. Jones, Rep. |
| 1847 1848, John P. Champlin | 1882 1888, F. P. Mueller, Dem. |
| 1849 1850, A. W. Preston, Whig | 1889 1892, Theodore Wolf, Dem. |
| 1851 1854, Frederick Salomon, Whig | 1893 1898, Julius Lindstedt, Dem. |
| 1855 1858, Albert N. Baker, Dem. | 1899 Bruno Mueller, Dem. |

## COUNTY CLERKS.

| | |
|---|---|
| 1839 1841, J. W. Conroe | 1865 1868, William Bach, Dem. |
| 1841 1844, Pliny Pierce | 1868 1871, P. P. Fuessenich, Rep. |
| 1845 1846, Charles H. Champlin | 1871 H. S. Pierpont, Dem. |
| 1847 1848, J. P. Champlin | 1871 1872, G. W. Burnet, Rep. |
| 1848 Charles Musson | 1873 1874, A. M. Richter, Rep. |
| 1849 1850, E H. Ellis, Dem. | 1875 1880, J. P. Wickert, Dem. |
| 1851 H. C. Hamilton, Dem. | 1881 1888, H. C. Buhse, Dem. |
| :852 Frederick Borcherdt, Rep | 1889 1894, Louis Senglaub, Dem. |
| 1853 1854, C. A. Reuter, Dem. | 1895 1896, Joseph Weinfurther, Dem |
| 1855 1856, Carl Roeser, Rep. | 1897 1898, Edward Schaffland, Rep. |
| 1857 1860, G. W. Burnet, Dem. | 1899 1900, Arthur Zander, Dem. |
| 1861 1962, J. W. Thombs, Dem. | 1901 Edward Schaffland, Rep. |
| 1863 1864, A. Wittmann, Dem. | |

HARBOR VIEW IN 1900.

MANITOWOC RIVER ABOVE BEND 1903

## CLERKS OF COURT.

1848 1849, Ezekiel Ricker, Dem.
1850      C. A. Reuter, Dem.
1850 1851, P. P. Smith, Whig
1852      F. Ulrich, Dem.
1853      Fred Borcherdt, Dem.
1854 1857, C. A. Reuter, Dem.
1857 1861, T. G. Olmstead, Dem.
1861 1863, Jere Crowley, Dem.
1864 1865, Joseph Francl, Dem.

1866 1867, P. J. Pierce, Dem.
1868 1869, Joseph Francl, Dem.
1870 1877, Adolph Piening, Dem.
1878 1886, Hubert Falge, Dem.
1887 1892, John Chloupek, Dem.
1893 1896, James P. Nolan, Dem
1897 1898, Gulic Hougen, Rep
1899      P. J McMahon, Dem.

## DISTRICT ATTORNEYS.

1849 1850, E. H. Ellis, Dem.
1851 1853, J. H. W. Colby, Dem.
1853 1854, James L. Kyle, Whig.
1854      N. Wollmer, Dem.
1855 1856, W. H. Hamilton, Rep.
1857 1859, George L. Lee, Dem.
1859 1862, J D. Markham, Rep.
1863 1864, W. M. Nichols, Dem.
1865 1868, George N. Woodin, Dem.
1869 1872, E. B. Treat, Dem.

1873 1874, William J. Turner, Dem.
1875 1876, Henry Sibree, Dem.
1877 1880, A. J. Schmitz, Dem.
1881 1886, William H. Walker, Dem.
1887 1892, A. J. Schmitz, Dem.
1893 1896, John Chloupek, Dem.
1897 1898, A. P. Schenian, Rep,
1899 1900, E. L. Schmitz, Dem.
1901      A. L. Hougen, Rep,

## SURVEYORS.

1841      David Giddings.
1844 1845, E. D. Beardsley, Dem.
1846 1848,, Pliny Pierce, Whig.
1849 1850, E. D. Beardsley, Dem.
1851      H. L. Allen, Dem.
1852 1856, Fayette Armsby, Rep.
1857 1858, C. Palmer, Dem.
1859 1860, P. Brennan, Dem.
1861 1862, Charles Wimpf, Rep.
1863 1864, P. Brennan, Dem.
1865 1868, J. B. Burke, Dem.

1868      P. Brennan, Dem.
1869 1872, Fayette Armsby, Rep.
1873 1874, John O'Hara, Dem.
1875 1876, C. Tiedemann, Dem.
1877 1882, John O'Hara, Dem.
1883 1884, C. Ertz, Rep.
1885 1896, John O'Hara, Dem.
1897 1898, Louis Pitz, Rep.
1899 1900 John O'Hara, Dem.
1901      Louis Pitz, Rep.

## CORONERS.

1848      O. C. Hubbard, Whig
1849 1850, Joseph Edwards, Dem
1851      C. W. Durgin, Dem
1852 1854, Lyman Emerson, Dem
1855 1856, Stephen Bates, Rep
1857 1858, Hansou Rand, Dem
1859 1860, Thomas Robinson, Dem
1861 1862, Jacob Halvorsen, Rep
1863 1866, Thomas Robinson, Dem

1867 1868, Franz Simon, Dem
1869 1870, John Oswald, Dem
1871 1874, Franz Simon, Dem
1875 1876, John Oswald, Dem
1877 1882, Franz Simon, Dem
1883 1896, F. S. Luhman, Dem
1897 1898, A. C. Fraser, Rep
1899 1900, F. S. Luhman, Dem
1901      J. E. Meany, Dem

## SCHOOL SUPERINTENDENTS.

1862    B. J. VanValkenburg, D    1880 1881, C. F. Viebahn, Rep
1862 1863, C. S. Canright, Rep    1881 1890, John Nagle, Dem
1863    J. W. Thombs, Dem         1891 1894, Conrad E. Patzer, Dem
1864 1869, Jere Crowley, Dem      1895 1896, A. Dassler, Dem
1870 1875, Michael Kirwan, Dem    1897 1898, E. R Smith, Rep
1876 1879, William A. Walker, Dem 1899     Fred C. Christianson, D

## MUNICIPAL JUDGES.

1895 1901, Isaac Craite, Dem      1901     A. P. Schenian, Rep

## CHAIRMEN COUNTY BOARD.

1839    J. G. Conroe,             1863     Alanson Hickok, Cato,
1840    Ben. Jones & R.M.Eberts   1864 1865, Jason Pellett. Gibson,
1841    R. M. Eberts,             1866 1867, G. Damler, Two Rivers,
1843    Oliver Clawson,           1868     Fred Schmitz, Newton
1844    Joel R. Smith,            1869     Louis Koehne, Mishicott,
1845    Oliver Clawson,           1870     Jacob Grimm, Cato,
1846    Joel R. Smith,            1871     Richard Donovan, Rapids
1847    Oliver Clawson,           1872     H. F. Hubbard. Rapids,
1848    Charles McAllister,       1873 1875, G. Damler, Two Rivers,
1849    J. M. Sprague,            1876     C. H. Walker, Rapids.
        Andrew J. Vieau, Man.     1877     Fred Schmitz, Newton,
1850    S. W. Sherwood, Rapids    1878     Thomas Thornton, Cato,
1851    William Bach, Man.        1879     Thomas Mohr, Kossuth
1852    Peleg Glover, Man.        1880     J. Lindstedt, Mishicott,
1853    John F. Sinns, Man.       1881     John Carey, Meeme,
1854    Peleg Glover, Man.        1882 1883, J. Lindstedt, Mishicott,
1855    Adam Bleser, Rapids       1884 1885, John Carey, Meeme,
1856    W. Aldrich, Two Rivers    1886     Thomas Mohr, Kossuth,
1857    C. W. Fitch, Man.         1887 1889, James P. Nolan, M. Grove
1858    H. C. Hamilton, Two R.    1890 1894, Henry Goedjen, Two R
1859    Alanson Hickok, Cato      1895 1898, Henry Lehrman, T.Creeks
1860 1861, A. C. Pool, Eaton,     1898 1901, W. C. Maertz, M. Grove
1862    Lyman Emerson, Rapids     1901 1903, Henry Lehrman,T.Creeks

## MEMBERS OF COUNTY BOARD.

### CATO.

1858 1859, Alanson Hickok         1885     B. Amunds
1860    Jacob Grimm               1886 1888, John Murphy
1861    W. H. Tucker              1889     B. Amunds
1870 1871, Jacob Grimm (x)        1890 1893, P. J. Conway
1872 1876, B. Amunds              1894 1895, Frank Wilhelm
1877 1878, Thomas Thornton        1896     M. Pankratz
1879 1881, B. Amunds              1897 1898, Riley Olson
1882 1884, John Halloran          1899 1901, L. P. Grimm
    (x) County system 1861-70.    1901     Peter J. Murphy

| | | |
|---|---|---|
| 1850 | Charles Koehler | |
| 1851 | J. Schwarz | |
| 1852 | Charles Ulrich | |
| 1853 1854, | M. Reiff | |
| 1855 | E. Eichoff | |
| 1856 | C. F. Uhlig | |
| 1857 | H. Poppe | |
| 1858 | F. Schulte | |
| 1859 | F. Greiner | |
| 1860 | Henry Poppe | |
| 1861 | Phillip Schneider | |

| | | |
|---|---|---|
| 1858 1859, | J. R. Weber | |
| 1860 1861, | John Touhey | |
| 1870 | Thomas Jaraneck | |
| 1871 1875, | John Touhey | |
| 1876 1877, | A Gauger | |
| 1878 | John Touhey | |
| 1879 | A Gauger | |
| 1880 1883, | John Touhey | |
| 1884 1885, | A. Gauger | |

| | | |
|---|---|---|
| 1852 | George Monroe | |
| 1853 | Ole Oleson | |
| 1854 | A. C. Pool | |
| 1855 | N. R. Johnson | |
| 1856 | S D. Clark | |
| 1857 | A McNulty | |
| 1858 | F. Boucher | |
| 1859 | M. McGuire | |
| 1860 1861, | A. C. Pool | |
| 1870 1872, | Anton Stoll | |
| 1873 | P. O'Shea | |
| 1874 1876. | Fred Swenson | |
| 1877 | J. Roemer | |

| | | |
|---|---|---|
| 1856 1857, | Alanson Hickok | |
| 1858 1859, | William Playfair | |
| 1860 | Michael Driscoll | |
| 1861 | James McIvor | |
| 1870 1872, | Peter Stoker | |
| 1873 1874, | William Playfair | |
| 1875 | Max Boehm | |
| 1876 1877, | M. Keehan | |

CENTERVILLE.

| | | |
|---|---|---|
| 1870 | | A. Mill |
| 1871 | 1873, | J. Mill |
| 1874 | 1877, | D. Schneider |
| 1878 | 1879, | Pe'er Werner |
| 1880 | 1881, | Jacob Kestley |
| 1882 | | J. Mill |
| 1883 | 1887, | Jacob Kestley |
| 1888 | 1891, | Joseph Schneider |
| 1892 | 1894, | Jacob Kestley |
| 1895 | 1901, | Fred Jacobi |
| 1902 | | John Reinemann |

COOPERSTOWN.

| | | |
|---|---|---|
| 1886 | 1887, | William Bruss |
| 1888 | | John Touhey |
| 1889 | | A. Gauger |
| 1890 | 1892, | J. W Wanish |
| 1893 | | Albert Krieser |
| 1895 | | Albert Arens |
| 1897 | 1899, | R. Drews |
| 1900 | | John Wanish |
| 1901 | | Albert Krieser |

EATON.

| | | |
|---|---|---|
| 1878 | | Fred Swenson |
| 1879 | | Fred Schwalbe |
| 1880 | 1882, | Fred Swenson |
| 1883 | 1886, | M. Rauch |
| 1887 | | Fred Swenson |
| 1888 | | Theodore Wolf |
| 1889 | 1891, | Thomas Hoppe |
| 1892 | 1895, | Fred Schwalbe |
| 1896 | 1897, | F. Schad |
| 1898 | 1899,, | J. Johnson |
| 1900 | 1902, | John F. Koeck |
| 1903 | | Fred Schwalbe |

FRANKLIN.

| | | |
|---|---|---|
| 1878 | | Peter Stoker |
| 1879 | 1880, | August Gans |
| 1881 | 1884, | Peter Stoker |
| 1885 | 1892, | P. Cahill |
| 1893 | 1894, | Charles Pinger |
| 1895 | | P. Cahill |
| 1896 | 1900, | J. A. Kellner |
| 1901 | | Charles Pinger |

| | | | | | |
|---|---|---|---|---|---|
| | | | GIBSON | | |
| 1858 | 1860, | Jason Pellett | 1884 | 1885, | Adam Tischer |
| 1861 | | A. J. Westgate | 1886 | | W. Zander |
| 1870 | | Luther Pellett | 1887 | 1888, | John Johnson |
| 1871 | | R. McCollum | 1889 | 1890, | C. Steinbrecher |
| 1872 | | C. Johnson | 1891 | 1892, | Pierre Burt |
| 1876 | | J. Shara | 1-93 | 1894, | William Schmidt |
| 1877 | 1878, | C. Steinbrecher | 1895 | 1900, | August Stueck |
| 1879 | | W Zander | 1901 | | Albert Honey |
| 1880 | 1882, | C. Steinbrecher | 1902 | | A Mathieson |
| 1883 | | W. Zander | | | |
| | | | KOSSUTH | | |
| 1852 | 1855, | William Eatough | 1883 | | P. McCarthy |
| 1856 | | G. W. Burnet | 1884 | 1885, | J. C. McCarthy |
| 1857 | 1859, | John Robinson | 1886 | 1888, | Thomas Mohr |
| 1860 | 1861, | Abraham Andrews | 1889 | 1892, | George Powell |
| 1870 | | Thomas Cross | 1893 | 1894, | Peter Kornely |
| 1871 | 1872, | W. Robinson | 1895 | 1896, | Thomas Mohr |
| 1873 | | Thomas Mohr | 1897 | 1899 | William Spencer |
| 1874 | 1876, | W. Robinson | 1900 | 1901, | Thomas Mohr |
| 1877 | 1879, | Thomas Mohr | 1902 | | W. H. Spencer |
| 1880 | 1882, | John Robinson | | | |
| | | | LIBERTY | | |
| 1858 | | Ole Oleson | 1878 | | James Taugher |
| 1859 | | James Taugher | 1879 | 1881, | K. K. Roble |
| 1860 | | W. Griebling | 1882 | 1885, | F. Hacker |
| 1861 | | Joseph Stephenson | 1886 | 1888, | Dan Tracy |
| 1870 | | J. Taugher | 1889 | 1890, | K. K. Roble |
| 1871 | | P. Mahoney | 1891 | 1894, | C. F. Hacker |
| 1872 | | P. Malloy | 1895 | 1897, | K K. Roble |
| 1873 | 1874, | J. Taugher | 1898 | 1902, | J. Finch |
| 1875 | 1876, | K. K. Roble | 1903 | | John Dunbar |
| 1877 | | M. Taugher | | | |
| | | | MANITOWOC | | |
| 1849 | | Andrew J. Vieau | 1875 | | John Hall |
| 1850 | | G. C. O. Malmros | 1876 | | E. J. Smalley |
| 1851 | | William Bach | 1877 | 1882, | F. Ostenfeldt |
| 1852 | | Peleg Glover | 1883 | 1885, | William G. Lueps |
| 1853 | | J. F. Zinns | 1886 | 1887, | F. Ostenfeldt |
| 1854 | | Peleg Glover | 1888 | 1889, | Jacob Fliegler |
| 1855 | 1856, | James Bennett | 1890 | 1891, | Ole Benson |
| 1857 | | Louis Sherman | 1892 | | John Hall |
| 1858 | | A. W. Preston | 1893 | | Ole Benson |
| 1859 | | C. Esslinger | 1894 | 1896, | Chris Muth |
| 1860 | | J. D Markham | 1897 | 1898, | John Hall |
| 1861 | | C. Esslinger | 1899 | 1901, | Chris Muth |
| 1870 | | W. F. Watrous | 1902 | | Joseph Roemer |
| 1871 | 1872, | E. J. Smalley | 1903 | | Chris Muth |
| 1873 | 1874, | Jacob Fliegler | | | |

## FIRST WARD—CITY

| | | | |
|---|---|---|---|
| 1857 | G. Kremers | 1881 1882, | Henry Greve |
| 1858 | J. F. Guyles | 1883 | John Franz |
| 1859 | Henry Baetz | 1884 | William Rahr |
| 1860 | Fred Schultz | 1885 | Henry Greve |
| 1861 | Henry Baetz | 1886 | Jacob Roemer |
| 1870 | R. Klingholz | 1887 1888, | Fred Schuette |
| 1871 | A. Wallich | 1889 1890, | G. Gelbke |
| 1872 | A. F. Dumke | 1891 | F. Haukohl |
| 1873 | A. Wallich | 1892 | John Staudt |
| 1874 | Fred Schuette | 1893 1894, | Henry Schmidt |
| 1875 | A. Bleser | 1895 1896, | John Mahnke |
| 1876 1877, | C Gelbke | 1897 1898, | John Staudt |
| 1878 1879, | Ernst Wagner | 1899 | F. C. Schultz |
| 1880 | A. Richter | 1900 | C. A. Groffmann |

## SECOND WARD—CITY

| | | | |
|---|---|---|---|
| 1857 | Charles W. Fitch | 1885 | Peter Johnston |
| 1858 1859, | J. D. Markham | 1886 | Thomas Torrison |
| 1860 | J. E Platt | 1887 | Peter Johnston |
| 1861 | S. Goodenow | 1888 | R. D. Smart |
| 1870 | W. W. Waldo | 1889 1892, | Joseph Willott |
| 1871 1872 | Edward Conway | 1893 | Stephen Bertler |
| 1873 | George Cooper | 1894 1898, | Joseph Willott |
| 1874 1876, | Peter Johnston | 1899 | John Chloupek |
| 1877 | C. E. Estabrook | 1900 1902, | William Frazier |
| 1878 1882, | Peter Johnston | 1903 | L. C. Senglaub |
| 1883 1884, | C F. Smalley | | |

## THIRD WARD—CITY

| | | | |
|---|---|---|---|
| 1870 | F. Bean | 1886 | A. Wittenberg |
| 1871 | George Pankratz | 1887 1889, | Daniel Bleser |
| 1872 | F. Bean | 1890 1892, | Henry Vits |
| 1873 | August Rosso | 1893 1894, | W. F Dicke |
| 1874 | F. Bean | 1895 1896, | C. A Gielow |
| 1875 1876 | C. H Schmidt | 1897 1898, | E. M. Carstens |
| 1877 | Henry Vits | 1899 | Joseph Staehle |
| 1878 1879, | George Pankratz | 1900 1901, | Charles Hartwig |
| 1880 | A. Wittenberg | 1902 | J. P. Nolan |
| 1881 1882 | J. Staehle | 1903 | Robert Uek |
| 1883 1885, | Henry Vits | | |

## FOURTH WARD—CITY

| | | | |
|---|---|---|---|
| 1870 1871, | J. W. Barnes | 1885 1887, | John Boecher |
| 1872 | M. Gilbert | 1888 | Oscar A. Alter |
| 1873 | F. Kostomlatsky | 1889 | John Boecher |
| 1874 | E. K. Rand | 1890 | Michael Kirwan |
| 1875 | J. W. Barnes | 1891 | E. J. Smalley |
| 1876 | E. K. Rand | 1892 1893, | E. K. Rand |
| 1877 | C. W. White | 1894 1896, | Oscar A. Alter |
| 1878 | George Cooper | 1897 | Frank Zeman |
| 1879 1880, | C. W. White | 1898 | W. Krainik |
| 1881 | J. E. Platt | 1899 | Frank Zeman |
| 1882 | George Cooper | 1900 1901, | Frank Vraney |
| 1883 | Sam Hall | 1902 | Frank Zeman |
| 1884 | A. J. Schmitz | 1903 | Frank Vraney |

## FIFTH WARD—CITY

| | | | |
|---|---|---|---|
| 1890 1891, | Henry Boettcher | 1898 1901, | Walter Pellett |
| 1892 1894, | J. Meyer | 1902 | Oscar Lindholm |
| 1895 | F. Gerpheide | 1903 | Ferdinand Veith |
| 1896 1897, | Otto Gerpheide | | |

## SIXTH WARD—CITY

| | | | |
|---|---|---|---|
| 1891 | Jacob Fliegler | 1896 1898, | J. Boecher |
| 1892 | John Boecher | 1899 | L. J. Nash |
| 1893 1894, | Gustave Torrison | 1900 | A. P. Schenian |
| 1895 | W. Beasant | 1901 | Edward Mohr |

## SEVENTH WARD—CITY

| | | | |
|---|---|---|---|
| 1892 | Peter Mazurkowitz | 1898 | C. Monk |
| 1893 | M. Pankratz | 1899 1900, | Frank Mrotek |
| 1894 | F Werner | 1901 | Gustav Mueller |
| 1895 1896 | C. Wachowitz | 1902 | C. Otto Schmidt |
| 1897 | John O'Hara | | |

## MANITOWOC RAPIDS

| | | | |
|---|---|---|---|
| 1849 | Charles McAllister | 1874 | Richard Donovan |
| 1850 1851, | S. W. Sherwood | 1875 1876, | Charles H. Walker |
| 1852 | T. W. Baker | 1877 | Richard Donovan |
| 1853 | C Klingholz | 1878 | Henry Wills |
| 1854 | Lyman Emerson | 1879 1882, | B. Roemer |
| 1855 | Adam Bleser | 1883 | R. Klingholz |
| 1856 | Wyman Murphy | 1884 | T. Osulson |
| 1857 | Adam Bleser | 1885 | R. Klingholz |
| 1858 | Richard Donovan | 1886 1892, | Charles Gustaveson |
| 1859 | Adam Bleser | 1893 1897, | David Sheldon |
| 1860 | Richard Steele | 1898 1899, | Oscar Lindholm |
| 1861 | Lyman Emerson | 1900 1901, | David Sheldon |
| 1870 1871, | Richard Donovan | 1902 | E. S. Bedell |
| 1872 1873, | Harvey F. Hubbard | 1903 | David Sheldon |

## MAPLE GROVE

| | | | |
|---|---|---|---|
| 1850 | M. C. Brown | 1873 | M. Connell |
| 1852 | D. B. Knapp | 1874 1875, | M. Finlan |
| 1853 1854, | A. Hickok | 1876 1879, | J. Miller |
| 1856 | D. B. Knapp | 1879 1882, | J. P. Nolan |
| 1857 | M. Roland | 1883 | James Noble |
| 1858 | John O'Hearn | 1884 1891, | J. P. Nolan |
| 1859 1861, | Edward Nolan | 1892 1893, | John Miller |
| 1870 | John O'Hearn | 1894 1901, | W. C. Maertz |
| 1871 | Edward Nolan | 1901 | J. P. Watt |
| 1872 | E. Regan | | |

## MEEME

| | | | |
|---|---|---|---|
| 1849 | T. Cunningham | 1876 1878, | John Carey |
| 1850 | B. Hansinger | 1879 | J. H. Bohne |
| 1851 | Thomas G. Jadwin | 1880 1882, | John Carey |
| 1852 | H. Mulholland, Sr. | 1883 | J. H. Bohne |
| 1853 | John Budemeyer | 1884 1885, | John Carey |
| 1854 | H. Simon | 1886 | C. E. Conway |
| 1855 1856, | Henry Mulholland | 1887 1888, | Q. A. Danforth |
| 1857 | Anton Walterbach | 1889 1890, | P. J. Conway |
| 1858 | Michael Herr | 1891 1893, | Q. A. Danforth |
| 1859 | E. Abrams | 1894 | John Hertel |
| 1860 | John H. Bohne | 1895 1896, | William Fenn |
| 1861 | E. Abrams | 1897 | John Hertel |
| 1870 | J. H. Bohne | 1898 1900, | Q. A. Danforth |
| 1871 | W. Danforth | 1901 1902, | P. J. Conway |
| 1872 1874, | J. H. Bohne | 1903 | Joseph Connell |
| 1875 | J. L. Edwards | | |

## MISHICOT

| | | | |
|---|---|---|---|
| 1853 | I Birdsall and A. Borcherdt | 1872 | C. Tisch |
| 1854 | Fred Ullrich | 1873 1880, | J. Lindstedt |
| 1855 1856, | W. B. D. Honey | 1881 | John Werner |
| 1857 | E. H. Shaw | 1882 1883, | J. Lindstedt |
| 1858 | W. B. D Honey | 1884 1886, | August Wagner |
| 1859 | J. Rankin | 1887 1889, | Peter Kaufman |
| 1860 | John Werner | 1890 1891, | August Wagner |
| 1861 | D. Van Valkenburgh | 1892 1897, | Bruno Mueller |
| 1870 | Ira P. Smith | 1898 1900, | J. Roemer |
| 1871 | H. Wehausen | 1901 | Herman Stehn |

## NEWTON

| | | | |
|---|---|---|---|
| 1850 | F. Hacker | 1878 | C. Wernecke |
| 1851 | Rudolph Von Carnap | 1879 1880. | H. Strodthoff |
| 1852 | J. Stevenson | 1881 | C. Wernecke |
| 1853 | William Griebling | 1882 | T. Teitgen |
| 1854 1855, | Fred Schmitz | 1883 1885, | Fred Schmitz |
| 1856 | William Griebling | 1886 | C. Wernecke |
| 1858 | Dan Shanahan | 1887 | J. Ruechoeft |
| 1859 | F. Hacker | 1888 1889, P. J. White | |
| 1860 1861, | Fred Schmitz | 1890 1895, A. Rodewald | |
| 1870 1873, | F. ed Schmitz | 1896 1897, Thomas Gretz | |
| 1874 1875, | C. Wernecke | 1898 1900, A Rodewald | |
| 1876 1877, | Fred Schmitz | 1901 | Thomas Gretz |

## ROCKLAND

| | | | |
|---|---|---|---|
| 1856 1861, | Louis Faulhaber | 1879 | F. Buboltz |
| 1870 | John Braatz | 1880 | E Thompson |
| 1871 | L Rusch | 1881 1884, George Miller | |
| 1872 | L. P. Nichols | 1885 1887, M. L. Cooney | |
| 1873 | L. Rusch | 1888 1893, T. Gleeson | |
| 1874 | Louis Faulhaber | 1894 1895, E. Thompson | |
| 1875 | M. Mason | 1896 1900, A. Moede | |
| 1876 1878, | E. Thompson | 1902 | Martin Rappel |

## SCHLESWIG

| | | | |
|---|---|---|---|
| 1856 1857, | H. F. Belitz | 1882 | J. D. Brockert |
| 1858 1859, | F. R. Gutheil | 1883 1884, John Barth | |
| 1860 | John Barth | 1885 | C. R. Zorn |
| 1861 | Herman Gutheil | 1886 1887, August Goerbing | |
| 1870 1871, | Louis Gutheil | 1888 | Louis Senglaub |
| 1872 | John Barth | 1889 | August Goerbing |
| 1873 1876, | C. R. Zorn | 1890 1894. F Zastrow | |
| 1877 1878, | John Barth | 1895 1898. C. R Zorn | |
| 1879 1880, | C. R. Zorn | 1899 1902, W. Reinhold | |
| 1881 | John Barth | 1903 | C. R. Zorn |

## TWO CREEKS

| | | | |
|---|---|---|---|
| 1860 | H. Luebke | 1877 1879 Fred Pfunder | |
| 1861 | J. C. Eggers | 1880 | G. Taylor |
| 1870 1871, | Fred Pfunder | 1881 1883, H. Johnson | |
| 1872 | Fred Vogel | 1884 1885, Joseph Immler | |
| 1873 | H. Reiss | 1886 1890, H. Johnson | |
| 1874 | I. Bartosch | 1891 1898, Henry Lehrman | |
| 1875 | J. Ruse | 1899 1900, J. C. Naser | |
| 1876 | W. Taylor | 1901 | Henry Lehrman |

## TWO RIVERS

| | | | |
|---|---|---|---|
| 1849 | John Stuart | 1872 | B. Wilkens |
| 1850 | Charles Kuehn | 1873 1876, | G. Damler |
| 1851 1852, | W. B. D. Honey | 1877 1878, | H. Goedjen |
| 1853 | Timothy Harrington | 1879 | E. Stollberg |
| 1854 | N. Kaufmann | 1880 1881, | H. Goedjen |
| 1855 1856, | William Aldrich | 1882 1883, | F. Schwartz |
| 1857 | H. S Pierpont | 1884 1885, | H. Goedjen |
| 1858 | H. C. Hamilton | 1886 | George Dicke |
| 1859 | C. Whitcomb | 1887 1894, | H Goedjen |
| 1860 | Conrad Baetz | 1895 1896, | T. J. McCarthy |
| 1861 | H. H. Smith | 1897 1900, | J. Sechrist |
| 1870 | B. Wilkins | 1901 1902, | William Zander |
| 1871 | H H. Smith | 1903 | Robert Schubert |

### TWO RIVERS VILLAGE

| | | | |
|---|---|---|---|
| 1870* | H. H. Smith | 1874 | B. Wilkens |
| 1871 1872, | G. Damler | 1875 1877, | Richard Mueller |
| 1873 | H. H Smith | | |

### FIRST WARD, CITY

| | | | |
|---|---|---|---|
| 1858 | William Aldrich | 1886 | J. Gagnon |
| 1859 | H. C. Hamilton | 1887 1889, | E. Mueller |
| 1860 1861, | H. S. Pierpont | 1890 1892, | U. Niquette |
| 1878 1883, | U. Niquette | 1893 1896, | Edward Courchene |
| 1884 | Edward Lamere | 1897 | J. Gagnon |
| 1885 | U. Niquette | 1898 | J. Geimer |

### SECOND WARD, CITY

| | | | |
|---|---|---|---|
| 1858 | H. B. Allen | 1883 1884, | E. Evans |
| 1859 | John H. Brown | 1885 1891, | Jonas Gagnon. |
| 1860 | J. G. Burns | 1892 1894, | Peter Schroeder |
| 1861 | B. J. Van Valkenburgh | 1895 | B Wilkens |
| 1878 | R. Mueller | 1896 | F. Schwab |
| 1879 | B. Wilkens | 1897 1898, | Jonas Gagnon |
| 1880 1882, | William Hurst | 1899 | William Boehringer |

### THIRD WARD, CITY

| | | | |
|---|---|---|---|
| 1878 | Peter Stout | 1888 | W. Wegner |
| 1879 | H. Wilger | 1889 1890, | William Luebke |
| 1880 1881, | G. Breunig | 1892 1893, | C. Hoffmann |
| 1882 | Henry Wilkins | 1894 1895, | W. Wegner |
| 1883 | M. Maloy | 1896 | F. Tegen |
| 1884 1887, | G. Breunig | 1897 | W. Wegner |

### FOURTH WARD, CITY

| | | | |
|---|---|---|---|
| 1897 | W O'Hara | 1900 | John J. Schroeder |
| 1898 1899, | Louis Hartung | | |

*From 1870 to 1878 the village of Two Rivers was represented by one member in the county board, although from 1858 to 1861 each ward had been represented.

FIFTH WARD, CITY

| | | | |
|---|---|---|---|
| 1897 | J. Tadich | 1900 | Anton Bonk |
| 1898 | J. P. Hoffman | 1901 | Charles Krause |
| 1899 | C. Krause | | |

VILLAGE OF REEDSVILLE

| | | | |
|---|---|---|---|
| 1892 | F. F. Stelling | 1898 1900, | A. C Maertz |
| 1893 1894, | F. C. Maertz | 1901 | J. E. Schulz |
| 1895 1897, | A. Mueller | | |

VILLAGE OF KIEL

| | | | |
|---|---|---|---|
| 1893 1898, | J. C. Mueller | 1900 1901, | W. J. Guetzloe |
| 1899 | A Dassler | 1902 | F. Zastrow |

# APPENDIX D.

## VILLAGE AND CITY OFFICERS.

### MANITOWOC.

| YEAR | PRESIDENT or MAYOR | TREASURER | CLERK |
|---|---|---|---|
| 1851 | George Reed | Gustavus Richter | S. A. Wood |
| 1852 | James Bennett | Gustavus Richter | S. A. Wood |
| 1853 | James Bennett | A. Wittmann | S. A. Wood |
| 1854 | William Bach | J. B. Dunn | N. Wollmer |
| 1855 | Charles Esslinger | E. D. Beardsley | Carl Roeser |
| 1856 | Charles Esslinger | E. D. Beardsley | Carl Roeser |
| 1857 | James Bennett | Oscar Koch | Carl Roeser |
| 1858 | Charles Esslinger | Oscar Koch | Carl Roeser |
| 1859 | S. A. Wood | Oscar Koch | J. W. Thombs |
| 1860 | S. A. Wood | Oscar Koch | Carl Roeser |
| 1861 | G. B. Collins | C. Hottelmann | T. C. Shove |
| 1862 | James Bennett | C. Hottelmann | T. C. Shove |
| 1863 | Oscar Koch | C. Hottelmann | A M. Richter |
| 1864 | A. D. Jones | C. Hottelmann | A. M. Richter |
| 1865 | Joseph Vilas | C. Hottelmann | A. M. Richter |
| 1866 | S. A Wood | Henry Baetz | A. M. Richter |
| 1867 | Henry Baetz | R. H. Hoes | E. Alter |
| 1868 | Henry Baetz | Otto Troemmel | Fred Borcherdt |
| 1869 | Charles Luling | Otto Troemmel | N. Nielson |
| 1870 | Peter Johnston | Otto Troemmel | W. Hempschemeyer |
| 1871 | Peter Johnston | A. M. Richter | Joseph Rankin |
| 1872 | Charles Luling | A. M. Richter | Joseph Rankin |
| 1873 | A. D. Jones | Fred Schulz | F. Stupecky |
| 1874 | A. D. Jones | Fred Harris | F. W. Borcherdt |
| 1875 | A. D. Jones | Joseph Staehle | F. W. Borcherdt |
| 1876 | A. D. Jones | Joseph Staehle | A. M. Richter |
| 1877 | A. D. Jones | A. Wittmann | A. M. Richter |
| 1878 | John Schuette | A. Wittmann | A. D. Jones |

| 1879 | John Schuette | Charles Gelbke | A. D Jones |
|---|---|---|---|
| 1880 | John Schuette | Charles Gelbke | A. D. Jones |
| 1881 | John Schuette | Charles Gelbke | Fred Heinemann |
| 1882 | John Schuette | Charles Gelbke | Fred Heinemann |
| 1883 | John Schuette | C. Haukohl | Fred Heinemann |
| 1884 | George Pankratz | C. Haukohl | Fred Heinemann |
| 1885 | George Pankratz | C. Haukohl | Emil Baensch |
| 1886 | Reinhardt Rahr | C. Haukohl | Emil Baensch |
| 1887 | Thomas Torrison | Francis Stirn | Emil Baensch |
| 1888 | Thomas Torrison | Francis Stirn | E. S Sherman |
| 1889 | Fred Schuette | Carl Hansen | Arthur Reichert |
| 1890 | Fred Schuette | Carl Hansen | Arthur Reichert |
| 1891 1893, | Fred Schuette | Fred Haukohl | Arthur Reichert |
| 1893 1895, | Joseph Vilas | C. Gielow | Arthur Reichert |
| 1895 1897, | Thomas Torrison | C. Gielow | Arthur Reichert |
| 1897 1899, | Thomas Torrison | C. Gielow | Arthur Reichert |
| 1899 1901, | William Rahr | C. Gielow | Arthur Reichert |
| 1901 1903, | William Rahr | John Mahnke | Arthur Reichert |
| 1903 | W. G. Kemper | John Mahnke | Arthur Reichert |

## TWO RIVERS

| YEAR | PRES. OR MAYOR | TREASURER | CLERK |
|---|---|---|---|
| 1858 | H. C. Hamilton | F. Bieling | J. C. Eggers |
| 1859 | H. S. Pierpont | C. Berger | J. C. Egers |
| 1860 | E Mueller | J. Oswald | J. C. Eggers |
| 1861 | J H. Burns | F Krause | Conrad Baetz |
| 1862 | David Smoke | G. Bieling | B. J.VanValkenburg |
| 1863 | John Oswald | G Bieling | Conrad Baetz |
| 1864 | John Oswald | John Franz | Felix Walsh |
| 1865 | John Oswald | John Franz | Felix Walsh |
| 1866 | Joseph Mann | John Franz | Felix Walsh |
| 1867 | E. Mueller | G. Berger | Felix Walsh |
| 1868 | John Oswald | F. Krause | Felix Walsh |
| 1869 | John Oswald | G Damler | Felix Walsh |
| 1870 | Andrew Baetz | Joseph Schwab | Felix Walsh |
| 1871 | J M. Conine | Joseph Schwab | Felix Walsh |
| 1872 | B. F. Richter | Louis Zander | Felix Walsh |
| 1873 | J. M Conine | Louis Zander | Felix Walsh |
| 1874 | J. M. Conine | Louis Zander | Felix Walsh |
| 1875 | Louis Zander | Nic Simonis | Felix Walsh |
| 1876 | J. M. Conine | Nic Simonis | Felix Walsh |
| 1879 | B. F. Richter | E. Hammel | Felix Walsh |
| 1878 | Michael Maloy | E. Hammel | Felix Walsh |
| 1879 | Michael Maloy | E. Hammel | Felix Walsh |
| 1880 | William F. Nash | H. Hansen | Felix Walsh |

| | | | |
|---|---|---|---|
| 1881 | Michael Malloy | H. Hansen | Felix Walsh |
| 1882 | Andrew Baetz | A. Kumbaleck | Felix Walsh |
| 1883 | Andrew Baetz | A. Kumbaleck | Felix Walsh |
| 1884 | William Hurst | John Ottow | E. H. Young |
| 1885 | William Hurst | John Ottow | E H. Young |
| 1886 | B H Wilkens | Peter Gagnon | William Hurst |
| 1887 | B. H. Vilkens | Peter Gagnon | William Hurst |
| 1888 | B H. Wilkins | Joseph Rehrauer | William Hurst |
| 1889 | B H Wilkins | H Hansen | William Hurst |
| 1890 | B F. Richter | H. Hansen | H. G. Wehausen |
| 1891 | Richard E. Mueller | H. Hansen | H. G. Wehausen |
| 1892 | Richard E. Mueller | H. Hansen | H. G. Wehausen |
| 1893 | J. E Hamilton | H. Hansen | H. G. Wehausen |
| 1894 | J E Hamilton | William Tegge | William Hurst |
| 1895 | Wm. Luebke | Henry Hansen | William Hurst |
| 1896 | Louis Zander | John Moseler | F. Althen |
| 1897 | Peter Gagnon | John Moseler | F. Althen |
| 1898 | Peter Gagnon | John Moseler | A. B. Leyse |
| 1899 1900, | Peter Gagnon | John Moseler | A. B. Leyse |
| 1901 | Peter Schroeder | J. Moseler | J. L. Klein |

ERRATA AND ADDITIONS.

Page 78  The Barry Line discontinued its west shore runs, north of Milwaukee in April 1903.

Page 80  8th line from bottom of page should read "1855"

Page 114  Should read "Judge Taylor" instead of "Judge Thayer."

Page 151  To last sentence of paragraph should be added "he being the candidate on the Populistic ticket for insurance commissioner."

Page 195  The present pastor of St Paul's M. E Church is Rev. C. E. Weed.

Page 201  Name should be "J. W. Thombs."

Page 206  The present pastor at Maple Grove is Rev. T. O'Connell.

Page 210  Last line, 33 instead of 13 feet.

Page 212  Rev. Joseph Chylewski is the present priest of the Manitowoc Polish R. C. Church.

Page 230  Should read in first line "membership in 1875 was 111."

Page 233  In February 1904 a large aerie of Eagles was established in Manitowoc.

Page 235  In 3rd line in last paragraph should read "Schmitz" instead of "Schmidt."

Page 298-9  The list of craft built at Manitowoc was compiled some six years ago for a local weekly and upon more recent investigation it has been found that several errors were made therein. Hanson & Scove builders, should have had credit for building the schooners Maxwell, Parker, McLaren, Linerla and Hall and the steamers Hinton and J. E. Hall. J. Butler superintended the building of the May Richards, Lalla Rookh and Rube Richards. To the list should be added

Schr. H. C. Albrecht (Thos. Hume) 309 tons, 1880, Hanson & Scove

Schr. Mary R. Ann, 20 tons, 1874.

Tug Dione, 9 tons, 1874.

Barge Daisy Day, 124 tons, 1880, Hanson & Scove.

Schr. Glad Tidings, 71 tons, 1883, J. Butler.

Scow Farrand H. Williams, 94 tons, 1883, Capt. Williams.

Tug Marinette, 30 tons, 1885, Rand & Burger.

Tug Grace Williams, 46 tons, 1885, Rand & Burger.

At Two Rivers during the early seventies the following schooners were built by Hanson & Scove: John Schuette 289 tons, Mike Corry 380 tons, Granger 366 tons and Bertie Calkins 256 tons.

# INDEX

Abbott, E. L............13, 19. 44, 153, 229, 244
Agricultural Associations............238, 239
Aldrich, Wm............89, 113, 136, 146, 187, 230, 271
Alverno............213
Ann Arbor Line............78, 79
A. O. U. W.............232
Arndt (family)............16, 21, 143
Athletic Organizations............236
Bach, W..46, 95, 124. 138, 148, 169, 172. 229, 233, 235-237, 242, 272, 275, 280
Baensch (family).45, 48. 129, 132, 142, 151, 164. 229, 240, 265, 273, 274, 285
Baetz, H..113, 115, 117, 122, 135, 138, 139, 148, 159, 161, 162, 172, 234, 235, ............ 264, 267
Banks and Banking............281
Baptist church............220-222
Barnes (family)............104. 113, 115, 136, 234, 282, 286
Beardsley, E. D............49, 91, 94, 113, 153, 155, 157, 228, 229 233
Bench and Bar............269-275
Benevolent Societies............240
Bennett, James............50, 60, 72, 115, 135, 144, 145, 168, 169, 171, 245
Bohemian Settlement............36, Societies 235, 237, 242
Borcherdt (family) 30, 32, 91, 98, 101, 113, 117, 121, 126, 144, 160, 198, 199 ............228, 247, 262, 264, 270
Boundaries............1
Branch............15, 26, 38, 40, 49. 51. 115, 186, 189, 231, 276. 289
Business Associations............240, 241
Business and Industry............288 292

Carey (family)..........................................54, 148, 150, 160, 225
Cato 1, 3, 13, 14, 31, 33, 34, 42, 46, 51, 54, 102, 106, 118, 125, 126, 146, 152,
..............................................................159, 231, 233, 242 245, 278
Centerville township 1, 3, 33, 35, 40, 125, 126, 146, 152, 155, 210, 216, 222,
...........................................................................................242, 245
Centerville village.............................40, 67, 51, 55, 83, 233, 237, 289, 292
C. & N. W. Ry.....................................................................77, 79, 85-111
Cholera........................................................................................351
Christian Church.............................................................................224
Christian Science.............................................................................225
Civil War.................................................................................114-128
Clark, T.............................................59, 95 98, 113, 117, 136, 146, 236
Clarks Mills...........................................37, 51, 53, 130, 187, 210, 212, 276
Cleveland......................................................................................52
Clover........................................................................................52
Collins..............................................................................52, 110, 217
Congregational Church..................................................................219, 220
Conroe (family).................20, 23, 27, 29, 42 44, 49, 133, 143, 152
Cooperstown 1, 2, 3, 4, 30, 31, 35, 37, 50, 102, 125, 133, 137, 146, 152, 158,
......................................................202, 206, 208, 223, 233, 242, 279
Creeks ........................................................................................4
Crowley, Jere..........52, 113, 138, 159, 160, 239, 242, 247, 2˙9, 260, 263
Dentists..................................................................................279, 280
Drainage....................................................................................53, 54
Dramatic Organizations........................................................................236
East Twin River..............................................................4, 9, 11, 28, 179
Eaton 1, 3, 34, 51, 53, 54, 102, 125, 126, 146 152, 155, 161, 201, 217, 223, 233,
.............................................................................................242
Eberts, R. M...........................................................27, 44, 154, 205
Edwards (family).............................................23, 28, 30, 47, 68, 70, 152, 191
Education.................................................................................243-254
Ellis, E. H..............................................47, 49, 154, 184, 225, 245, 270
Emerson, Lyman.........................................................30, 35, 145, 160
English settlements ..............................................................................34
Episcopal Church.......................................................................183 190, 246
Esslinger, C., 32, 47, 51, 60, 86, 88, 89, 94, 102, 114, 131, 135, 169, 170, 238,
...................................................................................242, 245, 275
Evangelical Association.................................................................223, 224
Fellows, M..............................................94, 104, 115, 186, 228, 240, 242
Fisheries......................................................................................28
Fitch, C. W............45, 47, 60, 87, 95, 137, 228, 229 234, 255, 257, 262
F. & P. M Ry. Co........................................................75, 77, 79, 100 107
Fourth of July.................................................................................130
Franklin..........................................1, 3, 33, 34, 53, 102 125, 146, 153, 242, 279
French Creek.................................43, 50 51, 202, 207, 208, 210, 211
French Exploration...........................................................................9-11

Geology ..................................................................................... 2
German Evangelical Church............................................... 225
German Imigration....... ......32, 34, Societies ......238, 235, 237, 231
German Reformed Chuych................................................33. 222, 223
Gibson 1, 2, 3, 4, 6, 11, 14. 31, 37. 51, 102, 125, 126, 133, 152, 159, 161, 195,
........................................................................................216, 233, 242
Glover (family).. .....36, 47, 86, 88, 95, 115, 130, 138, 227, 228, 234, 272
Goodrich Line .....................................................................70 79
G A. R........................................................................................128
Greenstreet..........................................................................5, 208
Grimms Station. ................................................... ... 2, 40, 51
Hamilton (family)..9, 47, 89, 91, 113, 121, 178, 181, 238, 241, 276, 286. 289
Harbors.......................................................................55 67
Hika ...........................................................................51, 279.
Hubbard (family) 20, 22, 27, 35, 45, 47, 49 ,58, 91, 124, 144, 152, 155, 201,
..........................................................................223, 229, 244, 279, 289
I O. G. T.................................................................230, 231
Indians....................................................................8 15
Irish Settlements..................34, Societies....................224
Jewish Church.......................................................242
Johnston, Peter.......................60, 149, 173, 200, 234, 254
Jones, A. D....................................20, 140, 171, 174, 253
Jones. Benjamin 17, 20, 22, 38, 43, 44. 87, 88, 94. 95, 98, 115, 152, 154, 159
.................................................................................186, 233, 270
Jones, K. K...,36. 45. 60, 70, 86, 115, 117, 120, 136, 144, 229, 233, 244, 245
.................................................................................................253
Jones, William...........................................................16, 17, 120
Kasson .....................................................................51, 211
Ke Inersville........................................15, 36, 51, 208. 210
Kiel..40, 48, 49, 51, 52, 106, 126, 128, 182, 213, 222, 229, 231, 233, : 35, 237,
..................................................................278, 280, 287, 289, 290
Kings Bridge......................................................................51
Kirwan, M . ................................... 106, 165, 248, 272, 275, 285
Klingholz (family) 47, 48, 68, 91, 94, 95, 97, 98, 115, 135, 234, 236, 237, 241
.........................................................................................242
Kossuth........1, 3, 6, 4, 30, 32, 34, 36, 61, 91, 102, 126, 146, 152, 155, 161,
....................................................................210, 222, 242, 244, 289
Kuehn, Charles.....................................47, 91, 95, 137, 145, 282
Labor Organizations ..............................................239
Lake Michigan........................................1, 2, 3, 10, 11, 55 84
Lakes.........................................................................5
Land Speculation.......................................................16, 17
Larrabee...................................................51, 217, 231, 279
Liberty 1, 3, 5, 33, 34, 53, 68, 102, 125, 126, 146, 152, 159, 161, 212, 242, 245
.........................................................................................246

Literary Organizations................................................233, 235
Louis Corners.............................................................52
Lueps, J...............45, 91, 92, 94 95, 97, 98, 101, 102, 104, 105, 234, 272
Luling, C........................61, 104, 105, 140, 141, 149 172, 174, 252
Lumbering ...........................................................16 31, 38
Lutheran Church...........................33, 214 218, 245, 247, 253
McAllister (family)................26, 38, 44, 46, 60, 86, 153, 155, 231, 238
Madsen..................................................................110
Manitowoc city...............................See topics and chapters
Manitowoc Rapids, township 1, 2, 3, 4, 5, 13, 34, 35 37 91, 120, 125, 126,
.........................................................146-52, 155, 189, 241, 242
Manitowoc Rapids, village 11, 16, 20, 23, 40, 43, 46-49, 135, 183-186 191,
........................................198, 202, 203, 212, 223, 224, 276, 289, 291
Manitowoc River.....................................3 11, 16, 57, 58, 190
Manitowoc & Mississippi Ry. Co............................85 111, 169
Mann (family)....................................66, 179, 239, 241, 2-2, 254, 289
Maple Grove 1, 3, 33, 34, 46, 50, 53, 91, 102, 106, 125, 126, 146-52, 155, 192,
................................................202, 206, 210, 217, 220, 231, 242
Marine Disasters ...................................................80-4
Markham (family) 62, 63, 98, 101, 104, 105, 113, 115, 122, 123, 126, 131,
.................................................................171 271, 274, 284
Masonic Orders......................................................227-8
Meeme 1, 3, 8, 34, 35, 38, 55, 102, 125, 126, 146-52, 155, 186, 202, 207, 210,
...............................................................224, 239 242, 245-6
Melnik............................................................52, 20 2, 275
Memorial Days..........................................................132
Menchalville............................................................52
Methodist Church....................................................190-8
Milhome.................................................................51
Militia System..............................................112, 113, 128, 129
Mishicot township 1, 3, 8, 33, 91, 102, 115-6, 133, 146-52, 155, 241 2, 244-5
Mishicot village 4, 30, 38, 48, 50, 73, 83, 114, 191, 213, 217, 231, 233, 237,
...................................................................278 279 289
Mound Builders.............................................................9
Mulholland (family) 35, 60, 122, 146, 148, 175, 177, 207, 234, 242, 245-6, 279
Munger, D. S.....................................................20, 22, 44, 153, 270
Murphy's Mills.....................................................4, 27, 44
Musical Organizations.............................................235, 236
Nagle, John..........................................142, 248, 250, 251, 254, 264, 267, 284
Nero....................................................................51
Neshoto..................................................4, 8, 16, 29, 38, 51, 73, 191
Newton 1, 3, 5, 32-3, 35, 40, 51, 91, 102, 118, 125, 126, 146-52, 155, 196, 211,
............................................................214, 216, 227, 235, 241, 242, 245
Niles.......................................................51, 202, 217, 231
Northeim........................................................51, 129, 211
Norwegian Settlement........................34, Societies 234

Odd Fellows Order..........229, 230
Olmstead, T G ..........115, 122, 255, 264, 272, 273
Oslo..........51
Osman..........52
Physicians..........275-279
Pierce (family)..........26, 31, 43, 47, 49, 112, 130, 135, 144, 148, 152-5, 163.
..........245, 270, 290
Pierpont (family) 32, 70, 124, 137, 138, 147, 159-61, 163, 178, 219 265, 291-4
Platt (family) ..........48, 50, 72, 91, 92, 94, 95, 98, 115, 121, 146, 168, 234
Polish Settlement..........40
Politics..........National 134-42, State 142-52, County 152-60
Postoffices and Pos Routes..........49-52
Presbyterian Church..........198 202, 246
Press, The..........255-68

Rahr (family)...47, 61, 97, 150, 164, 170, 175-7 235, 239, 254, 283, 288, 289
Railroads..........85-111
Rand (family) 72 5, 91, 94, 126, 136, 147, 170, 174, 199, 201, 228, 234, 240,
..........284, 285
Rankin, Joseph..........122, 140, 146, 148-50
Reed, George..........46, 86 103, 124, 138, 147, 158, 168, 181, 199, 271 3
Reedsville 4, 38, 40, 41, 46, 51, 181, 211, 216, 223, 224, 229, 233, 278 9, 290
Reif..........52
Rivers..........4
Roads..........42 9
Rockland 1, 3, 4, 5, 33, 35, 53, 54, 102, 125, 126, 146-52, 158, 161 223, 242
Rockville..........40
Roman Catholic Church..........33, 202-14, 247, 249, 253
Rosecrans..........51, 217
Rube..........217

Saint Nazianz..........33, 208, 210, 249 278, 279, 292
Saint Wendel..........52, 278
Salomon (family)..........91, 99, 113, 118, 122, 147, 229, 234, 255, 257 62
Schleswig...1, 3, 4, 5, 13, 14, 37, 40, 50, 102, 103, 107 118, 125, 126, 146-52,
..........158, 242
Schmidt (family)...118, 120, 131, 148, 164, 173, 237, 241, 255, 259, 264, 266,
..........267, 274 275
Schmitz (family) 32, 64, 106, 136, 141, 149, 151, 161, 165, 234, 242, 252,
..........272-5, 285
School Hill..........52, 220, 221, 233
Schuette (family) 49, 61, 63, 106, 149, 174-6, 239, 240, 254, 283-4, 291, 292
Sheboygan River..........4
Shove (family)..61, 114, 115, 117, 119, 126, 226, 208, 240, 248, 272, 282, 285
Smart, R. D..........51, 81, 131, 149, 163, 164, 175, 273, 274
Smith, H. (family)..29, 30, 35, 44, 47, 48, 50, 59, 89, 144, 149, 179, 242, 289
Smith, P. P. 2, 20, 22, 28, 47, 58, 60, 69, 88, 91, 112, 114, 120, 135, 138, 152
..........155, 190, 228, 229, 242, 244

Smith, S. W..................89, 113, 126, 138, 229, 234, 255, 257, 260, 262
Societies and Organizations...................................227-242
Sons of Herman.......................................................231
Spanish War.....................................................129, 130
Stark.................................................................52
Steinthal.............................................................51
Street Railways......................................................111

Taus..................................................................52
Telegraphs and Telephones.........................................52, 53
Timothy...............................................................12
Tisch Mills...............................................51, 209, 279
Torrison (fam ly).....34, 64. 72, 115. 175, 177, 229, 239, 254, 284, 285, 292
Transportation and Shipbuilding...................................67, 80
Treat, E. B..................................49, 101, 131, 162. 200, 263, 272, 273
Two Creeks1. 3, 11, 31, 37, 39, 51, 53, 61, 67, 102, 125, 126, 133, 146, 152,
..................................................159, 220 233, 242, 290
Two Rivers, city...........................................See Topics
Two Rivers, Township.....3, 33, 61, 102, 126, 127, 145, 163, 195, 244, 245

Valders..................................................52, 110, 217, 218
Vegetation..........................................................5, 6
Vieau, J.....................................................11, 28, 40, 155
Vilas, Joseph, 61. 63, 72, 100, 107, 110, 124, 126, 131, 138, 141, 147, 149,
........................................................171, 234, 241, 246, 290

Walker (family)..75, 95, 104, 120, 121, 141, 141, 145, 146, 161, 233, 234,
...............................................................241, 253, 270, 272
Waumegesako..........................................................13
Wells.................................................................52
Welsh Settlament............................................37, 220, 221
West Twin River...........................................1. 4, 9, 28, 29, 179
Whitelaw....................................................49, 52, 212
Windiate (family)......................49, 51, 82, 115, 127, 227, 234
Wisconsin Central Ry........................................78. 85-111
Wittman, A. 50, 113, 115, 124, 126, 131, 136, 138, 228, 234, 236, 245, 265, 267
Wood, S. A. 45, 47, 50, 60, 88, 91, 92, 94, 95, 97, 98, 101, 126, 138, 146 160,
...............................................168, 170, 174. 234, 242, 271. 285

Zander................................................................52

www.ingramcontent.com/pod-product-compliance
Lightning Source LLC
Chambersburg PA
CBHW060939230426
43665CB00015B/1995